POST-16
EDUCATION

POST-16 EDUCATION

Studies in Access and Achievement

Edited by **Clyde Chitty**

LONDON EDUCATION STUDIES
KOGAN PAGE
Published in association with
The Institute of Education, University of London

First published in 1991

Kogan Page Limited
120 Pentonville Road
London N1 9JN

© Institute of Education, University of London, 1991

British Library Cataloguing in Publication Data

A CIP record for this book is available from the
British Library.

ISBN 0 7494 0097 8

Typeset by DP Photosetting, Aylesbury, Bucks
Printed and bound in Great Britain by
Biddles Ltd, Guildford

Contents

Notes on Contributors

Eddy Adams has a background in teaching English as a second language and his previous work has included administering youth training programmes for bilingual students in East London. He is currently the Training Projects Officer for the London Docklands Development Corporation, although the views expressed in his chapter are not necessarily those of that organization.

Paul Barrow spent some time as a youth worker in Manchester before going into teaching. He is now a Senior Lecturer in Communications, and TVEI General Education Coordinator, at Epping Forest College, in Loughton, Essex.

Shane Blackman is a Research Officer in the Department of Educational Studies at the University of Surrey. He has previously taught in the Continuing Education Unit at the Thames Polytechnic and at the Institute of Education, University of London. He has published numerous papers on vocationalism, youth training and equal opportunities.

Clyde Chitty is a Lecturer in the School of Education at the University of Birmingham. He was previously a Lecturer in the Curriculum Studies Department at the Institute of Education, University of London. His recent publications include: *Secondary School Examinations* (with Jo and Peter Mortimore) and *The National Curriculum* (with Denis Lawton) (both Bedford Way Papers). He is co-ordinator of the educational journal *Forum*.

Martin Cross is Chief Executive of the Royal Society of Arts Examination Board. Before moving to the RSA in 1982, he worked in various colleges of further education, latterly serving as Vice Principal of the City and East London College. He was a member of the Review of Vocational Qualifications Working Group, is a member of the Board of Management of the Further Education Unit and was a member of the Speaker's Commission on Citizenship.

Andy Green has taught for many years in colleges of further education and in teacher education for that sector. He now works at the Post-16 Education Centre at the Institute of Education, University of London. He has many publications to his name.

Mavis Green has been an educational advice worker and counsellor since 1968, and has worked in the Careers Service, in Personnel, and in the Continuing Education Unit of a London polytechnic. She currently works in the Education and Training Department of the Chartered Institute of Management Accountants.

Pauline Greene has taught English in London comprehensive schools for the last 20 years, and has been the Head of Sixth Form in two schools in Haringey. In the autumn of 1991, she commences teaching at the College of St Mark and St John in Plymouth.

Janet Harland is a Lecturer in the Curriculum Studies Department at the Institute of Education, University of London. Her main interest is curriculum policy-making and its implementation with particular reference to the 14–18 age group.

Peter Mangan taught in the secondary and further education sectors in Northern Ireland before gaining a Masters Degree in Curriculum Studies at the Institute of Education (specializing in Access provision) and a Diploma in Access Studies at the South Bank Polytechnic. He set up a Modular Access Programme at a Tertiary Centre and is now Access and Progression Adviser at Croydon College.

Jack Mansell is a consultant on vocational education and training. Initially an engineer, he spent many years in further education, and was Chief Officer of the Further Education Unit from 1980 to 1987. He has served on many national committees, is a past-President of NATFHE and is currently a Visiting Fellow at the Institute of Education, University of London, and at the Oxford Polytechnic. He is the author of numerous articles and research reports.

Alan Payne trained as a geography teacher and taught in comprehensive schools in the Midlands and South Wales before moving to his present post as a member of the senior management team of a comprehensive school in East Anglia. His present responsibilities include coordinating INSET and TVEI in school and chairing local INSET groups.

Pamela Percy became a mature student in the expansive 1960s. During her career, she has developed continuing education in three institutions of higher education. Her main research interest is the Sociology of Technology. She is currently Head of Continuing Education at Westminster College in Oxford.

Sorrel Pindar has a background in developmental psychology and education. At the time of writing the chapter for this collection she was involved in educational research and development at the Centre for East London Studies, Queen Mary College in London. She is now engaged in civil liberties work for the London Borough of Southwark in their Community Rights and Safety Policy Unit.

William Reid is Visiting Scholar at the University of California, Riverside. He was previously Reader in Curriculum Studies at the University of Birmingham. The question of access to education has been an important theme in his research and writing over the last twenty years.

Ken Spours is a General Inspector for TVEI for the Tower Hamlets Education Authority and a Visiting Lecturer in the Post-16 Education Centre at the Institute of Education, University of London. He is the author of numerous publications on education and training.

Nanette Whitbread has taught in secondary schools in Middlesex, Essex and London and at the Leicester Polytechnic. She is now an Adult Education Tutor involved in Governor Training and Adult Basic Education. She has served on many national committees, and is a past-President of NATFHE. She is the author of numerous articles on the various sectors of education and is co-editor of the educational journal *Forum*.

Introduction

Clyde Chitty

The purpose and scope of the book

The purpose of this book is to present a collection of perspectives appraising the extent to which this country (mainly England and Wales) provides educational opportunities for its post-16 population. The emphasis is predominantly, although not exclusively, on the 16–19 age group; it is at this stage that almost irreversible decisions appear to be made, or accepted, regarding the continuation or otherwise of formal education.

General and specific perspectives are presented, and the index illustrates that there is a degree of overlap between the various contributions. In a sense, this reflects the congruence of opinion that emerges throughout the book since, almost without exception, the authors identify a far from satisfactory situation.

Whether the issues are comparative participation rates in post-16 education, the status of vocationalism, the adequacy of our secondary education, equal opportunities, or access to higher education, the respective analyses tend to suggest that progress has been limited. Similarly, recent solutions to problems such as low commercial competitiveness, inadequate training, restricted access, poor motivation and sheer neglect, appear to be more often than not distorted by cultural, political and economic pressures.

What clearly emerges from all these contributions is: that there is an urgent need for the widening of access to all forms of higher education; that this can be achieved only by moves towards a more coherent, unitary and integrated public system of 16–19 education and training; and that the tertiary college provides the institutional structure most ideally suited to a comprehensive system of post-compulsory provision. For a number of reasons, the 1988 Education Act has served merely to undermine the cause of enhancing access and achievement. But there are many signs that, despite this, teachers are finding their own ways of providing *genuine* equality of opportunity at the post-16 stage.

Post-war developments in 16–19 provision

The 1944 Education Act provided no clear definition of the structure of secondary education in this country, although it seems clear from the conclusions reached by the White Paper *Educational Reconstruction* (Board of Education,

1943a), and by the Norwood Report on *Curriculum and Examinations in Secondary Schools* (Board of Education, 1943b), that it was generally assumed that there would be a tripartite division of secondary education into grammar, technical and secondary modern schools. In the view of the Norwood Report, only two types of pupil were actually capable of advanced study leading on to success in higher education: first, 'the pupil who is interested in learning for its own sake, who can grasp an argument or follow a piece of connected reasoning', and second 'the pupil whose interests and abilities lie markedly in the field of applied science or applied art' (Board of Education, 1943b, pp. 2–3). Consequently, of the three types of school only the first two – grammar and technical schools– would have post-16 (sixth-form) provision.

As things turned out, priority was given to establishing an adequate number of secondary modern schools, while comparatively few local authorities opted for secondary technical schools. Their caution may have resulted from a certain amount of confusion as to the exact function of these schools, or it may have been due to the cost of the equipment required. Whatever the reason, as late as 1958 there were only 270 technical schools in this country, catering for less than four per cent of the secondary age group, and of these schools only 133 had sixth forms (Ministry of Education, 1959, p. 249; Rubinstein and Simon, 1973, p. 41).

The structure that had emerged by the end of the 1950s was in reality, therefore, a bipartite system comprising grammar schools on the one hand and secondary modern schools on the other – the former taking roughly one in five of all children at the age of 11. In the words of the 1959 Crowther Report commissioned to advise on the education of boys and girls between the ages of 15 and 18:

> Instead of a tripartite system, we have (if we may generalize about England as a whole) a two-sided system, based on the assumption, where maintained schools are concerned, that all boys and girls alike go to undifferentiated primary schools, and that from the age of 11 onwards, all go to a modern school unless they can show cause to the contrary and there is a place for them in a school giving a different kind of education. (Ministry of Education, 1959, p. 22)

The vast majority of secondary modern school pupils left school at 15, this being the statutory leaving age until 1972, so that the only types of school making any appreciable numerical contribution to sixth-form education were maintained grammar, direct grant and independent schools. Of these, the maintained grammar schools played by far the largest single part, accounting for around 60 per cent of all 17-year-old pupils in the late 1950s (ibid., pp. 199–201, 220). The comprehensive schools were as yet newcomers to the field, accounting for only two per cent of 17-year-old sixth-formers. Nevertheless, the Crowther Report confidently asserted that:

There is no reason to suppose that academic courses in the Sixth Forms of comprehensive or other new types of secondary schools, when they are developed, will differ substantially from the ones we shall be describing and discussing. (Ibid., p. 200)

While the grammar-school sixth form catered for the 'ablest boys and girls', another less favoured group of young students was being educated in technical colleges or colleges of further education under a variety of different headings.[1] Although, in the words of the Crowther Report, it was 'an alternative route' to 'the common goal' (p. 314), it was always looked upon by both parents and employers as an inferior type of provision. Many of the full-time students were there either because they had not done very well in school (which applied to a good number of the GCE students), or because the subjects they were anxious to study were not taught at all (for example, commerce), or were taught badly, in their particular school. The obvious need for some sort of alternative to the traditional school sixth form meant that the number of full-time students in further education increased by 70 per cent in the five years between 1953 and 1958; but this was by no means the factor chiefly responsible for the steady expansion of the further education (FE) sector in the 1950s. Under the new scheme of apprenticeships operating in a number of industries after the Second World War, apprentices were allowed to receive one day's release from work per week to attend courses at technical colleges for training in a specific trade. The great area of growth for these colleges in the 1950s and 1960s was therefore in part-time day courses, the majority of which were day-release courses for largely male apprentices.[2]

Despite the post-war rhetoric about the need to expand educational opportunities, it was still true that by the end of the 1950s, only one out of every eight young people in the 16 to 18 age range continued to be engaged in full-time education. At the same time, there were large numbers of school-leavers, 'many of them of limited intelligence', who entered industries that were not covered by apprenticeship schemes or who were not apprentices and therefore not eligible for day-release. Of those boys aged 16 who were not in full-time education in 1957-8, only 31 per cent received day release; and the corresponding figure for girls was negligible (ibid., pp. 179, 315, 349, 351).

One other form of post-16 provision deserves special mention at this stage in the analysis. This was the 'junior college' or 'sixth-form college', originally envisaged as 'a full-time institution without part-time students'. It was an institution officially recommended by the Crowther Report: 'providing an alternative form of education for those who had got incurably tired of school and for those whose schools had no sixth forms'. It would have 'the adult atmosphere of a technical college' but 'with a much wider range of curriculum and with terms of reference nearer to those of a school, in that equal weight would be attached by the staff to the subjects taught and to the personal development of the students' (ibid., pp. 422–3).

The concept then received official endorsement when the Labour Party was returned to power in October 1964 on a programme which included a promise to introduce comprehensive education. An arrangement involving 'comprehensive schools with an age range of 11 to 16 combined with sixth-form colleges for pupils over 16' was included in *Circular 10/65*, issued in July 1965, as one of six main forms of comprehensive organization that had so far 'emerged from experience and discussion' (Department of Education and Science (DES), 1965, p. 2). The circular gave three definitions of the sixth-form college: first, the college catering for the educational needs of all young people staying on at school beyond the age of 16 (the 'junior college'); second, the college making entry selective and, in effect, dependent on the satisfaction of certain conditions – five passes in the GCE O-level examination or a declared intention of preparing for A-level (the 'Advanced level academy'); and third, the expanded sixth form at a single secondary school, taking in pupils from local schools without sixth forms at the age of 16. This variant could take the form of either a non-selective 'junior college' or a selective 'Advanced level academy'. None of these arrangements received wholehearted backing in the circular, although it was argued that the merits and shortcomings of sixth-form colleges had been sufficiently debated to justify 'a limited number of experiments' (ibid., p. 5). In the event, few local education authorities (LEAs) chose to include separate sixth-form establishments in their plans for comprehensive reorganization, preferring alternative solutions that kept sixth forms attached to individual schools in the traditional way: by 1968, only 20 of the then 162 LEAs had submitted plans which included sixth-form colleges in their proposals (Corbett, 1968, p. 457).

Slater (1985, p. 180) has outlined some of the reasons why LEAs were initially reluctant to opt for sixth-form colleges in their plans for comprehensive reorganization. First, as we have seen, *Circular 10/65* itself was half-hearted in its endorsement of sixth-form colleges. Second, there was an expectancy of both a growing school population[3] and an increasing staying-on rate into the sixth form[4] which would mean that most comprehensive schools could support a viable sixth form in terms of numbers. Third, there was pressure from the comprehensive-school lobby itself for the prestige and points that the sixth form brought to the schools, giving the new comprehensives parity of esteem and status with the grammar schools they replaced – or, as was often the case, with which they existed side-by-side. Fourth, there were important ideological factors. Although the issue of sixth form colleges did not always divide the local education authorities along strictly party-political lines, it is true that for many Labour-controlled LEAs, this new type of college – whether overtly selective or not – simply perpetuated at 16-plus the divide that the comprehensive school was introduced to do away with at 11-plus. At the same time, sixth-form colleges, if selective, did have their attractions for some Conservative-controlled LEAs who saw them as an excellent way of preserving the standards and traditions of the grammar-school sixth form. As late as 1980, Andrew Fairbairn, at that time Director of Education for Leicestershire, was referring to the sixth-form college concept as 'the last refuge of the escapees from the selective grammar-school age' (Fairbairn, 1980, p. 8).

As Slater (1985) has also pointed out, it is significant that *Circular 10/65* made no mention of the FE sector in its discussion of six possible schemes for comprehensive secondary reorganization. Again, a number of reasons may be said to account for this. First, schools and further education were aiming at different markets: the FE sector was trying to cope with the growth of part-time day education connected with employers and training; while the schools saw it as their chief task to cater for the expanding school population. With demand outstripping supply, there was little or no competition for clients. Second, financial resources were available for both sectors, even at the risk of a certain degree of duplication. Third, there was, to use Slater's phrase, 'an educational divide' which had long held that schools and colleges served different educational purposes. This divide was reflected in the DES itself where policy on schools and on further education was separately devised in separate branches.[5] This was once referred to by a senior civil servant in the Department as 'the dialectic within the office' (Kogan, 1971, p. 123).

There was no mention of plans for the 16–19 age group in the key 1972 White Paper *Education: a Framework for Expansion* (DES, 1972) published during Margaret Thatcher's period as Education Secretary. This was a curious and revealing omission for which the DES was severely criticized in a report by a team of investigators from the Organization for Economic Cooperation and Development (OECD); appointed by the Department in 1974 to review educational planning in England and Wales.[6] This OECD team noted that, though designed to provide a 'framework for expansion' for the 'British educational service' the White Paper seemed to be rather more a 'framework of expansion' for 'certain pre-selected areas'. The problems associated with the areas chosen were said to be treated with 'admirable clarity, technical expertise, and straightforwardness'. There seemed on the other hand, to be certain other areas – such as provision for the 16–19 age group and for adult education – which had been wholly or partly omitted 'without adequate explanation of the selection criteria and procedure'. The White Paper did not address itself to 'the function of education in its relation to tasks such as vocational or industrial training'. Nor did it show any concern for those large numbers of 'disadvantaged youngsters' who left school at 16 without the prospect of any further education and/or training.

By way of explanation for the White Paper's obvious lack of interest in both the 16–19 age group and the academic/vocational dichotomy, the OECD investigators could only assume that after coping with a decade of expansion and change, and with its energies directed towards the raising of the school-leaving age to 16, the DES was quite content to leave in place the complex and apparently successful structure of post-16 qualifications and awards:

> One must . . . be aware of the factual situation in which this omission occurred: general education was to be raised to 16, and there was a long and proven system of ladder rungs through vocational professional diplomas and degrees from local, area or regional colleges right up to the university – a system so 'typically British' in its flexibility and empiricism which makes it hard to describe as a 'system' . . . Traditional English trust in the integrative powers of community and society as a whole, beside and beyond organized education, may also come into consideration. (OECD, 1975)

DES complacency about 16–19 provision was no longer in evidence when the Yellow Book was drafted in 1976. This was a 63-page confidential document compiled by DES civil servants in response to a request from Prime Minister James Callaghan for a memorandum covering some of the major issues in primary, secondary and further education.[7] The needs of the 16–19 age group, and particularly of those with no prospect of going on to higher education, were now depicted as being of central importance to the Government:

> The Government is committed to treating the educational needs of this age group as a priority. For those with academic ability, there are well-trodden routes through GCE 'A' level and technician courses to higher education, and for those combining average ability with practical interests through further education craft courses to various opportunities of skilled employment. A good deal of effort has been applied, with mixed success, to find suitable educational courses and aims for those who decide to stay at school after 16 but are not equipped to take GCE 'A' level courses . . . The greatest concern, however, is for the 40 per cent of school leavers who leave school at 16 and get no further education or vocational training. (DES, 1976, p. 14)

It was in July 1976 (the month that the Yellow Book was completed) that the Government announced its plans for a pilot programme of unified vocational preparation (UVP) as its main initiative in the further education sector for 'the less academically able 16–19s'. This was based on the idea that 'vocational preparation should be jointly planned and provided by the education and training services and should combine education and training elements inseparably'.[8]

The 1976–9 Callaghan administration was profoundly influenced by the view then being expressed by a number of employers, industrialists and right-wing politicians that pupils were being insufficiently prepared to enter 'the world of work'. The Yellow Book talked of the need 'to explore and promote further experiment with courses of a higher level of vocational relevance' (ibid., p. 22). It became fashionable to argue that the absence of effective vocational training for young people, both before and after the age of 16, was chiefly responsible for the economic decline of the nation. Yet there is evidence to suggest that, to begin with at least, the civil servants of the DES did not fully share the politicians' sense of urgency about the need to prepare youngsters for life and work in a capitalist society. Drawing on his experience as specialist adviser to the 1976–7 Education, Arts and Home Office Select Committee inquiry into the attainments of the school leaver, Professor Ted Wragg has concluded that the DES was 'singularly unenthusiastic about most aspects of the 16–19 school-to-work debate' (Wragg, 1986, p. 11). Those civil servants interviewed by the Committee apparently showed no appreciation of the importance of developing a coherent strategy for improving 16–19 provision. In Wragg's words:

> The DES tactic seemed to be: profess ignorance about the whole thing, mention a ludicrously long time-scale like twenty years, talk in telephone numbers about the cost and, with luck, the whole issue would waft away on the next breeze. (Ibid., p. 12)

This tends to confirm the earlier OECD finding that the DES resented outside interference and advice and was anxious to safeguard its status as an active and autonomous bureaucracy, 'largely in the position to determine itself the framework and the nature of its activity'.

By the mid-1970s, however, it was obvious to many that the country badly needed a coherent 16–19 policy.[9] And by that time, a new body had arrived on the scene, namely the Manpower Services Commission (MSC), that was to fill the vacuum created by DES inertia and would exert a powerful influence on the education and training of young people, particularly in the area of work-related, non-advanced further education.

The economic crisis and the rise of the MSC

The late 1950s and 1960s had been characterized by an expansionist mood at all levels of education. (Changes affecting higher education are dealt with fully in the next section.) It was a period when the country's economy underwent a major transformation as the old industries which had played such an important part in the prosperity of the nineteenth century tried hard to adopt to changing terms of trade and to the new demands of the post-war period. There was a marked shift towards the service industries and the professions which seemed to require a more highly-educated workforce.[10] It was generally assumed that education was desirable both for its own sake and as a way by which individuals could furnish themselves with necessary skills.

The evidence of the 1956 White Paper on technical education shows that David Eccles, Conservative Minister of Education from 1954 to 1957, was the first post-war Minister to assume that educational expenditure was economic investment. And, as Kogan has pointed out (1971, p. 21), the same assumptions were later to be deployed in the 1959 Crowther Report's assessment of the case for raising the school-leaving age. At the secondary level, arguments associated with economic growth were instrumental in supporting moves to avoid the wastage of talent resulting from a divided system.

It became an important feature of the Labour Party's bid for power in the early 1960s to emphasize the direct economic advantages that could be gained from a universal system of unsegregated education. This style of argument was very much favoured by Harold Wilson (Labour Party leader from 1963 onwards) who, in his famous 'Science and Socialism' speech to the 1963 Labour Party Conference, laid great stress on the point that the Party opposed a segregated, elitist secondary system, not only because it was plainly unjust and socially divisive, but also because by failing to capture talent at the point of entry to secondary education, it held back Britain's technological development and operated against our success on economic affairs.

As I have argued elsewhere (Chitty, 1989, p. 49), the policy-makers of the 1960s clearly saw a direct and indisputable correlation between educational reform and economic prosperity. It was generally assumed that a skilled and educated workforce would facilitate growth which would, in turn, constitute a firm basis for continuing educational expansion. This was the period when both Britain and America were under the spell of so-called 'human capital theory', which saw the production of a trained workforce as equivalent to investment in long-lived capital goods. In his 1960 Presidential address to the American Economic Association on the theme 'Investment in Human Capital', Theodore W. Schultz argued that the process of acquiring skills and knowledge through education had to be viewed not as a form of consumption, but rather as a productive investment:

> By investing in themselves, people can enlarge the range of choice available to them. It is the one way free men can enhance their welfare. (Schultz, 1961, p. 2)

According to this analysis, investment in human capital not only increased individual productivity but, in so doing, also laid the technical base of the type of labour force necessary for rapid economic growth. And this superficially attractive doctrine secured keen converts across the whole political spectrum in both America and Europe. As Karabel and Halsey have shrewdly commented, it even made a direct appeal to right-wing pro-capitalist ideological sentiments through its claim that:

> The worker is a *holder of capital* (as embodied in his skills and knowledge) and . . . has *the capacity to invest* (in himself). Thus in a single bold conceptual stroke, the *wage-earner*, who holds no property and controls neither the process nor the product of his labour, is transformed into a *capitalist* . . . We cannot be surprised, then, that a doctrine re-affirming the American way of life and offering quantitative justification for vast public expenditure on education

should receive generous sponsorship in the United States. (Karabel and Halsey, 1977, p. 13)

In Britain, human capital theory provided the intellectual justification for both comprehensive reorganization and the rapid expansion of higher education. Yet it would be wrong to give the impression that the educational advance of the 1960s was, in fact, based on minute and precise calculations of the cosy relationship between educational expansion and economic well-bring. Indeed, it seems clear that those calculations were never produced at all: that 'manpower' needs were never translated with any clarity into educational objectives. For the reformers of the 1960s, it was enough that the economic argument appeared to reinforce the more appealing and more significant objective of enhancing social justice. As Jones has pointed out, it was a vague belief in such slippery concepts as 'social justice' and 'a more equal society' that helped to keep the Wilson Government's superficially imposing 'edifice of policy' in being:

What helped to ensure that . . . cold figuring, with its implied assignment of students to particular occupational slots in an unequal division of labour, did not become central to educational planning was the active presence of other commitments and ideals. Among these was the combination of belief in equal treatment, objections to privilege, and protest at wasted potential that motivated the reform movement. This concern for social justice was rarely converted from a principle to a closely defined programme for reform – a failure which explains many of the subsequent problems of the comprehensive school. Yet it pervaded thought about education and provided a language in which to think its purposes. (Jones, 1989, p. 10)

It was the economic crisis of 1973–5, more than any other factor, that brought the 'edifice of policy' crashing down in an atmosphere of recrimination and doubt. The major world recession that erupted at the end of 1973 actually came at a time when the 1970–4 Conservative Government of Edward Heath seemed to be having some success with its economic policy. The Government had been prepared to risk inflation in order to promote growth. Yet its counter-inflation measures were proving remarkably successful in their initial stages, and looked like moderating the upward movement of prices and pay until such time as rising investment, profitability and output could contain them. At the same time, the British economy was suddenly expanding as fast as its rivals: its rate of growth in 1973 was 5 per cent, which equalled West Germany's. Yet by the end of the year, the Government's strategy had collapsed and the Conservatives were within a few weeks of losing office. As Professor Gamble has written:

The whole strategy suffered a spectacular shipwreck at the end of 1973, partly because of the internal crisis over pay caused by the miners' overtime ban and subsequent strike, partly by the loss of control of monetary policy, but mainly because of the abrupt termination of the world boom by the quadrupling of oil prices by OPEC (Organization of Petroleum Exporting Countries), which was the trigger for the commencement of a generalized recession and plunged Britain into a balance of payments crisis which dwarfed all previous experience. (Gamble, 1985, p. 124)

The economic crisis was accompanied by the growing problem of a falling school population. As Bernbaum has observed (1979), p. 11), central to the decline in schooling during the 1970s were 'the demographic changes, that . . . characterized most Western societies'. The birth-rate in Britain had been declining since the mid-1960s, and as the consequences of this decline began to be seriously felt in the mid-1970s, it was no longer possible for administrators and politicians to treat the clear manifestations of the fall as merely a temporary phenomenon. More seriously, from the point of view of 16–19 provision, there was no longer an increase in the staying-on rate into the sixth form which, according to DES figures, had hardly changed since the early 1970s (DES, 1979, p. 2). It was generally assumed by DES statisticians that the rate would remain constant in the future at the 1975 figure of almost exactly one in four pupils.

The falling birth-rate and the economic crisis led to renewed demands for both rationalization of 16–19 provision and a more effective strategy for dealing with those school-leavers who had no educational qualifications. In the area of institutional structures, there were many who argued in favour of the tertiary college as a way of bringing all post-16 provision together ·in one college under further education regulations.[11] Both Labour and Conservative governments became increasingly desperate about the extent of youth unemployment, and came to rely more and more on the MSC for effective, if short-term, remedies to overcome the problem.

The Manpower Services Commission (formally launched on 1 January 1974) was the creation of the Heath Government's 1973 Employment and Training Act which gave it power to make arrangements for 'assisting people to select, train for, obtain and retain employment, and for assisting employers to obtain suitable employees'. It was answerable to the Secretary of State for Employment who was given power to 'direct' the Commission and 'modify' its functions when necessary. But with control over its own budget, it enjoyed considerable autonomy and gained responsibility for a wide range of services and institutions including the industrial training boards (ITBs), the skill centres and the job centres.

Although the MSC's main function was initially to fund courses for adult retraining, the economic crisis of the mid-1970s soon shifted the bias of its work to the training of the unemployed – particularly the young unemployed. It was able to expand its role in financing training for 'the less academically able 16-19s' because it could work outside the conventional structure of central-local reltionships and the Rate Support Grant (RSG), by means of specific grants.[12] With its freedom of manoeuvre, it was in a good position to exploit the inertia and complacency of DES civil servants who placed the youth service, further education and adult education very low on their list of priorities. What very few people seemed to realize at the time was that the 1973 Employment and Training Act gave the Secretary of State for Employment powers of direct intervention in the education system of a kind that had never been available to the Secretary of State for Education.

It is clearly often the case that young people are affected disproportionately when the general unemployment level begins to rise. In July 1974, when the general level of unemployment was about 2.5 per cent, those aged under 20 formed about 5 per cent of the total. By July 1977, when the national percentage had increased to 5.5 per cent, those aged under 20 accounted for almost 30 per cent of the total. The number of school-leavers registered as unemployed had risen from about 10,000 in July 1974 to about 240,000 in July 1977.[13] This was the scale of the emergency which the MSC was rapidly expanding to deal with. The estimated rate of expenditure by the Commission during its first year of operation (1974–5) was around £125 million; by 1981–2, this has risen to over £1 billion.

By 1976, it was obvious that there was a real need for a reappraisal of provision for the young unemployed. A number of different schemes were now in operation: the Work Experience Programme, the Job Creation Programme, short industrial courses sponsored through the Training Services Agency, and sponsored apprenticeship award schemes run by some of the ITBs. In addition, there were the Community Industry Scheme and the Youth Employment Subsidy. The schemes varied in duration: from 12 to 13 weeks in respect of short industrial courses to 12 months' employment in the Job Creation Programme.

Increasing demands for the MSC to undertake an urgent review of the situation led to the setting up of a Working Party chaired by Geoffrey Holland to examine the whole problem of 'young people and work'. The Holland Working Party Report, with the title *Young People and Work* and published in May 1977 (Holland, 1977), ushered in the new Youth Opportunities Programme (YOP) which began life in April 1978 with an initial annual budget of £170 million.

This was designed to give 'disadvantaged young people' a six months' programme of work experience, with a limited commitment to additional education and training; but it was to come in for bitter criticism from a number of trade unionists and politicians. This criticism concentrated largely on three related factors: job substitution (employers were said to be making use of YOP trainees in situations which required the recruitment of 'normal' employees); cheap labour (a charge obviously linked with job substitution which claimed that YOP trainees were frequently undertaking the work of 'normal' employees); and the poor quality of the training on offer. Over the five years of the Programme's existence (1978–83), the number of work experience sponsors who provided the trainees entrusted to them with properly organized 'off-the-job' training in association with local colleges of further education, remained remarkably low. By mid-1983 YOP was being phased out, to be replaced by the new Youth Training Scheme (YTS), which similarly suffered much of the above criticism.[14]

As Low has shrewdly observed (Low, 1988, p. 220), 'the YTS was under way before the chickens of the YOP had come home to roost'. One of these roosters was the low proportion of young people who were actually in work six months after leaving a YOP scheme. The MSC was seen to be adept at moving with great rapidity from one programme to the next, 'from one three-letter initiative to another', without ever acknowledging the weakness of its own research and information base. The YOP scheme left a large pool of young adults unemployed which the adult training strategy, arguably the least successful of the MSC programme areas, did not properly cater for.

Two further MSC initiatives were to have profound consequences for the 16–19 age group. The first of these, the (New) Technical and Vocational Education Initiative (NTVEI), is an interesting example of the power and influence of the MSC in the period when David (now Lord) Young was its Chairman from 1982 to 1984 (see Chitty and Worgan, 1987; Low, 1988). Announced in a House of Commons statement by Prime Minister Margaret Thatcher on 12 November 1982, the new scheme started life with 14 pilot projects in the Autumn of 1983. By 1986, it involved 65,000 students in 600 institutions working on four-year programmes designed to stimulate work-related education, make the curriculum more relevant to post-school life, and enable students to aim for nationally-recognized qualifications in a wide range of technical and vocational subject areas.

The MSC's biggest incursion into the education field came in the area of non-advanced further education (NAFE).[15] The Department of Employment (DoE) White Paper *Training for Jobs*, published at the end of January 1984, proposed the extension of MSC responsibility for work-related, non-advanced further education by allowing it to take financial control of 25 per cent of work-related courses provided by LEAs through their further education colleges (see Thomson and Rosenberg, 1986, pp. 23–4). Prior to this proposal, MSC funding of further education had largely been limited to off-the-job YTS training and some provision through the Training Opportunities Scheme (TOPS). What was now being envisaged was that £200 million of spending should be transferred from the LEAs through the RSG, and disbursed through the MSC via bids from the LEAs themselves. The MSC could now 'purchase' courses as and when it wanted them from colleges. All this appeared to confirm the MSC in its new-found role as Britain's most influential quango. In the words of the 1984 White Paper:

The Manpower Services Commission . . . is already the main agency through which the Government institutes action and monitors progress in training . . .

The Government is now asking the Commission to extend its range of operation so as to be able to discharge the function of a national training authority. (DoE, 1984, p. 13)[16]

Yet within a matter of years, the MSC was dead and its legacy dissipated. Much to the surprise of many observers, the Commission did not long survive the third Conservative election victory in 1987. It may be that the period of its greatest power and influence owed much to the personality and drive of David Young and that it was useful primarily as a launching-pad for his career in the Thatcher Cabinet, first as Minister without Portfolio in 1984, then as Secretary of State for Employment in 1985. And it certainly lost a powerful and influential ally when Sir Keith Joseph was replaced as Education Secretary by Kenneth Baker in May 1986. In 1989 the Chairman of the Commission, Sir Bryan Nicholson, resigned: one of the key initiatives for adult training, the Job Training Scheme (JTS), failed to recruit the numbers envisaged and was recognized as being a costly mistake; and in November 1987 a radical restructuring of the MSC was announced. After the 1987 election, Kenneth Baker remained in place as Education Secretary, but Lord Young was moved from the Department of Employment, with its responsibility for the MSC, to the Department of Trade and Industry. In May 1988 the MSC became the Training Commission, which was itself then abolished in the following September.

The MSC's demise can also be explained by signs of a decline in youth unemployment in some areas of the country. However, and more fundamentally, the proponents of the so-called 'New Vocationalism' lost ground after 1986 to members of the Radical Right who resented the MSC's interference in the education service and saw little virtue in a vocationalized curriculum. The object was now to erect an hierarchical system of schooling subject both to market forces and to government by strict curriculum guidelines. The employers' critique of schooling was rarely heard or heeded. As Coles has observed:

> The concern about education in the mid-1980s came . . . from parents anxious about the education of their individual children, rather than from employers concerned about a whole generation of potential workers. The pressure of reform had thus shifted from the *collective consumers* of all education (employers), to the 'owners' of the *individual products* of education, parents. The latter are primarily concerned to make certain that *their* particular child has a competitive edge in gaining a firm foothold in an insecure world. (Coles, 1988, p. 197)

It can be stated with certainty that there was little sign of MSC influence in the final structure of the 1988 Education Reform Act.

Higher education: expansion and contraction

The post-war period was one of unprecedented expansion in higher education in this country, and of the various factors which can be held to account for this, two deserve special mention here. First, there was the demographic factor, critical for education. The high level of births in 1947 and the relatively high figures of the following years had obvious long-term implications for the demand for places in higher education.[17] Second, there was the trend for more and more pupils to stay on at school beyond the period of compulsory schooling and to then seek entry into one form or other of higher education. As Lowe has pointed out (Lowe, 1988, p. 152), 'this reflected both the increase affluence of the fifties and the growing realization that the economic transformation towards the service industries and the professions demanded a more highly educated workforce'. The late 1950s saw a sharp up-turn in the number of sixth-formers gaining two or more A-levels: from 25,000 in the mid-1950s to over 60,000 by 1964. The immediate result was a sudden fall in the percentage of school-leavers able to take up available university places – from 80 per cent in 1956 to 65 per cent in 1961 – which prompted demands for a general expansion of facilities (ibid).

At the same time, the period saw significant changes in the catchment allocation of the main civic universities, which ensured that they became more truly 'national' in character. Before and immediately after the Second World War, almost a half of all university students lived at home. Of the rest, many were studying at their regional university. The greater availability of awards by the end of the 1950s meant that it became possible for growing numbers of first-generation university students to move away from their home area. Before the war, only about 40 per cent of students in the universities of England and Wales received financial assistance from public or private funds. By 1957–8, around 80 per cent of students in England and over 90 per cent in Wales were receiving some kind of financial support; and the proportion of students living at home had dropped to just over 25 per cent (Dent, 1961, p. 95). For a privileged group of young people, going to university became associated with a fair degree of freedom and independence. But, as Lowe observes (p. 154), 'it was luxury shared to a lesser degree by the teacher training colleges and hardly at all by the technical sector'.

The first phase of university expansion in the 1950s was largely confined to existing institutions and was most marked in the most recent creations. Growth was particularly dramatic in the new universities, four of which – Exeter, Hull, Leicester and Southampton – had received their Charter by 1957.

But none of this was sufficient to meet the needs of the expanding number of suitably qualified sixth-formers – particularly in southern and eastern England – with the result that in the late 1950s and early 1960s, plans were drawn up for the establishment of seven new universities. These new universities, situated at Norwich (East Anglia), Colchester (Essex), Canterbury (Kent), Lancaster, Brighton (Sussex), Coventry (Warwick) and York, were soon able to prove that the number of young people able and anxious to benefit from higher education was not finite.

This was certainly the view taken by the Robbins Committee, whose 1963 Report launched the most massive expansion of higher education ever seen in Britain. As Layard, King and Moser have commented (1969, p. 22), 'few official reports in British history, and certainly in educational history, have led to such immediate changes in government policy'. The main quantitative recommendations were accepted in a White Paper published within 24 hours of the Report's appearance. It is of course true that 1963 was a good year for the Report to be published, with a general election in the offing; and this, more than mere elitism, may help to explain why it was acted upon so quickly. But, to quote Layard, King and Moser again, 'more important was the imminence of the bulge and the Government's genuine belief in the importance of higher education on both social and economic grounds'.

The Robbins Report anticipated that the number of home and overseas students in full-time higher education would rise from 216,000 in 1962–3 to 558,000 in 1980–1. To meet the increased demand it was proposed there should be six more new universities in addition to those already in process of formation. Furthermore, the Colleges of Advance Technology (CATs) should be given full recognition as 'technological universities'; and within the university sector there should be developed as soon as possible five Special Institutions for Scientific and Technological Education and Research. Underpinning all these proposals was the so-called Robbins principle that 'courses of higher education should be available for all those who are qualified by ability and attainment to pursue them and who wish to do so' (Robbins, 1963, p. 8).

To cope with the issues raised in the Robbins Report, and the upsurge of entrants into universities and colleges anticipated in the later 1960s, the Wilson Government developed what is usually referred to as the 'binary policy' for higher education. This was enunciated by Anthony Crosland (Education Secretary from 1965 to 1967) in speeches first at Woolwich Polytechnic in April 1965, then at the University of Lancaster in January 1967. It sanctioned the development of higher education in two major sectors: an 'autonomous' sector consisting mainly of universities and a 'public' sector under local authority control. But it was and is an over-simplification to think of each of the two sectors as being basically homogenous, since the public sector contained a number of institutions in addition to the powerful polytechnics, and the universities, although relatively few in number, were also very diverse.[18]

The binary policy can be seen as a rejection of the basic Robbins principle that higher education provision was virtually synonymous with university education. In addition to giving the CATs university status, the Robbins Committee had recommended the creation of a number of new universities and the virtual absorption of the teacher-training colleges into the university system. This part of the Robbins Report was rejected by the Labour Government which decided that there were to be no more universities in the immediate future and that the colleges of education (as the teacher-training colleges were to be known) were to remain under local authority or voluntary body control. As Elliott has pointed out (Elliott, 1985, p. 205), 'Robbins had gone in for university empire-building on a grand scale, and Crosland was preventing this from happening by developing the Advanced Further Education (AFE) sector as a respectable counterweight'. This objective was, in fact, largely accomplished since the university sector was prevented from expanding: the statistics show that the number of full-time students studying in universities was 60 per cent in 1962–3 and 58 per cent in 1980–1 (ibid).

Crosland clearly felt that the binary policy was infinitely preferable to the university controlled system for higher education recommended by the Robbins Report. He was anxious to avoid a situation where the universities would be responsible for the vast majority of degree courses, with all other institutions left with sub-degree or part-time work. Yet the binary policy was still criticized for perpetuating an elitist system, falling far short of the undifferentiated comprehensive system of higher education recommended by, among others, Robin Pedley and Eric Robinson.[19] The polytechnics were attacked for aping the universities in much the same way that the secondary modern schools had once sought to emulate the grammar schools.

If self-confidence and expansion were the dominant characteristics of higher education in the 1960s and early 1970s, this was certainly no longer true by the early 1980s. By then, as Scott has pointed out (Scott, 1988, p. 134), 'the golden age of Robbins seemed so remote that it now appeared irrecoverable'. The debate was now all about how universities, polytechnics and colleges could, in Scott's words, 'adjust their practices and their expectations to live within their newly restricted means'. There was a new set of priorities:

> Value-for-money efficiency, managerial hierarchy instead of collegial consensus, performance indicators to enforce political accountability, the extension of the old customer–contractor principle beyond its original home in applied research to determine the future shape of all higher education priorities – these were the new elements in the debate which political circumstances had made obligatory.

DES obsession with the phenomenon of falling rolls had already caused the wholesale closure of the colleges of education from 1975 onwards, as well as prompting a programme of merging and closing schools in the maintained sector to preserve their efficiency and viability. This thinking was then carried over into higher education generally with the prospect of a 30 per cent decline in the number of 18-year-olds in the later 1980s and 1990s. Both universities and polytechnics were placed under great pressure by the public austerity imposed by the Thatcher Government. The dominant view was that higher education must be restructured in a way which would maximize its contribution to the nation's prosperity. This is clearly evident in a letter sent by Secretary of State Sir Keith Joseph to Sir Edward Parkes, then Chairman of the University Grants

Committee (UGC), headed 'Development of a Strategy for Higher Education' and dated 1 September 1983:

> The Government would like to see a shift towards technological, scientific and engineering courses and to other vocationally relevant forms of study throughout higher education . . . I hope that the Committee will consider what measures might be taken to increase the resources devoted to fundamental scientific research, and to applied research and development, and to encourage their most effective use, for the sake of the quality of our science and for its contribution to the economy. (Reported in *The Times Higher Education Supplement*, 16 September 1983; quoted in Elliott, 1985, p. 214)

Here we have a classic statement of the idea that higher education is necessary for the creation of wealth.

The present situation

Of the many related themes in post-war educational history, two have been shown to have particular significance for the quality of post-16 provision: first, the recognition that spending on education is investment as well as consumption; and second, the idea that educational advance is a powerful means of creating a more just society. Former Conservative Education Minister Edward Boyle argued in 1971 that in the 1960s there had been two traditions in the DES:

> . . . the social justice tradition, wanting to widen opportunity, giving people the greater opportunity to acquire intelligence, and the technical college tradition – education for investment, education for efficiency. (Quoted in Kogan, 1971, p. 123.)

Economic prosperity and pressure of numbers made it possible, and indeed desirable, to satisfy both of these traditions in the 1960s. As Hunter has observed, with reference to the secondary sector and isolating economic prosperity as *the* determining factor:

> In a period of growing GNP, it was possible to support the two potentially opposing objectives: that secondary schooling should work towards creating greater social justice and equality within society *and* be an investment in creating a more efficient workforce. (Hunter, 1984, p. 274)

Neither of these traditions survived the traumas of the 1970s in their original form, and little is now left of the somewhat naive optimism they epitomized. Indeed, it is hard to determine what the social engineering of the 1960s actually achieved in a lasting way. In an article published in October 1983, Richard Hoggart argued that the socially privileged character of higher education had hardly been challenged over the years: 'the great body of working-class people have been left almost untouched' (*The Times Higher Education Supplement*, 28

October 1983). The statistics certainly show that the proportion of working-class students entering university has not significantly changed since the Second World War, while the proportion of children of manual workers among university students actually *fell* from 26 per cent in 1973 to 23 per cent in 1978 (Labour Party, 1982, p. 3). In an article published at the beginning of 1988, Andy Green was able to claim that:

> We have the highest rate of early school leaving, the lowest rate of achievement in nationally recognized qualifications, and the lowest rate of participation in higher education of almost any country in Europe, except Portugal and Spain. (Green, 1988, p. 25)

Including both universities and polytechnics, Britain has around 15 per cent of the relevant age group in higher education, compared with the United States where 30 per cent study at degree level, with Japan where 37 per cent are in university or college education, and with Germany where 20 per cent are in universities or polytechnics (ibid).

Doing something to remedy this situation would require a great effort of political will. One of the key problems for the Thatcherite project was how to represent the ideals and aspirations of an upwardly-mobile, materialistic bourgeoisie without alienating the ranks of the Establishment. In educational terms, this meant advocating parent power and grant-maintained schools, without challenging the position of Oxbridge or of the top public schools. It is indeed hard to see how the Government's education programme could be said to promote genuine equality of educational opportunity for all, or to widen access to those parts of the system hitherto reserved for a select few. Recent well-publicized initiatives such as the 1981 Assisted Places Scheme, together with the setting up of a small number of City Technology Colleges, will provide a privileged education experience for a minority of middle-class pupils and for an even smaller number of those of working-class origin. At the same time, nothing is being done to alter a situation where key posts in the British establishment are monopolized by that small proportion of our society (around 7 per cent in 1988) which went to independent, fee-paying secondary schools. And the recent rejection of the Higginson Report (DES, 1988b) shows that even a government which prides itself on its radicalism is not prepared to tackle the entrenched 'A' level structure with its in-built assumptions about specialization and rigour.

In a speech at Lancaster University in January 1989, the then Education Secretary, Kenneth Baker, called for a doubling of the proportion of young people going into universities or polytechnics (to around 30 per cent) over the next 25 years. But he made it clear that the expansion he anticipated in higher education should be based on American models of private funding rather than on the Western European system of increased public finance. Since then, his immediate successor John MacGregor, in an interview with *The Guardian* (24 November 1989), abandoned the target of 30 per cent, and added that he was still committed to *some* expansion of student numbers but 'only on a realistic and affordable basis, with funding coming from a variety of sources'.[20]

Turning to the other end of the political spectrum, the Labour Party appears to have recently been making a new commitment to the concept of education as economic investment. Speaking to the Labour Party's Annual Conference in Brighton on 3 October 1989, Party Leader Neil Kinnock claimed that education and training were now the 'commanding heights' of every modern economy. He went on to say:

> Now and for all time in the future, human skills and human talents will be the major determinants of success or failure – not just for individuals but for a whole society in all of its social, cultural and commercial life. (Reported in *The Independent*, 4 October 1989)

More than one commentator (see, for example, the *Independent* editorial of 4 October), likened these sentiments to Harold Wilson's more grandiose, though ill-focused, flirtation with 'the white heat of the scientific revolution' in his 1963 conference speech which came to nothing. This may be less than fair; but Labour clearly needs to develop a coherent strategy for the 16–19 age range and to show how its education policies will provide increased opportunities for girls and black and working–class students.

In this respect, Labour would do well to take note of the recommendations contained within *A British Baccalauréat* (1990), a report published by its own think-tank, the Institute for Public Policy Research (IPPR), set up in 1988. Here the key proposal is for a new, unified, system of education and training leading to a single 'Advanced Diploma' or 'British Baccalauréat'. The new system would be designed to encourage substantially greater full-time participation post-16, and also to guarantee education-led opportunities for those who do not stay on full time. In the words of a *Times Educational Supplement* editorial (6 July 1990), the Report 'leapfrogs the IPPR to the forefront of thinking on the well-trodden post-16 education and training disaster scene'.

Many now accept that Britain's post-16 education system is elitist and confusing. The 1987 White Paper *Higher Education: meeting the challenge* (DES, 1987a) urged higher education institutions to widen access, in part in response to the demographic decline in the number of school-leavers predicted for the early 1990s. It was felt that greater priority should be given to recruiting non-traditional entrants and then supporting them on their chosen courses more effectively. An HMI report, *The Widening of Access to Higher Education* published in July 1989, found that exciting initiatives were underway in a number of institutions, but that these tended to be 'ad hoc, disparate and uncoordinated, and . . . often inadequately underpinned by wider institutional policy' (DES, 1989).[21]

In a letter to the Chairman of the School Examinations and Assessment Council (SEAC), dated 28 November 1989, the then Education Secretary John MacGregor recognized the need for 'a more coherent approach to qualifications for all 16–19 year olds' and for a policy which would give all young people 'a clear spectrum of opportunities'. Yet there is no indication that either MacGregor or his successor Kenneth Clarke has understood the importance of ending the division between education and training. And sadly the divisive nature of the 1988 Education Act, with its clear attempt to break up the comprehensive system of secondary schooling, makes it less likely that in the near future we will achieve a broad, unified and open system at 16-plus.

Notes

1. The terms 'technical college' and 'further education college' are often used synonymously to cover the whole of this period, though it was not until the 1960s that the latter term came into common use.
2. This type of provision was usually referred to as PDR (part-time day release). Attendance at the classes was normally made a condition of the release, and the students were often also required to attend on one or two evenings a week in their own time.
3. In England and Wales, the total population in maintained nursery, primary and secondary schools grew from five million in 1946 to a peak of nine million in 1977. Growth was almost continuous throughout this period, although for some years in the early 1960s numbers in the compulsory age range showed a small decrease (DES, 1979, p. 1).
4. The staying-on rate increased steadily: by 1975, 25 per cent of the maintained secondary-school population stayed on in the sixth form for one year, and 16 per cent for two years. This information was contained in a written reply from Minister of State Rhodes Boyson to a question from Jim Marshall MP in the House of Commons on 28 July 1980, reported in *Education*, 8 August 1980.
5. The Department of Education and Science was created as a single department – responsible for education, science and the universities – in April 1964 when the Ministry of Education and the Office of the Minister for Science were amalgamated and took on various responsibilities from other departments. There were ten Under-Secretaries of State in the 1960s, each responsible for a particular aspect of the Department's work: schools, teacher supply, teacher training, further education, universities, etc.
6. The 1975 OECD Report was first published in *The Times Higher Education Supplement*, 9 May 1976 and is reprinted in P. Raggatt and M. Evans (eds) (1977), *Urban Education 3: the political context*, pp. 149–169.
7. The Prime Minister met Fred Mulley, the then Secretary of State for Education and Science, in May 1976 and raised with him several areas of concern. It is commonplace to argue that on that occasion, Mulley undertook to prepare a lengthy memorandum on the matters that were causing Callaghan anxiety, but some commentators believe that work on the document had already begun before the May meeting took place, since the finished product was on the Prime Minister's desk by the beginning of July. For a fuller discussion of the origins and scope of the Yellow Book, see C. Chitty (1989), *Towards a New Education System: the victory of the New Right?*, pp. 72–90.

8. The Unified Vocational Preparation Programme was not particularly successful in improving the career prospects of young people in jobs with little or no prospect of further education. The DES had problems both in finding the money for the programme and in paying the money directly to local authorities, with the result that, early in 1982, control was virtually handed over to the Manpower Services Commission (MSC): the role of the DES was changed from a 'sharing' one with the MSC to a 'helping' one (DES, 1982).

9. For example, Edward Boyle, Conservative Minister of Education from 1962 to 1964, had argued in 1971 for a new Education Act which would provide in particular a new framework for the 16- to 19-year-olds. And this view was endorsed, up to a point, by Timothy Raison of the Centre for Studies in Social Policy who argued, in an influential pamphlet published in 1976, that while 'major changes' in dealing with the 16–19 age group were obviously 'immediately desirable', it might be that they would be 'better launched when there are more obviously the resources to back expansion' (Raison, 1976, pp. 11, 76).

10. Between 1951 and 1964, the numbers employed in distributive trades and other services rose from 8.5 to 10.5 million (Times Newspapers, 1971, p. 9; see also Lowe, 1988, p. 152).

11. The first tertiary college was opened in Exeter in 1970. By 1977 there were 12 in operation, and by 1980, there were 15.

12. It was not until the passing of the 1984 Education (Grants and Awards) Act that the DES was able to pay education support grants to LEAs for specific 'innovations and improvements' that it wished to encourage. The 1985–6 financial year saw the introduction of these grants.

13. These figures are contained in an *Education* Digest, 'MSC: the first decade', published in July 1983; see also Low, 1988, p. 216.

14. For an interesting and perceptive account of the transition from YOP to YTS, see Dan Finn's *Training Without Jobs* (1987), especially pp. 131–59. The shortcomings of YOP are frankly acknowledged in the *Education* Digest referred to above.

15. NAFE comprises the provision offered by LEAs, through colleges of further education, of qualification levels below degrees, higher diploma, higher certificate and professional courses of equivalent level.

16. The proposals outlined in the 1984 White Paper aroused strong opposition from the local authorities. For the further development of the NAFE scheme and a description of the compromise reached, see Janet Harland's chapter in this volume.

17. The birth-rate stood at 16.2 per thousand in 1945, but increased suddenly, peaking at 20.7 per thousand in 1947 and only falling slowly back to 15.8 by 1951. Moreover, this was accompanied by a sharp decline in infant mortality, which between 1935 and 1938 had averaged over 43,000 deaths per year, but had fallen to only 24,800 in 1951 and to less than 21,000 by 1954 (see Lowe, 1988, p. 9).

18. England's first three polytechnics – Hatfield, Sheffield City and Sunderland – were born on 1 January 1969. *The Times Higher Education Supplement* marked their twenty-first anniversaries in 1990 with a special article charting their progress: see MacGregor, 1990, p. 8.

19. In 1965 Boris Ford asked Lord Robbins whether he would have modified his Report in the light of what had then transpired. Robbins was amazingly forthright: 'If I had

known that anything so reactionary and half-baked as the binary system was going to be propounded, I certainly would have suggested adding a few paragraphs to the Report, dealing with this as it deserves' (quoted in Halsey, 1990). Edward Boyle, interviewed by Maurice Kogan in December 1970, saw the binary system as: 'inherently unstable . . . any attempt at precise articulation of the difference between what a university is for and what a polytechnic is for doesn't stand up' (Kogan, 1971, p. 128).

20. More recently, in April 1990, the Government published figures drawn from an inter-departmental review of supply and demand for graduates, and a study of employers' predicted demand, carried out by the Policy Studies Institute and the Institute for Employment Research, indicating that the number of new graduates would rise by about 26 per cent between 1988 and 1993.

21. The whole question of access courses is dealt with in the chapters by Mavis Green and Pamela Percy, and by Peter Mangan.

Part I
General Perspectives

Chapter 1

The Ideology of Access in Comparative Perspective

William A Reid

I begin with the point that quantitative, economic accounts of access to education are inadequate as explanations either of existing situations or of policies for change. Figure 1.1 compares enrolments of 17-year-olds in secondary education in England and Wales with graduation rates from American high schools over the period 1870–1970, with both statistics given as percentages of the 17-year-old cohort. The figures stand at the same low level until 1890, then over a 50-year period a huge gap opens up: the percentage for England rises a little, but that for America soars to 50 per cent. No account based on economic factors alone can explain such a wide divergence. And where future policies are concerned, there is an equal lack of congruence. The latest wave of reports on reform in the American high school is in broad agreement about the importance

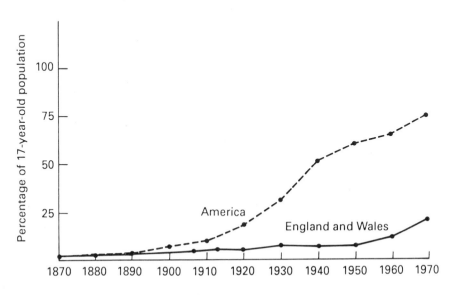

Figure 1.1 *Growth in enrolment of 17-year-olds in full-time secondary education compared to that of American high-school graduates (1870–1970)*

(Adapted from Reidd and Filby, 1982, p. 256)

of continuing to offer access to general education to all up to the age of 17 or 18, while in Britain, vocationally-biased courses are officially advocated for the majority of students (Reid, 1988). It seems unlikely that the needs of the two countries are so wildly different as to justify such a contrast in policies on purely economic and demographic grounds. I have to agree with Fritz Ringer who concluded, after a searching survey of the development of national systems of education in England, France, Germany and the United States, that 'social conventions have at least as much to do with the demand for education as any supposedly objective requirements of the economy' (Ringer, 1979, p. 261).

Ringer uses the term 'social conventions' to refer to factors over and above economic ones which help determine who will be educated. Rhoades (1987) following Turner (1960) uses the term 'folk norms', while I have had recourse to the words 'ideology' and 'tradition' (Reid and Holt, 1986). What all these expressions hold in common is an emphasis on social rather than economic phenomena, and an implication that these are rooted in unexamined assumptions. Rhoades, in his study of efforts to reform the GCE/CSE system of public examination, 1966–76, gives an example:

> A folklore emerged in the interviews about the poor specialist who could not work outside his specialty, stories of the whiz in physics or classics who was a washout in literature or maths. It would be an outrage, people said, to hold such students back for failing a subject outside their specialty, or even to force them to take such a subject. No mention was made of the need for well-rounded individuals or the need to prepare people for life. (Rhoades, 1987, p. 50)

In contrast to 'folklore', 'ideology' and 'tradition' allow a little more flexibility: ideologies can at least be contested and argued over, while, if we follow Popper (1963, pp. 120–35), tradition is something that can (and should be) reflected on and modified – though not, I would argue, ignored or abandoned. I am not making a plea here for a reinstatement of the economists' project, which I regard as misguided, but for an effort to move away from the strait-jacket of ideology (or Popper's 'first-order tradition') and towards what MacIntyre (1981, p. 206) calls 'traditions in good order', since they are 'partially constituted by an argument about the goods, the pursuit of which gives them their particular point and purpose' (Popper's 'second-order tradition'). In the quotation from Rhoades above, the folklore (ideology) sees the licence to promote the specialist as an end in itself, and gives no consideration to the more fundamental educational 'goods' that might be served or negated by endorsement of the cult of specialism. A tradition in good order is one that responds to changing circumstances by fostering deliberation on relationships *of ends and means* within evolving social and cultural contexts. Nevertheless, it respects the power of tradition and realizes that new structures and policies will be effective only in so far as they themselves can become part of the developing tradition (Reid and Filby, 1982, Chapter 12).

The importance of this last observation hinges on the fact that traditions are directive of practice not only through their inculcation of cultural norms, but also because they are lastingly embedded in social arrangements.

Understanding of the interaction of tradition and social arrangements is important in a discussion of access to education, since access is heavily dependent on curriculum structure and organizational structure. Let us look at an example of how educational ideas have influenced structure, and how structures have, in turn, sustained and promoted ideas. When state support for secondary education was instituted in England and Wales by the Education Act of 1902, it seemed that many choices were opened about how schools should be organized and what they should teach. In fact, as I have argued elsewhere (Reid, 1985), these decisions were determined by a tradition which, at that point, had already become an ideology – that is, which promoted norms without enquiring into the 'goods' which normative practice was supposed to secure. One of the norms espoused by the ideology was that of subject specialization. The approved curriculum for the new secondary schools was centred on the study of academic subjects and, although a general programme was proposed from the age of 11 to 14 or 15, no attempt was made to insulate older students from the effects of the demands of the universities for specialization in one, two, or at the most three academic subjects. Thus, the idea of specialization became instituted in the school curriculum and subsequent generations of educators absorbed the idea through their studies: it brought them success, status and rewards. But specialization also shaped the organization of secondary schools. Subjects became administrative units for resource allocation and served as the principal reference point in shaping teachers' careers. Heads of schools, who had the greatest influence over practice, owed their positions to their success in rising through a hierarchy of subject-based positions.

All of this was heavy with implications for access to upper secondary education. First of all, curricular and institutional bias towards specialization served to control the pool of those likely to attempt to continue their education beyond the age of 14 or 15. Not only were those who did not show commitment to some academic study likely to be discouraged from continuing, but the judgement about access would be made by teachers who were experts in subjects rather than in education; the fact that subject learning was sequential and spread over courses lasting three or four years ensured that anyone not already enrolled in the secondary school could definitely be excluded. Secondly, those who did want to continue were rigorously selected on the basis of examination results in academic subjects. Thirdly, those who were seen as admissible had no choice but to grapple with a diet of two or three subjects, taught as preparation for following a specialist degree course in a university. Specialization, as embodied in curriculum and organization, helped to ensure that access was negatively rather than positively construed: the question was not who could be persuaded to join, but who would be left when all the principles of exclusion had been applied.

So far, my account has been mainly historical. Today it might be supposed that things have changed dramatically: the traditional school sixth form, with its trappings of uniforms and prefects, has given way to more democratic institutions such as sixth-form and tertiary colleges; new types of course have been introduced to cater for those not pursuing A-level programmes; the boundaries between education and training have been blurred. Factually, all of this is true. But behind the facts of new institutions and new curricula, the old ideology still holds sway. New policies have had only very limited impact on the implicit assumptions within which education at 16-plus is carried on: institutions remain internally divided between academic and non-academic students; A-levels preserve the specialist curriculum as it has existed from the beginnings of state secondary education; courses with a vocational bias are widely seen as inferior. All of this emerges much more clearly for the observer who is not already familiar with the norms of the system. Rhoades, in his study of examination reform from a transatlantic viewpoint, comments that 'an American would find it astounding that . . . target group divisions were drawn within a cohort of less than 50 per cent of the age group'; and that 'American educators are principally concerned with prodigal children and rejoice most when they return. The English encourage them to leave' (Rhoades, 1987, p. 49).

Comparison between English and American policies on access is instructive. As we have seen, over the period 1890 to 1970 the American senior high school became hugely more accessible to the age cohort than was the case with the English sixth form. But numbers alone do not tell the whole story. As Ringer (1979) points out, at least two other criteria have to be taken into account – 'progressiveness' and 'segmentation'. Progressiveness is a measure of the extent to which access is random in terms of the social class or ethnic origin of entrants. For example, growth in enrolment could take place which signalled greater probability of higher social class students remaining in education, while the probability of attendance by lower class students was unchanged. This, I have argued, is to a large extent what happened in periods when sixth-form numbers rose (Reid and Filby, 1982, p. 137). However, in situations where enrolment exceeds 80 per cent, as is currently the case for grades 11 and 12 in America, class bias in the composition of the student population is unlikely to be great – which is not to say that it does not exist. On the other hand, there is no reason in principle why low enrolment should not reflect progressiveness in access, though in practice this is hardly ever the case since low enrolment typically results from rationing of a scarce and valued resource which middle- and upper-class families are better placed to exploit. This rationiong may occur either through limitation of total enrolment for a particular age group, or from segmentation (Ringer's second additional criterion) *within* the overall enrolment. That is to say, where schools and colleges are internally divided into sub-units offering different kinds of educational experience to the students within them, with only a limited number gaining entry to high-status curricula. Here again a sharp distinction appears between students in grades 11 and 12 in the American high school and 16-plus students in England. The former are participants of a relatively unsegmented curriculum system; study units are in principle open to all, the same rules for satisfying graduation requirements apply to all, and almost all complete their secondary education in the same way – by becoming a high school graduate. The latter, however, are enrolled in many quite distinct curricula – A-levels, BTEC, CPVE, various specialist vocational courses, and so on – with little or no overlap of content or possibility of transfer, and emerge at the end with different and barely comparable qualifications. Clearly, some of these curricula are seen as more desirable than others and so questions of access and progressiveness of access have to be asked in relation to segments of the system, as well as in relation to the system as a whole. Again it must be emphasized that I am not arguing that the American high school is free from segmentation, but simply that it is relatively less segmented than institutions of 16-plus education in England and Wales.

When contrasts in terms of total enrolment, progressiveness and segmentation are made between schools in England and America, supporters of the British system often point to evidence of racial bias in access to American upper secondary education and of tracking among senior high school students, as well as to the allegedly lower standards demanded of them. However, the claim that the difference between the two systems is of great significance does not depend either on demonstrating that American high schools eliminate relationships between social class, curriculum and achievement (clearly they do not), or on assertions that access rates can be changed without implications for what students learn. What *is* central to consideration of the question of access is that whereas conflicts of purpose in England have tended to be resolved in favour of policies supporting restriction of opportunity and increased segmentation, such conflicts in America have generally resulted in solutions which give priority to extension of access and commonality of experience (something which American writers periodically complain about).

A conflict found in all systems of upper secondary education is that between the need to prepare students for entry to courses of higher education and the need to provide suitable courses for those not intending to proceed further. In the late nineteenth and early twentieth centuries, heated debates around this issue took place in the United States (Krug, 1969). Advocates of the college preparatory curriculum pressed for the claims of academic subjects in general and of Latin in particular. By 1910 however, American high schools were firmly set on the path of electives (subject choices) and the unit system which are the basis of the high school curriculum today. While it remains perfectly possible for students to follow an academic curriculum, this is a variant of the fundamental curriculum rather than the exclusive embodiment of it. As Ringer has said, 'Differences of academic and social standing in secondary . . . education [were not] reinforced by curricular distinctions' (1979, p. 258). In England, however, the conflict was resolved in the opposite way. Confronted by one model for an academic curriculum derived from the public and endowed schools, and another for a general curriculum offered by the higher grade schools, the framers of the 1904 regulations for secondary schools adopted the first model with no concessions at all to the second.

In recent years, there has been a feeling in America that high schools may have moved too far away from the academic model. A 1983 national report (US Department of Education, 1983) complained that 'school curricula have been homogenized, diluted, and diffused to the point that they no longer have a central purpose'. However, debates on what might be done to improve matters have taken it as axiomatic that high-school graduation must be available to all and not to a sub-set of students seen as having special talents. As the report itself said, 'Our recommendations are based on the beliefs that everyone can learn [and] that a solid high school education is within the reach of virtually all'. Contrast this with the situation in England in the late 1960s – a period of high tide in educational reform – when the Schools Council set out to produce proposals for change in the curriculum of the sixth form. The work was undertaken by two quite separate groups, one of which was exclusively concerned with the curriculum for college-bound students while the other considered what might be done for the 'new sixth-formers', but within a framework defined by the perceived needs of those served by A-level examinations. The procedure adopted in setting up two working parties was in itself significant, but so too was the fact that this was seen as a 'natural' way of dealing with the problem and not one that was in need of special justification.

Different bases for the resolution of conflict are to be found not only at the level of policy-making for the system but also in schools and classrooms. Rhoades has observed that teachers too tended to divide students into 'target groups':

> The distinctions are hierarchical and value-laden. They are part of the language, appearing in terms such as *goats* and *sheep* (and *supersheep*). Compared to the neutral language American educators use, this terminology appears and is derogatory. The labels connote different degrees not just of ability but of worth. (Rhoades 1987, p. 49)

This finding is in sharp contrast with the conclusion of Cusick's study of teachers in American high schools. He claims that his teachers' curricular choices were guided by an 'egalitarian principle':

> The bottom line was keeping the students in school and in a state of order, and the way for teachers to do that was to get along with them on a personal basis and use that personal basis as the center of instruction. But that meant that the

curriculum was always laced with the teacher's opinions, approach, background, and predilections. (Cusick, 1983, p. 112).

Note that Rhoades and Cusick are equally critical in their comments: resolutions of conflict are always ambiguous and leave something to be desired. But perhaps what they found most disturbing was that neither group was able to throw off the shackles of the prevailing ideology – meritocratic in the one case, and egalitarian in the other. National level policies, it can be argued, are every bit as much in thrall to unexamined assumptions, but their promoters have more interest and skill in presenting a face of polished argument and reasoned discussion to the world. Teachers and principals are more prone to give unguarded responses, and easier to observe in situations where behaviour is more eloquent than anything that is said.

There seems to be little doubt that differences in policy and practice between Britain and America over access to education are better explained in terms of tradition and ideology than they are in terms of response to economic conditions. But how are we to understand such radical differences? To what do meritocratic and egalitarian principles relate? Where do they come from? And how do they become institutionalized? If we can make some progress in understanding these matters, we may be better placed to appreciate the implicit assumptions with which we approach decisions affecting access, and be enabled to move from the ideology or 'first-order tradition' which asks no questions about inherited values, and towards the 'second-order tradition' which, at least some of the time, concerns itself with the 'goods', the pursuit of which gives education its point and purpose.

National education systems are inherently political in the broad sense of the word. Whatever claims can be made about the pursuit of ends which are purely educational, the involvement of groups with political power in the provision of schools inevitably results in the establishment of systems with structures which reflect political goals and values. In particular, what we see reflected are the goals and values dominant when the systems were founded. The founding era for America was that immediately following the Revolution, when schooling was very consciously identified as a prime means of preserving and transmitting the core values of the new Republic. Education was established as a public responsibility through the new state constitutions which, in referring to support for schools, typically cited the need 'to preserve democratic values and the spirit of the Revolution'. Once monarchy, aristocracy and the church were rejected as sources of authority, the proposition that the people themselves were the ultimate repository of power had to be treated seriously. In the preamble to his *Bill for the More General Diffusion of Knowledge* (1779), Thomas Jefferson presented the case for regarding education as a bastion of democracy:

Whereas it appeareth that however certain forms of government are better calculated than others to protect individuals in the free exercise of their natural rights, and are at the same time themselves better guarded against degeneracy, yet experience hath shown, that even under the best forms, those entrusted with power have, in time, and by slow operations, perverted it into tyranny; and it is believed that the most effectual means of preventing this would be to illuminate, as far as practicable, the minds of the people at large, and more especially to give them knowledge of those facts, which history exhibiteth, that, possessed thereby of the experience of other ages and countries, they may be enabled to know ambition under all its shapes, and prompt to exert their natural powers to defeat its purposes.

Jefferson himself can safely be categorized as a meritocrat, but the implications of his political position were unavoidably populist and egalitarian. Rejection of monarchy and aristocracy in favour of democratic republicanism, coupled with the need to promote nationalist sentiment within a federal system of government, inevitably led to the identification of the common school as a prime means of securing unity around the concept that the people, collectively, were the source of political and social authority. The values implied by this were to guide the development of nineteenth-century elementary education, which was the first manifestation of the common school. As public secondary education began to be generally available towards the end of the century, the predominance of these same values ensured, as we have seen, that questions of curriculum and structure were resolved in favour of forms which fostered access and encouraged universal enrolment through to grade 12. The high school became the common school of the twentieth century. Today, it could be argued, the way is being prepared for university and college to become the common school of the twenty-first century. Already enrolment exceeds 50 per cent of the age cohort and, just as in the case of the high school of 80 years ago, debates about curriculum and structure are, in spite of heated controversy, tending to produce solutions guided by the ideology which was the legacy of the founders of public education in America.

The history of the national education system in England and Wales yields a different story. The political context for the development of the system was basically the same – the challenge presented by pervasive ideas of democracy. Also similar was the recognition that schools could have an important part to play in resolving the social and political problems posed by a changing world. Matthew Arnold and J.S. Mill both felt that the key to how the growth of democracy should be handled lay in education, but they were very far from seeing the issue in the same terms as Jefferson. Like the leading historians, lawyers and constitutionalists of the day – Buckle, Maine and Bagehot – the educators were interested in preserving traditional sources of authority. For them, the ultimate disaster which could befall the country was for it to be 'Americanized' (Reid and Filby, 1982, p. 46). Arnold defended the legitimacy of traditionally derived 'right reason' to decide for society as a whole what is good and what is bad. The necessary extension of access to power was to be accomplished by co-opting selected outsiders into the prevailing culture of the governors:

> *Culture and Anarchy* was the prime social text of the new English ruling class of the later nineteenth century, for it provided more persuasively than anything else the intellectual basis upon which the aristocracy and bourgeoisie could adopt a common style. (Shannon, 1974, p. 34)

And the values expressed in *Culture and Anarchy* were reflected in the independent and endowed schools of the era. Questions of curriculum and structure were settled in ways that strengthened the legitimist and hierarchical aspects of the system and which favoured segmentation and selection. The curriculum was a curriculum of 'high culture' centred on academic subjects, and progress in it was linked to examinations. Heads of schools, teachers and senior students wielded authority. Competition was instituted as the driving force in the academic, social and sporting life of the schools. There was no question, then or later, of the secondary school becoming a ready inheritor of the common-school aspects of elementary education, as in America.

The essential difference between the two systems was captured by Cyril Norwood:

> European education which began in the universities has always known the meaning of intellectual values, for it has begun at the high levels and percolated down to the low. American education, which has of necessity been based upon the primary school, has never had the same standards, for the proper process has been reversed, and the movement has been from the lowest levels upwards. (Norwood, 1929, p. 330)

Those who accept it as a premise, explicitly or implicitly, that true education is defined from above will always tend to resolve questions of access in line with values which favour exclusion and segmentation, since they will identify with, and accept the legitimacy of, those who are employed in the 'higher' part of the system. On the other hand, those who assume that progress in education is built from below will resolve such questions according to values which stress incorporation and commonality of experience, since their reference point will be the practice of the 'lower' stages of education. As Rothblatt explains:

> Whereas in Europe, high school teachers in the advanced secondary sector valued their ties to universities and identified with the academic community above them, taking pride in their inter-institutional associations and common professional interests, in the United States the identity of high school teachers remained closer to that of teachers in the lower schools. (Rothblatt, 1988, p. 15)

Thus, English secondary school teachers talked about sheep and goats (and 'passing' O-levels a decade after the 'pass' was abolished) and agreed with admissions tutors' judgements about candidates for entry to universities, applying A-level criteria even more strictly than the tutors themselves (Reid, 1972, p. 99). But for the American teachers studied by Cusick, 'the bottom line was keeping the students in school' and their efforts were directed to devising curricula which ensured that almost any student who wanted to could graduate and claim a place in a state university.

The problem with these teachers, as with Cyril Norwood, is not so much that their views are wrong or misguided as that they are based on unexamined ideologies. We can be less critical of Jefferson and Arnold because they were consciously thinking through the implications of social, cultural and political developments, and making choices of courses of action relevant to the prevailing situation. But, in spite of all the injunctions daily pressed upon us to be responsive to the modern world, my sense is that today policies affecting access to education in Britain and America are being determined by unreflecting responses stemming from the value systems of the last century. How else do we explain how the National Curriculum enshrined in the 1988 Education Reform Act repeats almost to the letter the curriculum laid down in the grant regulations of 1904, while the prescriptions of *A Nation at Risk* (US Department of Education, 1983) mirror the 1894 recommendations of the Committee of Ten? As I have already suggested, there is no reason to suppose that national level policy-makers in education are any more sophisticated than teachers when it comes to the examination of basic assumptions. Indeed, the more policy-makers are seduced by the possibilities of economic forecasting and of projections of employment requirements, the less likely they are to pay attention to fundamental questions of what education should be for and who should be getting it. In this they follow the regrettable example of the Crowther Report of 1959, which was produced by an economist anxious to respond to future demands but which totally accepted the ideology of the nineteenth-century sixth form.

What are the fundamental questions concerning access to 16-plus education which we should be deliberating over? I have argued in this paper that access is determined by the basic structure of educational provision and of the curriculum. As we consider the significance of this in more detail, we must realize that the 16-plus question cannot be considered in isolation: who is available for what kinds of learning after basic secondary education depends on the curriculum up to age 16. Similarly, the experience of the curriculum for those who are enrolled after 16 depends on how it is shaped by what follows – higher education and employment. The central curriculum issue was well and simply explained in the Cockroft Report (1982):

> Syllabuses now being followed by a majority of pupils in secondary schools have been constructed by using as starting-points syllabuses designed for pupils in the top quarter of the range of attainment in mathematics. Syllabuses

for pupils of lower attainment have been developed from these by deleting a few topics and reducing the depth of treatment of others; in other words, they have been constructed 'from the top downwards'. (p. 133)

This passage illustrates the pervasive influence of the ideology of 'right reason' on curriculum. The adjustment of curriculum content to students' goals or interests is hardly a practical proposition since the value orientations of those with decision-making power predispose them to shape syllabuses in line with the requirements of experts in the disciplines. The new AS-level syllabuses, for example, are simply slices of an A-level. Content is reduced but the curriculum becomes only marginally more accessible: it continues to be rejected not only by students who think they are likely to fail, but also by many who see the curriculum as serving a specialized interest which they do not share. Thus, extension of access, in so far as it is a goal, has to be secured by curricula segmentation. Attractive arguments for this are built around the proposition that it is 'good' for students who have been unsuccessful in the 'top-down' curriculum to have the chance of a new start on something designed for their 'needs'. This is a revised version of the 'separate but equal' tripartite policy which failed so disastrously following the 1944 Education Act. Then, as now, what might have been a reasonable argument in the abstract was vitiated as a practical proposition because it completely accepted existing ideologically-sanctioned structures: in the first case, the grammar-school curriculum and the existing percentage enrolment in it; in the second, the A-level curriculum and its highly restricted target population. The meaning of a curriculum for students enrolled in it can never be created from scratch as if no other curriculum existed. Just as secondary modern students were as much defined by the curriculum from which they were excluded as by the one which they were following, so 16-plus students in vocational courses are identified by themselves and others as 'non A-level'. (There is no suggestion in present government policies that 16-plus students in independent schools should be doing anything but A-levels.) We should also note that where alternative curricula are encouraged, they too tend to be determined by outside 'higher' influence, in this case that of employers rather than disciplinary experts, however much this is disguised by the use of labels such as 'pre-vocational'.

One question, then, that we should be deliberating over is how disciplinary content and vocational skills and knowledge can be transformed into materials for the achievement of educational goals rather than imposed upon students as ends in themselves (for discussion of the issues that this would raise, see, for example, Fensham, 1985 and Keitel, 1987). We also need to deliberate who should receive the kinds of education that such materials would make available. Questions of this kind can never be totally divorced from considerations of ideology or tradition, but they have practical aspects which cannot be sensibly addressed unless the limitations which ideology puts on research and discussion are recognized. The 'accessible' curriculum would be different from the 'top-down' curriculum, but it need not fall into the trap of dilution and diffusion complained of in *A Nation at Risk*. International research into mathematics achievement, for example, suggests that other solutions are possible. Figure 1.2 shows that increased enrolment in grade 12 in America, compared to England and Wales, may be bought at the price of lower achievement within what is still a small proportion of the age cohort. The experience of British Columbia, however, indicates that high enrolment can be combined with good levels of attainment to yield overall higher productivity, and IEA research provides pointers on how curricula might be designed for this purpose (McKnight et al., 1987).

Of course, the possibility of realizing such an outcome depends not just on knowledge about how to plan a curriculum, but also on the overall structuring of the educational system within which the curriculum is to be implemented. Thus, the British Columbia results can be related to a lower grade curriculum which avoids sharp peaks in the introduction of new content, but they also depend on the relative insulation of secondary curricula from the curricula of higher education, as compared to the situation in Britain. If policies on access at 16-plus are to be chosen, rather than be dictated by the inertial influence of ideology, then Britain must follow other countries in treating this stage of education as an integral part of the system as a whole and applying rules for

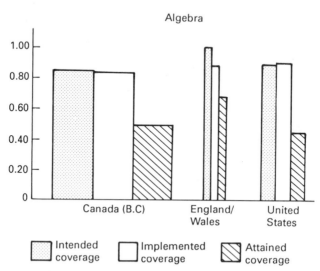

Figure 1.2   *Achievement in Algebra at Grade 12 in Canada (BC), England and Wales and America*

(Adapted from McKnight et al., 1987, p. 60. Achievement (attained coverage) is shown in terms of mean score (height of bar) and proportion of students enrolled (width of bar). Enrolment in British Columbia is 30 per cent, in England and Wales 6 per cent and in America 13 per cent.

transfer to university which are in the interests of all parties and not just of teachers in higher education. An accessible mathematics curriculum is not compatible with demands for 'double mathematics' at A-level.

Organizational structure, as well as curriculum structure, must be a subject of deliberation if rational policies on access are to be evolved. At least since the Taunton Report in the 1860s, which distinguished three levels of secondary education, differentiation of curricula has been enshrined in school buildings and in the principles of administration found within them. Lately, this differentiation has been pressed to extremes. Sixteen-plus students are to be found in selective school sixth forms, comprehensive school sixth forms, sixth-form colleges, tertiary colleges and technical colleges. Within these institutions, they are enrolled in many different and separate courses; moreover, a given course may be found in a number of these institutions which are only specialized to a degree. And now students may be enrolled in YTS-type courses which may or may not be associated with an institution which is part of the educational system. Segmentation has run riot. It is impossible, even using published DES statistics, to construct a comprehensive table showing how many students are enrolled in what courses and what institutions. This, as I have argued elsewhere (Reid and Holt, 1986), is a result which inevitably follows from the ruling ideology which regards the goals of high-status education as immutable. Challenges raised by increased demand for access on the part of students, or by the need to counter increased levels of unemployment by boosting enrolment in courses of education and training, have been met by a proliferation of courses and administrative structures which leave the A-level curriculum intact. One does not have to be totally opposed to differentiation in any form to be disturbed by the lack of ground for serious debate which is caused by this *ad hoc*, uncontrolled and largely unmonitored extension of provision. The sixth-form curriculum of the nineteenth century, limited and elitist as it was, had a point and a purpose; 16-plus education in England today lacks that point and purpose because it is still shackled by an ideology bequeathed by the era of the founders. It is time to turn that ideology back into a living tradition by considering alternative possibilities for the structure of the system and for the curriculum it supports. Looking at the contrasting ideologies which influence policies on access in other nations may be one way of achieving this desirable result.

Chapter 2

Upper Secondary Education in England and Wales: An Overview of Curriculum Pathways

Janet Harland

Either side of the boundary

In many countries the term 'upper secondary education' refers to the years from 15 onwards. In Britain, 16 has long been the crucial boundary. There are three main reasons for this: first, no matter when pupils chose to leave, from 1902 the basic secondary course was seen to cover the five years from 11 to 16; second, the end of this course was, and still is, marked by a complex system of public examinations (soon to be reinforced by a system of national testing) which, though they have over time changed in range and style, still remain a crucial rite of passage into the years beyond; and third, the tradition of the English sixth form – in origin, a two-year experience of specialized academic study leading towards higher education – remains a powerful influence on national thinking. For all these reasons, the break at 16 has come to seem to most people in this country somewhat akin to a law of nature. For example, when David Hargreaves wrote an influential and much-quoted book, *The Challenge for the Comprehensive School* (Hargreaves, 1982), the one element which received little serious attention was the proposal that there should be a common course to 15 and that thereafter pupils should follow more divergent tracks; and this, despite the popularity of 15 as a moment of choice in many European countries.

Of these reasons, the mythology of 'staying on in the sixth form' has been the most potent. Reid and Filby (1982) have traced the origins of the sixth form from its roots in schools for the social elite in the nineteenth century, via its institutionalization after 1902 in a state-sponsored system of secondary education in the Morant grammar schools, into the comprehensive schools of the 1960s. The grammar schools survived the grafting process and became themselves bastions of the sixth-form tradition. The Report of the Crowther Committee, which sat from 1956 to 1959 to consider how to advise the Education Minister on the education of girls and boys between the ages of 15 and 18, stands as a testimony to this assimilation (Ministry of Education, 1959). Although the Report's overall message was about expansion, including an immediate rise in the leaving age to 16 and the need for at least a four-fold expansion in the participation rate of those under 18, it is now chiefly remembered for its panegyric of the sixth form. In so doing, it identified the five 'marks' of the sixth form: close links with universities; specialization and 'subject-mindedness'; independent study; 'intellectual discipleship'; and social responsibility. As Reid and Filby say, 'Historically and empirically most of the statements don't stand up'; but they nevertheless characterize a tradition which still has the support of many, particularly many influential, people in Britain. However, this model of the sixth form was essentially selective. It worked on the assumption that those not fit for, or suited by, the academic sixth form would be 'eliminated' from the school system by, or at, the age of 16. For some, of course, there was to be vocational education and training in separate institutions; but for many more, there would be little or nothing. Into the early 1980s, Britain had a spectacularly poor showing in terms of the high percentage of young people who never received any form of education or training after the minimum leaving age.

The comprehensive schools of the 1960s and 1970s had more of a problem with the dominant tradition of the sixth form. Most modelled their curriculum from the age of 11 on the grammar school, since the fundamental rationale of non-selective secondary education was most often construed as equality of access to the opportunities offered by a grammar-school education. All those comprehensives that could manage it developed sixth forms which were also as close to the traditional pattern as possible. In particular, those which were based upon reorganized grammar schools successfully developed A-level programmes and their sixth forms exhibited all or most of the 'marks' identified by Crowther.

However, selection by elimination is hard to reconcile with comprehensive principles. Throughout these decades, there was growing concern about the 'new Sixth', meaning those young people who elected to stay in school after 16 and who needed and demanded courses other than the traditional academic studies of the sixth form. This provision mainly took the form of either a second opportunity to tackle the 16-plus examinations, or a low-level vocational course (shorthand and typing were particularly common for girls), or a combination of the two. Despite individual successes, there was an overall sense of dissatisfaction and frustration with these options, especially the first.

By the 1970s, there was a noticeable widening of the institutional setting for sixth-form studies. Thus, increasing numbers of students were turning to the further education (FE) colleges for their O- and A-level courses, resulting in the inevitable duplication of provision. Research evidence demonstrated that these students were often expressing a positive preference for the more adult atmosphere of the college as compared with the school (Dean et al, 1979). Of course, the colleges also continued to provide conventional vocational courses, many of which were formerly part-time or sandwich courses linked to apprenticeships, but which increasingly became full-time as the number of apprenticeships shrank during the decade. Thus the colleges were now catering for both the academic and the vocational tracks. However, yet another significant area of activity was opening up. As youth unemployment rose, more and more were developing 'pre-employment' courses for those young people who neither wished to continue their general (academic) education, nor were qualified to enter directly into a vocational course because they lacked the 16-plus examination passes required for admission. This group was often euphemistically referred to as the 'vocationally uncommitted'. Some of these young people had previously been 'hiding' in the school sixth forms, though the majority had tended to drift somewhat aimlessly around various forms of unskilled work until they found a comfortable niche. But as unemployment increased their numbers, and since schools also benefit financially from large numbers of sixth-form students, they increasingly developed courses for this group (usually beginning with the City and Guilds of London Institute (CGLI) foundation courses which were available from 1974). Thus schools and colleges came to be in direct competition for the same students.

But what these varying developments show is that despite changes in clientele, institutions and courses, the 16-plus boundary has survived as strongly as ever. Furthermore, for increasing numbers of students this boundary has been reinforced by an institutional break, in some cases as a result of voluntary flight to the FE college, but in many others by a local authority decision to provide all 16-plus education in either a mixture of FE and sixth-form colleges, or in a new all-purpose institution, the tertiary college. And of course, 16 remains the age at which young people may legally leave full-time education and training, as well as the time at which society awards them some of the other 'privileges' of adulthood – the right to marry, buy cigarettes and face criminal prosecution!

Yet if the boundary itself has been maintained, it is arguable that its nature is changing. Firstly, selection by elimination is notably declining. Of the 53 per cent who left full-time education and training in 1988, 22 per cent are described as being 'in employment' – (all figures taken from the DES Statistical Bulletin 14/88, December 1988). But for the others it was a choice between unemployment (7 per cent) and participation in a government training scheme (24 per cent). This last comprised the two-year Youth Training Schemes (YTS) which offered a trainee allowance of £29.50 per week, up to 20 weeks off-the-job training and, possibly, some form of recognized qualification. Government has put pressure on young people to participate either in this scheme, or to remain in full-time education or training, by denying welfare payments to those who prefer to opt out. When we remember that the exclusive ethos of the sixth form (though still strongly entrenched in some sectors and particularly in the independent schools), has been stretched and buffeted by widened participation and changed patterns of vocational education, and that both schools and colleges offer pre-vocational courses to all, it has to be said that there is now no young person for whom there is nothing on offer. However, it remains a fact that nearly one in three appear not to want to know.

The second reason why the boundary is changing is that despite the apparent egalitarianism of comprehensive schools, the installation of the 'common' GCSE examination to replace the two-tier GCE and CSE, and the establishment of a national curriculum for all, reinforced by a national system of testing, the obvious effect of much recent government policy will be to increase the degree to which pupils are differentiated during the period of compulsory schooling. Looking very briefly at each of these indicators, it is difficult to avoid the view that the object of the Education Reform Act is to sustain the rhetoric of common schooling while simultaneously allowing substantial variations to develop: locally-managed schools, variously advantaged or disadvantaged by the requirement to publish unadjusted test scores; City Technology Colleges with a distinctive curriculum and ethos, not to mention a resource base which bears no relation to that of neighbouring schools; and opted-out schools whose very motivation for independence is to be other than what the LEA would wish them to be. All these developments imply less rather than more parity of experience, let alone parity of esteem. The GCSE exam system, so lately and painfully installed, is already under threat because of its manifest disjunction with 16-plus testing: recent talk is of half or three-quarter GCSEs, and even of 'super GCSEs' which will 'stretch the bright'. The cumulative impact of strenuous testing against graded attainment targets is as yet far from clear, but without doubt one result will be to further the arguments for, and the practice of, ability grouping and curriculum tracking. We may even see the end of promotion by age – for so long a standard feature of British education – due to the increasingly refined grouping of children according to their positions on the various ladders.

Young people are therefore likely to reach the point of transition already pre-selected for the various levels of course available after 16. There should be little surprise at this situation. For some years, increasingly prescriptive government statements stressed differentiation as a key principle in the planning of the 5–16 curriculum (see for example, *Better Schools*, Department of Education and Science (DES), 1985). The 1979 Conservative election manifesto specifically condemned mixed ability teaching, a teacher-initiated development extant in many comprehensive schools; most educational policy moves since that time can be seen to incorporate this concern to eradicate what was seen as naive egalitarianism.

To this argument about differentiation pre-16, some commentators have added the charge that government has endeavoured to create a division at around 14 into general and vocational tracks (see for example, Chitty, 1986): education for some, preparation for employment for the rest. Since the early 1970s, schools have increasingly offered various vocational and pre-vocational courses to lower attaining pupils from the age of 14. But the key move was the introduction of the Technical and Vocational Education Initiative (TVEI) for 14–18s in schools and colleges, funded by the Manpower Services Commission (MSC), an agency of the Department of Employment (see McCulloch, 1987, for a revealing account of the origins of this scheme). Many people thought that this scheme would create a middle-ability 'technical' stream, oriented towards an early commitment to a vocational goal. To add to this, evidence about the pupils recruited to

TVEI pilot schemes suggested that the intake was skewed towards the less able, and this fuelled the view that a curriculum cross-roads would soon be well established at 14. But more recently this has come to seem less likely. In the first place, from its outset in 1987, the extension phase of TVEI has required, as a condition of grant, that *all* pupils in participating schools should study some kind of technology within their curriculum and should, in addition, have some personal experience of the links between school and working life. And secondly, Technology is established as a 'foundation' subject for all pupils at all ages, thus subsuming the curriculum requirement of the TVEI extension programme. Indeed, in the new environment of the Education Reform Act, the TVEI scheme is still searching for a secure niche: as in other areas of government education policy, there would seem to be some real contradictions between different elements in the total package. In my view, the argument for bifurcation at 14 is not proven: one has only to look at current initiatives aimed at incorporating elements of 'enterprise' education into higher education courses (MSC, 1987) to see that government attempts to modify the allegedly 'anti-industrial' character of Britain (Wiener, 1981; Barnett, 1986) are not exclusively aimed at the less academically able.

To summarize, there are many paradoxical and ambiguous developments in the pre-16 years which bear upon the issue of differentiation. On a superficial level, it might seem that the move towards a national curriculum represents a commitment to less differentiation, not more. After all, the system of option choice from 14 has given rise to much criticism that pupils were being allowed to make decisions which could result in premature specialization, unbalanced curricula and *de facto* ability grouping, all factors which meant that for many, upper secondary tracks and indeed much beyond was determined at far too early a stage. As Maurice Holt wrote in a memorable phrase, 'the old bi-partite structure is alive and well and living in the option columns' (1978, p. 13). Schools have progressively retreated from the notion of choice as a self-evident virtue and have increasingly adopted curriculum structures characterized by terms such as 'restrained options' and 'protected cores'. Now government policy appears to have moved in the same direction, though it is arguable that the motive relates more to social investment and efficiency rather than to social cohesion and equality.

Thus, it is important to recognize how young people stand at the boundary of the upper secondary years. The changes which are taking place post-16 are not divorced from the pre-16 experience. As we shall see, divergent views about differentiation and separation in the upper secondary years reflect parallel disagreements about policy trends in the lower secondary phase. The purpose of my digression into that earlier phase has been to demonstrate the increasing impact of arguments about differentiation, even within a near-universal comprehensive system. The meritocratic ideology of Conservative education policy has found a means of expression, even through the rhetoric of common schooling, common curriculum and common examinations.

Dale (1983) has suggested that these policies represent a strain of populism within Thatcherite thinking which aims to open doors to the 'deserving', those 'able and willing to make the most of opportunities offered to them'. And such policies are essentially hostile to social democratic principles of the kind so often denigrated by Conservatives as 'sixties liberalism' and exemplified in the establishment of comprehensive schools and the search for a genuinely common curriculum within a genuinely common school (Skilbeeck, 1982). Dale sets out what he sees to be the Tory critique of the social democratic state:

> It tries to bring about unnatural things, like social justice. This involves upsetting the natural hierarchy – or even meritocracy – which it is the legitimate task of the state to maintain . . . It may even be a part of the state's job to make sure that the natural hierarchy of talent is properly attuned to national, economic needs through the education system. Indeed it is in this way that the national education system can be most effective, both for the individual and the nation. (Dale, 1983, pp. 242–3)

Staking out the territory

It has already been suggested that the clear divisions and effective exclusiveness of post-16 education in the decades following the 1944 Education Act have been substantially challenged and at least partially demolished since the early 1970s. The result has been a growing confusion of courses, institutions, sponsors and students which, in turn, appear to have encouraged a passion for categorial thinking. Thus reports, policy statements and other commentaries on 16-plus provision are full of taxonomies, maps and lists. One of the most useful was that produced by Beryl Pratley for the Further Education Unit (FEU), *Signposts*, (1st edn, April 1980; 2nd edn, September, 1985a). In the Introduction to the second edition, Pratley says:

> In 1980 . . . it was common to hear the arrangements for the education of 16–19 year olds referred to as a 'jungle'. Looking back from the position in which we now find ourselves . . . the map of 1980 seems like highways through a desert – clear for miles, and a model of simplicity – compared with the tangle of paths now produced by competing planning authorities. (FEU, 1985, p. 1)

Pratley originally classified young people 'on the basis of whether or not the student is committed to a particular occupation' (FEU, 1980, p. 1), though by 1985 she had to recognize that choice was often deferred through lack of employment, and she therefore gave more space to vocational preparation (itself a curiously illogical product of the lack of work opportunities). Her modified categories now covered:

1 Students not yet committed to a specific career and therefore likely to be following a general education course.

2 Young people who have made a career choice and who are following a vocational course, and also those on YTS which have replaced the traditional apprenticeships (for example in the engineering and construction industries).

3 Young people who wish (or are forced) to delay occupational choice and follow pre-vocational courses of some kind: this category includes the majority of those on YTS. Pratley suggested that here 'the jungle is most impenetrable' with pre-vocational courses reaching down to 14-plus in the schools and new courses developing for students with special needs in the colleges)

Another important attempt to classify the age group was produced in 1980 by a joint group of local education authority (LEA) representatives and the DES. This was the Report of the Macfarlane Committee which addressed 'the major challenge in developing the opportunities needed by 16–19 year olds' in terms of 'the range and quality of education, its provision at reasonable cost and its development in directions reflecting the well-recognised need for more vocational education' (DES, 1980a). Their report said that 'differences in needs, aspirations and abilities of young people . . . are rightly reflected in the variety of types of course, their purposes and modes of attendance'. The resulting classification of young people contained seven groups, divided into three who leave full-time education and four who do not. An abbreviated version follows:

- those who enter employment and who receive no structured part-time education or training;
- those who enter employment but do not receive such education or training;
- those without work;
- those in full-time education aiming for higher education;
- those seeking a vocational education and aiming to begin work at some stage up to 18;
- those 'not committed to a specific vocational objective but who wish to continue their general education, personal development and pre-employment preparation';
- those who require remedial education.

The report goes on to advocate that provision be planned to meet the needs of each group.

A further attempt at classification is made in a pamphlet produced for the Schools Council in 1982 by Locke and Bloomfield, significantly titled *Mapping and Reviewing the Pattern of 16–19 Education* (Schools Council pamphlet, no. 20). The authors develop a graphical approach to producing route maps for individual students and more general maps for specific geographic, vocational or subject areas. After unsuccessful attempts to provide more comprehensive maps, they concluded that 'it would not be practicable or helpful to produce a national map as an instrument of review or guidance', thus demonstrating that the jungle had defeated them too. In all the sample maps that they produced, they begin with an initial classification of students by their 16-plus qualifications, ranging from 'no formal qualifications' through to various levels of success in CSE and O-level examinations. However, they later admit that admission of young people to specific courses is regulated by colleges and schools rather than by examining boards. The increasing use of profiles and graded tests has complicated the picture still further since the time this study was produced, and the issue of progression through the routes is still one of acute concern.

These three exercises in classification enter the problem through an attempt to rationalize on the basis of student characteristics, such as their vocational plans, their immediate destinations or their initial qualifications. This might broadly be called a 'bottom up' approach, although there is something inherently predictive about such categories. If categories exist, people will be found to fill them. More recently, official statements have increasingly employed classifications according to 'the variety of courses which has to be developed to meet the needs of 16–19 year olds' (DES, 1987b). This Circular lists the courses which are thus needed:

1 GCE A-levels, to be supplemented by AS-levels (the new Advanced Supplementary level, which represents one half of an A-level course).
2 Full-time and sandwich vocational courses leading to qualifications offered at present by the Business and Technician Education Council (BTEC), the Royal Society of Arts (RSA) and other bodies.
3 The Certificate of Pre-Vocational Education (CPVE).
4 Resat or additional O-levels and CSEs, or both (now replaced by GCSEs).
5 Off-the-job provision for YTS trainees.
6 Part-time courses leading to qualifications offered by BTEC, CGLI, RSA and other bodies.
7 Courses for young people with special educational needs not leading to formal qualifications (DES, 1987b).

The Circular goes on to say that 'the Secretary of State believes that a sound framework of courses is being established within which local education authorities can effectively, efficiently and economically meet the needs of the 16–19 age group'. Particular mention is made of the National Council for Vocational Qualifications (NCVQ). The NCVQ was set up in 1986 to 'recommend a structure of vocational qualifications in England and Wales' which would be 'relevant, comprehensible and geared to progression'. In its initial report (NCVQ, 1986), the Council recommended the establishment of a national framework' to incorporate and embrace existing vocational qualifications up to and including higher levels of professional qualifications'. The NCVQ accordingly proposed a five-level structure and of these five levels, at least three were to be accessible to students up to the age of 19. All the numerous examining and validating bodies – who between them certificate a multitudinous array of different courses for this and older age groups – are now in the process of seeking endorsement of their qualifications as exemplars of a specified level. Many questions as yet remain unanswered, such as the issue of progression between levels and the links between GCSE, A- and AS-levels and the new National Vocational Qualifications (NVQs). But their relevance to the current argument is the degree to which they contribute to the further systemization of course provision and the further delineation of categories, stages and differences.

So far we have looked at various attempts to classify students and the tracks available to them. Another set of classifications emerges when we examine how those varied tracks are the responsibility of different agencies: different kings rule in different parts of the jungle.

In the first place, let us look at the academic courses leading towards higher education, notably A- and AS-levels. For many years, this sector has been dominated by the university examining boards and all proposed syllabus changes have been the object of minute scrutiny by their representatives, who have tended to judge the adequacy of each proposal in terms of its supposed impact upon first-degree courses. In recent years, the DES has reasserted its right to shape and to control the school examination system; in the Joseph years, the reconstruction of the 16-plus examination into the GCSE shaped by national criteria rather than the university examination boards and teachers was a notable advance in this direction. The position of GCE A-levels (with their new satellite, the AS levels) is less clear. In this respect, the fate of the Higginson Report (DES, 1988b) is perplexing. This was the work of a committee set up by the Secretary of State to 'recommend the principles that should govern A level syllabuses and their assessment'. After taking much advice and evidence, it recommended a broadening of the A-level track to include five 'leaner' subjects rather than the normal three. These proposals were firmly rejected by Kenneth Baker, who saw the new and optional AS-levels as an adequate strategy for broadening the sixth-form experience, especially where they were used to provide a vocationally useful supplement to specialized study, such as might occur through the addition of maths or a modern language. Thus the Secretary of State effectively defended the *status quo* whereby A- and AS-levels remained the province of the university boards, and appeared to be indicating that the government did not relish a dilution of the specialized and academic nature of the present A-level track. More recently, however, there are signs of change: the newly established Secondary Examinations and Assessment Council has offered advice to the Secretary of State specifically on the development of 'general principles to govern A and AS examinations with a view to having an improved system in place by 1994' to include 'controls on standards, syllabus development and progression from GCSE' (DES press release, 268/89, 22 August 1989).

Turning now to vocational and pre-vocational education and training, we find a diminished DES presence, although this is contested ground and the picture is far from clear-cut. Vocational courses are traditionally strongly shaped by those bodies who examine and validate them and indeed it is sometimes said that they are insufficiently close to industry and other employers. Some of these bodies, such as CGLI and RSA, are independent organizations with charitable status, solely dependent for their very survival on the revenue they receive from examining. Others, notably BTEC, are semi-autonomous government agencies. Although the DES and other government departments have considerable influence over these bodies, on a day-to-day basis they operate with substantial independence. This has been clearly demonstrated by the vigour with which they have extended their reach into pre-vocational education.

Over the past decade, courses in non-advanced further education have increasingly been influenced by the FEU, a semi-autonomous curriculum development body within the DES. The FEU has promoted styles of pedagogy, assessment and course construction which have deeply influenced both low-level vocational and pre-vocational courses. This impact has been as keenly felt in schools as in colleges and is therefore affecting not only provision for 16-plus but also for many at 14-plus. Although the Unit does not exercise direct control over any courses or institutions, its development work has been significant for curriculum initiatives across the board from TVEI to the YTS, and, moreover, its strategies for institutional and staff development are increasingly influencing practice well outside the world of the FE Colleges (Harland, 1987).

Nowhere is FEU influence more apparent than in the development of CPVE. This course grew out of an FEU-devised framework for one-year, pre-vocational courses, set out in the report *A Basis for Choice* (FEU, 1979). The FEU recommended that such courses should be based on a common core, expressed as 12 broad aims to be achieved through a range of 'observable performances to be expected of students and learning experiences which they should be offered'. The core was to occupy 60 per cent of the time, the remainder to be filled with 'vocational studies' and 'job specific studies'. The proposals were taken up by the CGLI who developed their '365' course in conformity with the ABC framework, and a system of assessment by profile to go with it. In October 1980, when the DES issued the policy document *Examinations 16–18* (DES, 1980a), they announced their preference for a national 17-plus examination based on the FEU/CGLI pilot rather than upon the further development of the Certificate of Extended Education (a teacher-devised sequel to the CSE examination, which was essentially subject-based and did not lend itself to the development of a vocational focus). The new qualification, which became known as the CPVE, was developed jointly by BTEC and the CGLI, with only marginal participation by either the DES or the university examining boards. It was quickly established in schools and colleges, most of which had prior experience of the 365 course. However, the law of this particular jungle is already causing problems since

BTEC has been busy undermining the edifice which they themselves helped to build. CPVE was formally launched in 1985. But already in 1986, BTEC were offering their vocationally-specific 'First Certificate' courses which are likely to attract many of the better qualified 16-plus students on the grounds that they give more assured access to the sought-after BTEC national courses at 17-plus than do the more broadly-based CPVEs.

The net effect of DES authority over general academic education, and of the validating bodies plus the FEU over vocational and pre-vocational courses, has been to reinforce a deep division between students on each side of this line. Whereas those following A-level courses (or retakes of O-levels) have remained in the tradition of subject-based courses, frequently attended by an emphasis on reception learning, didactic pedagogy and terminal examinations, those on the vocational and particularly the pre-vocational track have experienced course-based programmes with an emphasis on transferable skills, integrated assignments, experiential learning and continuous assessment which invariably includes profiles. This difference in approach naturally underlines the categorial distinctions between upper secondary students.

So far I have not specifically discussed the extent of the Manpower Services Commission's (MSC's) influence over the 16–19 sector. In the 1970s this influence was largely confined to special programmes for the young unemployed, a series of measures which culminated in 1983 with the YTS, described as a work-based programme with off-the-job training. The YTS was extended to a two-year scheme in 1986, and described by the DES as 'a permanent feature of the vocational education and training system' (DoE/DES, 1986). As such, YTS is increasingly concerned with the acquisition of specific vocational qualifications, and more elaborate arrangements are being made to secure the 'quality of training' provided. Much of that training has been and will be provided by 'sector training organizations and individual providers' but some is found inside the education system, especially where YTS has replaced the traditional apprenticeship route. However, we are concerned here with the overall structure and curriculum for the age group. The Government claims that up to half a million places are now available under the YTS, and they are putting increasing pressure on all young people not otherwise engaged in work or education/training to participate. So YTS is now covering up to 20 per cent of the age group and is therefore a very significant element of the total provision.

By the early 1980s, the MSC had moved into a more active relationship with the mainstream providers of education and training. In September 1983 the Commission began to fund the TVEI, already discussed in relation to the last two years of compulsory schooling. The pilot TVEI programmes were designed to cover a four-year span, from 14–18, and the MSC was anxious to see cooperation between schools and colleges, particularly where there was an institutional break at 16. But although new forms of collaboration could be observed in many parts of the country, TVEI at 16 became less defined than in the 14–16 age bracket. Students could not be restrained from choosing all forms of post-16 courses, including ones which bore little or no relationship to the specifically TVEI elements of their pre-16 experience; some moved across boundaries to further education colleges in other authorities; and it appeared that no more were deciding to stay on in full-time education than was the norm for the area in which they lived. Thus, although the initiative had a very considerable impact, the attempt to create coherent routes and greater continuity through the years from 14 to 18 was not spectacularly successful. Nevertheless, the MSC persisted in its attempts to influence the 16–19 curriculum: borrowing a term from HMI, their advisers sought to promote the notion of an 'entitlement' curriculum for those still in full-time education with specialist studies of whatever kind being supported by various forms of enrichment, including counselling and work experience which served to reinforce the TVEI orientation towards the world of work.

TVEI is the biggest curriculum development programme ever undertaken in Britain, with an estimated expenditure of £900 million in the mid-1990s. It has been a matter of continuing concern that such an enterprise has been in the hands of an agency of the DoE rather than of the DES. What is more, the MSC worked hard to achieve a similar dominance in relation to non-advanced further education (NAFE); in other words, that part of upper secondary education which was either vocational or pre-vocational. In 1984 the government decided that 25 per cent of NAFE should in future be contracted and directly funded by the MSC. The LEAs protested strongly and a compromise was reached. Under this agreement the MSC could provide 25 per cent of the funds, but not directly for an identified quarter of the total provision. Instead the Commission was given oversight over the *whole* of each LEA's NAFE programme and had to approve the total plan before providing its share of the funds. This 'knight's move' left the MSC in an exceedingly influential position. Furthermore, although the validating bodies still certified the actual courses, they did so in the interstices of a net where the warp was held by the MSC and the weft was increasingly gripped by the NCVQ, itself answerable to the same department as was the MSC.

In sum then, there is nothing in the overall situation which might lead us to think that the often impenetrable landscape of 16–19 provision has been sorted out since it was first described as a jungle. The student population is described in terms of what sets them apart from each other; once embarked upon a particular track, the surrounding undergrowth is so thick that a sideways jump is almost inconceivable; and there are far too many mutually competitive safari companies out there seeking to bring clients into their itinerary and nobody else's. When we add to that the growing conviction that travellers in this wilderness often seem to have arrived on a particular track by chance rather than by rational decision, we may well conclude that this territory is still frontier land.

Institutional categories: unoccupied territory?

There is perhaps only one area in 16–19 education within which a serious challenge to differentiation can be made, and in some cases is being mounted; that is in the area of institutional structures.

Some mention has already been made of significant changes in the location of 16–19 studies, as the old dichotomy of academic studies in the school-based sixth form and vocational studies in the college has broken down. This restructuring has, in many authorities, gone much further than the mere rationalization of course provision across schools and colleges. Two new types of institution have appeared: the sixth-form college, which brings sixth-formers together from a number of 'feeder' schools; and the tertiary college, which replaces both sixth forms and FE colleges, offering within one institution all those courses which may first be taken at 16-plus, and catering therefore for academic and vocational studies, for full- and part-time students, and for older students who want these same courses. The implication of both systems is that all young people leave school, as such, at 16.

In a review of the structure and ideology in upper secondary education, Reid and Holt claim that 'the greatest challenge to orthodoxy at the 16–19 level has come about not in terms of curriculum policy . . . but in the matter of organisation which is the province of agencies of local government' (Reid and Holt, 1986). The extent of this challenge is evident, therefore, in the rapid growth in the numbers of reorganized colleges. Yet in many authorities, the arguments for reorganization have been frankly resource-based. Pressures created by declining school rolls, disappointing participation rates in full-time study, and wasteful duplication of courses have necessitated the changes.

Some LEAs have come very reluctantly to this conclusion. Take, for example, the Inner London Education Authority, which long defended the principle of all-through 11–18 schools. Declining rolls forced an acknowledgement that many schools could not offer an adequate post-16 curriculum and that teaching groups were often too small to be justified on either educational or resource grounds. So elaborate consortia arrangements were established to enforce cooperation and shared teaching arrangements among groups of neighbouring schools. But the logistics of annual bargaining and daily travelling between schools proved intolerable and in the two years before its abolition in 1990, the Authority was moving towards tertiary reorganization. For the purposes of this argument, the most interesting aspect of this change of heart was that once the commitment to tertiary had been made for manifestly resource-based reasons, the educational rationale was moved in behind it.

In part the reasons are obvious, for clearly an authority must use people who are known to favour the tertiary model to lead such a restructuring process. However the conversion process is not as crude and calculating as might at first appear. The significance of multi-causality cannot be ignored, for major changes rarely come about as the result of one factor and one factor alone. Expediency produces different solutions in different settings; decisions are often shaped by left-over ideas, and constrained by such realities as left-over buildings, themselves the product of earlier (expediency-based) policies. Thus, as we review the increasing trend towards the reorganization of upper secondary education, it is probably pointless to seek to determine what precise forms of justification underpin any particular decision. And certainly a major factor has been the contribution of radical thinking about the evolution of 16–19 education.

For many people, the restructuring of the 16–19 sector represents an opportunity to extend the comprehensive principle into the post-compulsory years. Some of the arguments rest on social grounds: thus Reid and Holt (1986) say that the development of post-16 education should be towards structures which are 'more inclusive, more progressive, and less segmented' in order to combat elitism and promote equality. This argument for greater inclusiveness has clear political overtones: 'the main purpose of an educational system is . . . to provide a means of incorporating citizens' (Maden, 1987), and 'educational systems [should] encourage in all people feelings of full membership in the commonwealth rather than show on what grounds membership is to be confined or limited' (Reid and Filby, 1982). Other arguments are more explicitly educational such as the plea for 'a more gradual transition from general to intensively specialized programmes' (Whitfield, 1980). Moreover, it is said that the tertiary colleges allow for more varied combinations of general and vocational education and also simplify the process of changing early decisions. Yet other arguments concern the characteristics of the age group who are said to share a 'communality of concerns and pre-occupations' which relate directly to their transitional status between childhood and adulthood (Maden, 1987). In addition, there is a powerful pragmatic argument based on the successes of the existing colleges (see, for example, Janes et al, 1985).

As more and more reorganization takes place, the spaces in which the prevailing categories might come to be challenged are increasing. One must not over-state the case because there have been notable instances where government has resisted LEA proposals in the interests of preserving traditional school sixth forms where they are large and well-supported, and has thus thwarted attempts to develop a coordinated system within a given area. But the imperatives of Conservative economic theory must, ultimately, favour supply side arguments and the chances are that the long-term future lies with the unified institutions.

Differentiation can, of course, survive the rationalization process if exclusive categories are sustained by college procedures and structures. Yet the aspirations of shared experience, equal respect, and an emphasis on personal and social development, are in large measure within the sphere of institutional discretion. There is absolutely no reason why they should not be pursued on the ground.

Conclusion

The story told in this chapter is manifestly one which embodies the *leit-motif* of English education in the twentieth century. That theme is one of the struggle between two competing principles: namely, the endorsement of existing inequalities versus the promotion of increasing equality. In the 1970s it seemed that the site for this contest might shift to the upper secondary years; indeed Reid and Holt argue that it is crucial to contest the issue of segmentation in the 16-plus years, for without progress in this sector, 'the way is open for assaults on the progress which has been made towards a common curriculum for 11–16 year olds in comprehensive schools (Reid and Holt, 1986, p. 100). But I have attempted to show that over the past few years, not only has segmentation post-16 increased, but also that the Conservative cause of differentiation during the compulsory years has been, and is being, notably advanced. Thus is seems that the tide of ideological confrontation between meritocracy and communality has once again receded to the lower secondary years and any discussion of 16–19 issues had better start from that fact. Yet it has left behind some useful flotsam in the form of new institutions for the 16–19s. For it is here that educators may find space to explore how we can have legitimate differentiation without intolerable division.

Chapter 3

The Education Reform Act: A Missed Opportunity for 16-plus

Nanette Whitbread

For over a decade before the Education Reform Bill was thought of, it was becoming clear that legislation was needed to facilitate the responsive evolutionary changes in educational provision for the 16–19 age group that were occurring in many parts of the country to improve access and widen opportunity. Existing regulations were being bent, pragmatically reinterpreted and even flouted to accommodate curricular change and piecemeal government initiatives that necessitated more coherent provision across schools and colleges of further education. Even so, retention and age participation rates in Britain lagged alarmingly behind those in competitor industrial countries.

The Macfarlane Report, *Education for 16–19 Year Olds* (DES, 1980a), reviewed the diverse patterns of post-compulsory educational provision that had evolved by the end of the 1970s and concluded that there was urgent need for coherent policies and planning for the 16–19 age group by each local education authority (LEA). The variety of linked courses, local consortia, tertiary schemes and colleges has continued to evolve since then in parallel with the considerable curricular change which prompted such links and structural reorganization in the first place. Innovation continued to be constrained, however, by the persistence of traditional attitudes and structures which separate school and further education cultures. Meanwhile, the demographic imperative of declining numbers in this age group encouraged schools and colleges to develop curricula to attract and cater for a wider clientele, just as the prospect of unemployment encouraged some of those who would otherwise have quit education to consider continuing in the hope of improving their prospects by gaining marketable qualifications. The Further Education Unit (FEU), established in 1977, gave a lead through a Study Group set up a year later, which led to a joint Working Party and then a pilot project with the City and Guilds of London Institute (CGLI), developing an innovative curriculum concept to encourage informed vocational choice. The report on this work was published as *A Basis for Choice* (FEU, 1979). In 1982, the DES announced the Government's intention to introduce the Certificate of Pre-Vocational Education (CPVE) at 17-plus, designed to lead directly into courses for recognized qualifications awarded by the Business and Technician Education Councils (BTECs), and the Royal Society of Arts (RSA). In September 1983, the first pilot schemes for the 14–18

Technical and Vocational Educational Initiative (TVEI) launched by the Manpower Services Commission (MSC) began in schools. Both CPVE and TVEI required collaborative curriculum development across schools and further education locally.

The need identified by the Macfarlane Report was fast becoming more urgent in the years immediately following it. Yet 16-year-olds had to contend with a system that was still failing to meet their diverse needs and aspirations flexibly and responsively enough in the context of rapid change in the economy and labour market, despite curriculum innovation. It would have been reasonable to expect such a major piece of educational legislation as the 1988 Education Reform Act to address the matter.

The 1987 Education Reform Bill was seriously flawed by coming about as an accretion of disconnected proposals to which the Government had become committed. These included populist reformist measures combined with anti-progressive pressures from the Hillgate Group and their erstwhile Black Paper antecedents, all largely in the schools sector; a determination to curb the power of LEAs, particularly the ILEA; and somewhat more developed ideas for restructuring higher education so as to make it more amenable to market forces and more directly subservient to the supposed needs of the economy. None of these commitments related directly or specifically to post-compulsory education from 16-plus, but most impinged on it in significant and potentially damaging ways. These interconnections and implications were consistently ignored by Ministers and civil servants.

Legislation on higher education had been on the political horizon for some time and was heralded by the White Paper *Higher Education: meeting the challenge*, published on 1 April 1987 (DES, 1987a), and two more detailed DES consultation papers in April and May. The 1987 Conservative Election Manifesto and various postscrips on schools during the election campaign provided the agenda for the Education Reform Bill. Meanwhile, the DES issued Circular 3/87 *Providing for Quality: the pattern of organization to age 19*, on 6 May (DES, 1987b). This revived the Macfarlane Report's notion of coherent planning for 16–19 provision as a whole, asking LEAs 'to review their non-advanced provision for the whole of this age group and to take any appropriate action in the interests of educational effectiveness and value for money'. A tertiary perspective with improved access seemed clearly in view. 'New arrangements should offer an education better suited to the needs of pupils and students of all abilities than would be offered by those they replace'. Given the timing of this Circular, the Bill might have been expected to take some cognizance of the need to plan coherently for 16-plus education. This should at least have been on the agenda.

Of the four main consultation papers concerned with legislative proposals in the schools sector issued in July 1987, two contained obvious implications for education at 16-plus but neither drew attention to this aspect. The proposals for financial delegation to individual schools clearly implied that the LEAs could lose their ability to plan 16–19 provision and resources across the system, and the procedure whereby an individual school could decide to opt out from the local authority to direct grant-maintained status would entirely remove its 16-plus provision from the scope of LEA planning.

In August 1987, as an apparent afterthought, the DES issued a consultation paper *Maintained Further Education: financing, governance and law* (DES, 1987d). While proposing financial delegation to individual colleges, this paper recognized the problem of reconciling such autonomy with the need to plan overall provision, especially at 16–19, but failed to resolve it. Instead it postulated 'a continuing framework of strategic planning by the LEA' without elucidating how this might be achieved. Indeed, the problem was further confounded by a suggestion that 'it would be appropriate for some colleges to have corporate status – while remaining within the local authority FE sector'.

The organizational and personnel structures of the DES and LEAs reflect the traditional division between schools and further education. It is seldom if ever any department's, committee's or individual official's responsibility to view 16–19 educational provision as a whole. Ironically, the Manpower Service Commission (MSC) came nearest to doing so, but from a training and employment, rather than from an educational, viewpoint. As a result, its successive interventions via the Youth Opportunities Programme (YOP) through to the two-year Youth Training Scheme (YTS) distorted the scene, further fragmented provision, and competed with educational opportunities. Paradoxically, the MSC's own other initiative, the TVEI for the 14–18 age group, has itself had to compete at the 16-plus stage with the short-term financial attraction of YTS.

It is against this background of long identified need, outmoded administrative structures, missed opportunities and political priorities that the Education Reform Act's contribution to improving access and achievement at 16-plus must now be assessed.

The Act might, on the face of it, seem to give greater security of educational opportunity and choice at the end of compulsory schooling. Section 120 makes it the unequivocal 'duty of every local education authority to secure the provision for their area of adequate facilities for further education'. Moreover, this is redefined to cover full-time and part-time post-compulsory vocational and recreational education and training. Thus, provision of further education is now on a firm legal basis, and is more broadly defined in a manner that should extend opportunities for 16-year-olds, even though 'adequate facilities' are no better defined than before.

It might seem, too, that explicitly absolving LEAs from any duty to provide higher education – transferring to the new Polytechnics and Colleges Funding Council (PCFC) sector those colleges whose courses are predominantly at higher education levels – may encourage them to focus more clearly on what has become known as non-advanced further education (NAFE) without the distraction of responsibility for extensive status-conferring advanced courses in expensive and elite institutions of higher education. In some parts of the country, some limited and specific provision for 16-plus – mainly foundation art courses – is located in a predominantly higher education institution, which will acquire corporate status within the PCFC sector outside the LEA's strategic control. This is an anomaly, further fragmenting 16–19 education. Such courses must be brought within the scope of LEA planning.

Significantly, LEAs' legal duties have been extended to include provision of continuing vocational education 'to persons already in employment' and their obligation has been strengthened in respect of 'persons over compulsory school age who have learning difficulties'. These additional specific responsibilities should benefit young school leavers who go straight into work, often without qualifications, and those who had special educational needs (SEN) while at school and who therefore still need extra help either in the basic skills of literacy and/or numeracy or in acquiring recognized qualifications.

The Education Reform Act seems to have taken account of the DES 1981 review of the legal basis of further education and criticism of a significant weakness in the 1981 Education Act's failure to cover young people over 16 who were not at school. The broadened scope of further education and its obligation to provide for young people with learning difficulties were noteworthy improvements on the original Bill, as a result of intense lobbying during the parliamentary process. In response to Circular 3/87, LEAs were already in the process of undertaking major, wide-ranging reviews of 16–19 provision across their schools and further education colleges even before the Bill began its progress through parliament. These reviews will presumably now encompass their extended responsibilities under the Act, particularly regarding young people over 16 with learning difficulties but not at school. Educational prospects for 16-year-olds reaching the crucial decision-making age when compulsory schooling ends might seem to have been enhanced.

But the Act created significant discontinuities with recent and rapid evolutionary developments in 16–19 educational provision and initiatives within many LEAs. Important local initiatives are consequently now in jeopardy. Particularly at risk are plans for tertiary systems and tertiary colleges, intended to make for more coherent and comprehensive 16–19 educational provision, being more responsive to local needs and individual aspirations than the traditional division between sixth form and further education. As these boundaries became increasingly blurred and artificial at the same time as total numbers in the age group declined, more LEAs heeded the Macfarlane Report's advice that 'it is vital for authorities to review the pattern of 16–19 provision in their areas, and in doing so treat it as a whole'. Tertiary colleges or consortia schemes were being planned in various parts of the country even before Circular 3/87. But, far from facilitating their implementation, the Act puts obstacles in their way.

It repeats the separatist approach of the consultation papers and poses the same problems. Part I of the Act concerns the schools sector, Part II deals with higher and further education without cross reference to Part I, even though 16- to 19-year-old students attend institutions governed by regulations pertaining to sections in each Part. Chapter IV of Part I enables schools to opt out of their local authority and acquire grant-maintained corporate status, while Section 105 of Chapter V covers the creation of independent City Technology Colleges (CTCs). Neither type of institution, being outside LEA control, can be effectively within any coherent pattern of planned 16–19 provision. Nor can an LEA ever be sure, when proceeding with an on-going planning review, that a key school may not opt out or a CTC be set up within its area. Either eventuality would undermine sensible planning for local access, even though it need not affect opportunities for individual 16 year olds in the short term.

It was already apparent before the end of 1988 that an individual school would be able to torpedo an LEA's plans for tertiary reorganization by deciding to ballot parents on a proposal to opt out. This opens up the possibility of using the threat of opting out as a form of blackmail to prevent tertiary reorganization. In the event of a ballot, the parents of pupils over 16 in an 11–18 secondary school, who might feel that the proposed tertiary scheme or college was in their children's best interest, would themselves constitute a minority even if all of them voted against opting out. There is no means whereby 16- to 19-year-old students at the affected college, or their parents, could express their views in a ballot. This cannot reflect natural or social justice.

Local management of schools and further education colleges, with their budgets delegated to their individual governing bodies by the LEA in accordance with a formula for determining each institution's share of the LEA's general budget for that sector, has now been explained in considerable detail in Circulars 7/88 and 9/88 respectively (DES, 1988c,e). It is evident that LEAs will lose significant overall planning power for both sectors and, as they must initially determine separate general budgets for each sector, their scope for planning across the two sectors will be minimal. This probably makes sense for much that is included in the delegation requirements except 16–19 education. While there is provision for the LEAs to hold back part of their general budgets for certain costs, these are specified for each sector and the percentage restricted to a specified limit. There is no scope for discretionary exception related to 16–19 expenditure other than in respect of capital on building projects and major structural repair and maintenance. Both school and college governors will, in future, be able unilaterally to determine staffing requirements within their institutional budgets, even though the LEA remains the employer. This is but one of several ambiguities to be resolved.

There may be a possibility for some limited planning and budgetary protection of students with special educational needs. LEAs will be allowed 'to except some or all provision for statemented pupils so that it is clearly earmarked and targeted on the needs of the individual pupils concerned' in schools, and may classify special educational needs, and remedial literacy and numeracy, as areas for specific provision when allocating student numbers within the budget weighting for colleges. As it is usual for little more than 2 per cent to be statemented under the terms of the 1981 Act, it is difficult to envisage how the Warnock Report's notional further 18 per cent, likely to need some kind of special provision, can be attained.

Some attempt has been made in Circular 9/88 'to allow the authority to express its strategic intentions for the broad pattern of work in the college'. Similarly, the LEAs still have a duty under Section 17 of the Education Act (no. 2), 1986, to determine and make up an up-to-date statement of their policy for the secular curriculum in their schools. To what extent they will be able to exercise these powers, so as to plan educational provision at 16–19 across schools and colleges in such a way as to ensure open access to comprehensive tertiary provision, remains to be seen. It seems likely to be more difficult than hitherto, largely as a consequence of local management and financial delegation compounded by school opting out arrangements.

A strategy for planning the curriculum as available for all students to choose from at 16-plus is an essential prerequisite for genuine access and student choice. In the context of decreased numbers in the age group, this means tertiary planning across school and further education sectors, so that reasonably comprehensive choice can be available overall. This makes it possible for individual students to decide which institution to select for the course and subject components on offer there. For such curriculum planning to be effective, there must be curriculum-led staffing, at least some of it planned across institutions, so that appropriate specialist expertise is available, particularly for those subjects that attract a minority of students. Minority foreign languages are an obvious example, and will otherwise disappear.

Many problems very largely disappear where all post-compulsory education is provided in a system of strategically located, comprehensive tertiary colleges. But it seems likely to be extremely difficult to establish such a system now. It may be that over time, as school and college governors and managements struggle to match their budgets with parental and student demand for course and subject choice at 16-plus, there will be increased recognition of the advantages to be gained from tertiary planning. However, as financial delegation will not be completed until about 1993, there is likely to be a fairly general planning blight in the meantime.

Cooperative curriculum development across and between schools, and with colleges of further education, will inevitably become more difficult as institutions are distanced from one another by local financial management and the consequent need to work out how to apportion the cost of this, including the hidden costs in terms of staff time and other resources, as each institution becomes a cost centre. The criterion of educational benefit for students cannot be readily costed, and moreover is calculated by and for each separate institution. Yet, inter-institutional curriculum development and course planning are now crucial for 16–19 education. This is particularly the case for the one-year CPVE course taken at 16 plus to 17 plus, and the four-year TVEI courses for 14- to 18-year-olds which require collaboration even during the last key stage of the national curriculum.

It is in relation to TVEI that a remarkable example of discontinuity occurs with the Education Reform Act. A venture by the MSC into the schools sector, announced late in 1982, and with the aim of influencing the curriculum at 14–18 across schools and further education so as to encourage thereby more students to continue their education and training to at least 18 and gain recognized qualifications in the process, was always intended not only to span the two sectors but to bring them closer together in working collaboration. From the first pilot 14-plus schemes started in 100 schools in 14 LEAs in September 1983, TVEI is now well-established nationally across schools and colleges of further education in all 104 LEAs, potentially catering for much of the 14–18 age group as intended. More than any other curriculum development it has promoted, and indeed necessitated, collaboration between schools and colleges through linked courses and modules, often bringing about consortia arrangements. It has opened up access to a range of qualifications including GCE/GCSE, BTEC certificates and diplomas, City and Guilds, A- and AS-levels, various secretarial certificates, or the CPVE – which itself can lead directly into various vocational qualifications. Where collaboration has been most problematic, the result has been an unsatisfactory 2 + 2 (14–16, 16–18) version, from which many more students drop off than envisaged. TVEI encourages tertiary systems to evolve locally by bringing participating schools and colleges closer together for curriculum development and teaching. Now, the Education Reform Act seems set to make tertiary systems and TVEI collaboration more difficult by distancing institutions from each other and restricting LEAs' ability to plan. The problem of 'ownership' of students – which of the institutions they are registered with, and thus counting in the weighted units of budgetary income – is likely to become even more of an issue with financial delegation under the Act than hitherto.

The relationship between TVEI and the national curriculum at 14–16 is still unclear. Despite the assertion in the July 1987 consultation document that the latter 'will allow curriculum development programmes such as the TVEI to build on the framework' of the ten 14–16 foundation subjects, there must be some doubt about conflicting pressures, ethos and direction as well as time. The bottom-up, grass-roots curriculum development that has characterized much of TVEI, as teachers, schools and colleges took it over, would seem to fit uncomfortably with top-down, externally-designed Standard Attainment Tasks (SATs), as the national curriculum edges into the 14–16 stage. This does not bode well for the notion of 14–18 coherence, so important to TVEI, and its role in encouraging 16-year-olds to continue into further education.

In view of the announcement by the National Curriculum Coucil towards the end of 1988 that science is to be offered at two levels within the national curriculum – 12.5 per cent or 20 per cent of national curriculum time – TVEI will need to operate its equal opportunities criterion stringently and watchfully to ensure that girls do not suffer discrimination. Students taking the 12.5 per cent option pre-16, leading to a single instead of a double GCSE in science, will find themselves debarred from A-level science post-16. School governors will also need to be attentive, and must insist on monitoring how this system operates. It seems clear that in some respects the DES has at last begun to come to terms with the 16–19 issue. Paragraph 2.7 of Circular 9/88 is worth quoting in full:

A primary need will be to ensure proper coordination between provision in FHE colleges and 16–19 provision in schools and sixth-form colleges. The DES circular 'Providing for Quality: The Pattern of Organization to Age 19' emphasized the importance of considering provision for 16 to 19 year olds as a whole. Whether authorities choose to think in terms of a single planning procedure covering all their post-16 provision or separate but related procedures for schools and FE, the pattern of provision for the 16–19 year old age group needs to be coordinated. Authorities will, for example, need to take account, as they enter on the extension of the Technical and Vocational Education Initiative (TVEI) across all their secondary schools and FE colleges, of the strategy they are developing for the 16–18 phase of that initiative.

For the first time the issue is also briefly considered with reference to planning the schools sector. Paragraph 49 of Circular 7/88 states:

In planning the global amount of their expenditure available for schools, LEAs will need to have regard to the interaction of schools' 16–19 provision with provision in the FE sector. This will be part of the LEA's broader responsibility for managing the service, and will continue to be a key element in its overall strategy.

It is also true that building a firm and effective partnership between the LEA and the governing bodies of schools and colleges will henceforth be crucial. Only by working in genuine partnership with the LEA will governors come to appreciate that the interests of students, and their real access to a wide range of educational opportunities at 16-plus, must be paramount and transcend misconceived vested interests of individual institutions. LEAs, for their part, will need to develop more open communication and better public relations so that the public, especially parents and governors, understand the benefits of 16–19 overall planning.

Coordination and planning for 16–19 provision as a tertiary system across schools and colleges has never been easy. It requires determination and much good-will from the teachers and lecturers involved as well as active support by the LEA, and furthermore is time-consuming. Some local initiatives pre-date CPVE and TVEI and have provided models of good practice on which others have drawn. An example originating in 1980 illustrates some of the steps taken by the City of Bradford Metropolitan District.

A joint Working Party drafted a framework document for viable groupings of schools and colleges, setting out aims, criteria and intended coverage. It had to coordinate time-tabling sufficiently for some course packages to be made up across pairs of institutions; and involved the careers service and other personnel from the LEA. The scheme was financed by contributions from each institution's capitation and some additional central funding. Initially, each participating institution designated a senior staff member as link-person to what became, in effect, an embryo academic board for each geographical area; and two years later the LEA appointed a tutor coordinator on FE terms whose prime allegiance was to the consortium as a whole. A small core of administrative and secretarial staff was also assigned to service the consortium. Some such area liaison board, properly constituted and serviced, is clearly essential for sound management. Course and subject sub-committees can then function within a structure, while student counselling and pastoral work can be effectively incorporated. As a scheme develops it may be appropriate to make some teaching appointments to the consortium and to write commitment to working within it into job descriptions for some appointments at institutional level. An important outcome is publication of a single comprehensive brochure to enable students to make informed choices from a wide range of options which have been put together in coherent patterns of provision (see Anderson (1981), p. 71).

A prime objective is, of course, the enrichment of student choice. The number of minority A- and AS-levels that can be offered greatly increases through shared provision, and is further facilitated by the three-session day in the further education colleges and in-fill with part-time students. Those students for whom it seems individually appropriate can more readily combine A- and/or AS-levels with, for instance, BTEC or CPVE. A bonus is that some part-time courses can be integrated into the scheme, thereby adding the option of entering employment and pursuing a part-time route to further qualifications for some students who might otherwise lose contact. Indeed, it has even proved possible to incorporate a 'mode A' YTS.

To secure existing, and initiate new, schemes will require even more attention to the management structure and involvement of school and college governing bodies. Some form of liaison board of management will be essential to represent and coordinate the institutions forming a consortium, and to administer a budget contributed by them and the LEAs. It will be a real test of effective partnership between governors and LEAs. This is a matter for careful consideration in devising delegation schemes under the Act as there is not explicit provision for such tertiary systems.

The benefits of participation will have to be understood by the governors, especially by parent governors of schools and business/industry governors of colleges. Under Section 152 of the Act, at least 50 per cent of a college's governors must represent 'business, industry or any profession or . . . other field of employment relevant to the activities of the institution' or be so employed. The new governing bodies were to be appointed by September 1989, or soon after, taking on full powers under delegation schemes by April 1990. Where governors of secondary schools and colleges can be inspired by a vision of cooperative venture for coordinated 16–19 provision, their delegated powers offer them an unprecedented opportunity.

At 16-plus students need coherent, comprehensive, open access tertiary systems – a tertiary college where this is locally feasible, or some form of tertiary consortia. The object of such arrangements has to be to offer a wide and rich choice of academic, pre-vocational and vocational subjects and courses, both full-time and part-time, with flexibility to mix and match to individual needs and aspirations. That choice has to be supported by accessible and effective careers advice, and counselling for students and their parents: indeed, provision of this is an obligation on LEAs under the 1973 Education and Training Act. When it can be provided in the context of a planned tertiary system, rather than within and by individual schools or colleges which are in competition for students, it is more likely to be objectively informative and student-centred. The integrity of educational and careers counselling for students at 16-plus will be best assured as an excepted, LEA-wide service excluded from delegated budgets.

Conclusion

Increased blurring of the old curricular demarcation at 16-plus between school sixth forms and colleges of further education through curriculum development in both over the last dozen or so years – accelerated by CPVE and TVEI from the mid-1980s – made it ever more evident that reform of institutional structures was needed to match curriculum change and better serve more students in the 16–19 age group. A new tertiary phase was emerging which straddled the structural divide. Schools, colleges and LEAs struggled to develop inter-sectoral collaboration through consortia and new types of tertiary institution in the interest of students, and efficient use of scarce resources, despite regulations designed for traditional organizational structures. The DES urged LEAs to plan their 16–19 provision as a whole. Legislative reform was clearly needed to facilitate sensible tertiary reorganization to suit local circumstances.

When a bill to reform the education system came onto the political agenda, there was an opportunity to bring some degree of coherence into the confused and divided 16–19 phase. But the Education Reform Act was silent on this, while creating discontinuity, fragmentation and new obstacles to planned reorganization. The consequential circulars ostensibly required LEAs to play a strategic role yet reduced their power so to do. The losers are young people, who should be entitled to progress without hindrance at 16-plus and embark on the post-compulsory stage of education and training which can equip them for adult life. Their ability to make sensible decisions risks being constrained by LEAs' inability to plan sensibly within the new constraints created by the Education Reform Act.

As hitherto, initiatives will depend on those who appreciate the potential of coherent provision for 16–19s in some form of local tertiary system, and who are committed to trying to meet the diverse educational needs of this age group within the locality. Sadly, an opportunity was missed to encourage and facilitate such developments.

Chapter 4

The Politics of Progression: Problems and Strategies in the 14–19 Curriculum

Ken Spours

Crisis of the curriculum and structure

At the beginning of the 1990s we are confronted by two interrelated developments in the 14–19 curriculum. First, the persistence of a confused and divided structure and contradictory initiatives in education and training in England and Wales, and second, the continued interest in issues of progression. These are quite clearly linked – the more complex the structure, the greater the need to create student pathways through them. But the issue is more than one of complexity and confusion of courses and initiatives typical of the post-16 scene in England and Wales. The essential problem is concerned with the new forms of division which have arisen as the result of the vocationalization of the curriculum and the participation of new types of students in post-16 education and training in the 1980s. The 'politics of progression' is an attempt to analyse the dynamics of this division in the curriculum and in the process of certification in order to evaluate ways in which practitioners have addressed the question.

Our starting-point is the fundamental problem of stratification reflected in the ranking of different types of certification into levels of prestige. This involves the stereotyping of the award and therefore the abilities of the students involved. The stereotyping attitude can be summed up as 'judging the course rather than the student'. Those involved in learning directed towards academic qualifications are largely regarded as more able than students who are undertaking vocationally-related courses. At the same time, those taking the Certificate of Pre-Vocational Education (CPVE) have often been deemed as least able to cope with examinations and graded assessment.

The process of stratification is a complex one and goes beyond the simple academic/vocational divide of mental and manual labour. Full-time courses in post-16 education appear to reflect divisions within the labour market (see for example, Gleeson, 1985, Raffe, 1985). There are advanced academic courses for those who wish to delay entry into the labour market until the completion of higher education, for example those courses leading to A-levels. There are broader vocational courses for 'technician' and junior managerial functions reflected by a range of Business and Technician Education Council (BTEC) First and National Awards. The City and Guilds of London Institute (CGLI) and the

Royal Society of the Arts (RSA) on the other hand, offer more occupationally-specific operative and craft-related courses at several levels. Finally, there is CPVE which has often accommodated the 'undecided student' unprepared for an academic or vocationally-specific award.

These problems of stratification adversely affect to one degree or other all those students who do not attain two or three A-levels. It has had the most significant impact on the bottom 50 per cent of the cohort who find themselves in pre-vocational or basic vocational provision either at school, college or in a Youth Training Scheme (YTS). The overall effect has been to create barriers to movement between courses, and to encourage the repetition of learning which, in turn, depresses participation rates in 16–18 provision such as courses leading to A-levels or BTEC National Diplomas.

The problems of progression are a reflection of a structural crisis which embraces certification, delivery organizations and the curriculum itself, and is one of the main contributors to the low participation, attainment, and progression equilibrium which characterizes our 14–19 system. The manifestations of this crisis of structure centre upon the relationship between certification, training initiatives and providing institutions in four main areas of 14–19 provision:

1 There is a sharp break at 16 presenting problems of discontinuity for all students. In England and Wales there are discontinuities between a general subject-based curriculum leading to the General Certificate of Secondary Education (GCSE) and narrow A-level specialization; discontinuities involved in the transition between institutions, school to Further Education (FE) or work, and the lack of a systematic development of both knowledge and skills. The greatest problems are experienced by those making a transition to vocational courses or to training schemes at 16. The Technical and Vocational Education Initiative (TVEI) has aimed to develop continuity for the 14–18 age range, but the emergence of the national curriculum, with its emphasis upon a general education subject-based approach has, at least until now, re-emphasized the break at 16 rather than a longer period of transition.

2 The duplication of certification, particularly for those staying on full-time at 16 who do no A-level courses, is illustrated by the competition between CPVE and BTEC First Awards. The absence of a common foundation framework for one-year provision at 17-plus has encouraged barriers to movement to higher awards such as BTEC National and A-levels, with learning delays. There is also a high incidence of the repetition of learning where students are directed from pre-vocational to basic vocational courses.

3 There is a conflict found in the area of YTS between basic work-based occupational training, as a response to youth unemployment, and gaining

qualifications for progression to further study. The work of the National Council for Vocational Qualifications (NCVQ) should be evaluated to see if it can resolve this issue.

4 The problem of access and attainment for 16- to 18-year-olds is due to highly exclusive and specialized A-levels with norm-referenced assessment systems, which result in a high failure rate and therefore narrow patterns of recruitment. There is still a large gap both in terms of curriculum and progression potential between the prestigious A-levels and the 'equivalent' vocational awards of BTEC and CGLI which has adversely affected participation rates in comparison with our European partners.[1]

This paper focuses upon two of these areas, which have been central to changes in education and training in the 1980s. First, the emergency initiatives in relation to youth unemployment and the ways in which these brought into the full-time education system those who would previously have found unskilled jobs. Second, the focus upon work-based training and accreditation and the divisions between this and academic awards. The immediate roots of both of these developments can be found in the New Training Initiative of 1981 and the agenda which it created for the rest of the decade.

At the beginning of the 1990s, as the focus begins to move away from the young trainee to adults, and from basic training to the wider problems of attainment 14–19 and academic awards such as A-levels, there are new problems to be confronted. The focus is now less upon skills for unemployment and more upon high skills and knowledge for new technological and work developments. The spotlight is therefore increasingly turning to the division between the academic and the vocational courses as Britain has to compare its 14–19 system (and therefore participation and attainment levels) with other European nations. A wide variety of organizations and commentators are critical of the relationship between academic and vocational learning and certification, though there are a variety of solutions being offered (see Baker, 1989; CBI, 1989; SEAC, 1989; TUC, 1989).

It can be argued that one of the most pressing tasks now is how to forge a pathway to a more unified framework of certification which embraces the dualities academic and vocational, part-time and full-time study, 14–19 and 19-plus. The first step involves an evaluation of both the forces and processes which have promoted and inhibited the development of such a policy in the 1980s if we are to be able to develop coherent and detailed strategies in the 1990s.

The concept of progression in the early and late 1980s

The concept of progression, both as a policy objective and as a set of explicit practices, is a relatively recent innovation and is immediately associated with both the qualifications and client groups of the so-called 'new vocationalism'. Previous to the New Training Initiative (1981), progression had been a series of implicit practices around established qualifications systems and was seen very much in terms of movement *within* academic and vocational systems of qualifications (largely associated with apprenticeship), which had little connection with one another. The other dominant issue was transition from school to jobs in the labour market. The system could be basically described as stable but divided in which the bottom 50 per cent simply progressed by 'job hopping'.

The economic crisis of the early 1970s began to erode this situation. The growth of mass youth unemployment in the late 1970s and the early 1980s decimated jobs for 16-year-olds and brought a further decline in apprenticeships. The Government responded with the extension of training and post-16 opportunities, in part to keep 16- and 17-year-olds off the unemployment register. The quantitative extension of vocational education and training resulting from these initiatives was designed for those young people who would not necessarily have been able to travel the academic or apprenticeship routes, and who were most affected by the drop in demand for relatively unqualified labour. Whatever the motive, the creation of YTS and the 17-plus qualification CPVE nevertheless raised wider and more complex issues of access and movement within public provision than had previously been the case. There was now need to develop progression routes not only between different types of qualifications but also from YTS and work-based learning back into full-time provision. It was the sudden inclusion of the bottom 50 per cent in post-16 provision, intensifying a trend which had begun in the mid-1970s, that led to a new-found interest in the concept of progression.

But the progression focus shifted throughout the 1980s in response to different vocationalizing initiatives. Since 1985, and in view of its relative success in politically containing unemployment, the Government has been chiefly concerned with the reform and modernization of the vocational education and qualifications system. This led to the establishment in 1986 of the National Council for Vocational Qualifications (NCVQ). An important element of the analysis of this paper is to examine the consequences of this extension of state intervention which aims to offer a wider basis of training but through competitive and privatized means of delivery. The task of a 'politics of progression' involves an examination of the ways in which all these factors have affected progression opportunities in recent years: the mixture of intervention and market forces; the role of the Department of Education and Science/ Training Agency (DES/TA); and the relationship between exam boards and between the examining and validating bodies (EVBs) and delivering institutions.

There are two historical questions which must be asked if we are to learn lessons from the 1980s:

1 What kind of impact did the *contextual* issue of the relationship between the delivery agencies have upon the coherence of provision? And to what

degree do these problems still persist and continue to provide the operational context for future reform?

2 To what degree did decisions about the *content* of the curriculum affect the chances of producing a more coherent system? And in retrospect, are there mistakes in curriculum design worth avoiding?

Progression as a fragmented perspective in a fragmented system
A unified system requires a unifying perspective. The concept of progression has the potential to provide both an overview and connective thinking because it emerged out of a criticism of division. But even the concept of progression itself is not immune to division.

Reference to progression is now found in most post 14- and 16-plus educational documents. There are, however, a variety of perspectives and a diverse terminology. A range of terms and concepts can be included under its umbrella, and these are: access to courses and institutions, continuity of learning, recurrence of education, transition to the labour market, maturation of intellectual work, movement between types of qualifications, movement between different levels within a qualifications system, vertical and horizontal progression associated with the workplace, and credit accumulation and certification. The diversity of terms reflects not only the real complexity of the concept but, more practically, the fact that there are different notions of progression in relation to different problems and locations in the 14–19 and 19-plus curriculum. The concept itself appears to reflect the fragmentation of the system it is meant to cohere.

One of the most important differences applies to whether the term 'progression' is seen in an individualized or structural way. It can be used to describe personal progress through a complex and confusing system. Or it can be a series of perspectives to examine the policy and practices of a system of certification, its delivering institutions and the degree to which these facilitate individual progression. A broader structural analysis can draw upon four interlocking dimensions:

- movement between different types of qualification;
- movement between levels within a qualifications system;
- transition between different institutions;
- continuity of learning.

As we will see, all of these dimensions are present in all four areas of the progression focus outlined earlier, but in each case one or other of these dimensions predominate. In an analysis of two of the areas – duplication of provision at 16-plus and the movement towards work-based accreditation – I want to refer in particular to problems of progression which make it a concept of the 1980s; the problem of movement between different types of qualifications (first discussed in the vocational preparation debates of 1981) and movement within a qualifications framework (arising out of the work of the NCVQ in the mid-1980s).

Duplication of certification and problems of progression at 17-plus

CPVE is now on the decline, with less than 30,000 registrations out of a year cohort of over 400,000. It has declined most rapidly in FE colleges but the take-up is more stable in schools. This increasingly marginal role in post-16 is, however, in an inverse relationship to its educational significance. Due to its aims of providing a framework for the curriculum, accreditation and institutional collaboration, CPVE was, and still is in many ways, the most important post-16 curriculum development of the last decade. There are, however, other reasons for reflection on the CPVE experience. From 1985 onwards it has been the most focused rallying point among teachers for the development of progression routes and practices in local education authorities (LEAs) and institutions; and more than any other initiative, it has enabled progression to become part of educational common sense.

However CPVE has been both victim and cause of the duplication and fragmented provision and of the competition between exam boards and institutions. It is no longer a serious contender as a framework for the rationalization of certification. With the stringent efforts to preserve its small part of the market, the Joint Board and CPVE itself have become part of the problem. As we will see, the same phenomenon of duplication of provision appears to be happening with NVQs and AS-levels. So to go back to our original question: what underlies this fragmenting tendency and to what extent have these been affected by curriculum decision-making? The main attempt to provide an explanation is the notion of tertiary tripartism.

Tertiary tripartism: the system of delivery and content of the curriculum
The phenomenon of stratification and differentiation has been referred to as 'tertiary tripartism' (Ranson, 1984; Green, 1986; Radnor et al, 1989). The concept has been discussed largely from the viewpoint of social control and the division between types of knowledge, or as reflections of the labour market (Gleeson, 1985; Raffe, 1985). Green, however, takes the discussion of tripartism into an analysis of more detailed issues of curriculum differentiation in FE. I would like to take this analysis further and reflect upon the efforts of the past eight years or so to 'promote progression' in particular from the tier referred to as the 'tertiary modern'. Like Green, I am interested in exploring curriculum differentiation but specifically in relation to the problems faced by practitioners in opening up movement between courses. Facilitating progression can be seen as a means of challenging stratification which is seen to 'lock students into pre-existing class and gender divisions' (Raffe, 1983). Tertiary tripartism is, in fact, a metaphor to describe a complex process of stratification in 16–19 provision; in reality, there

are more than three strata of courses and many more barriers. Tripartism analysis has therefore to be developed to take into account the specific form of barriers to progression, as a strategic guide to practitioners and planners in their attempts to overcome them.

Specific inhibitors of progression are the differences between content of learning, methods of assessment and structure of courses and the ways in which these differences are reinforced by institutional organization. Moving between pre-vocational, vocational and academic provision is made more difficult by the lack of comparability of not only content (extensively discussed by both Ranson and Green), but above all, patterns of assessment and the structure of course organization (see Spours, 1988a). A well-known example is the suspicion that many admissions tutors have of summative profiles because of the assumption that high grades in GCSE are the most accurate indicator of general ability and that profiling takes place in 'unregulated' conditions. Suspicion is at its highest when students are arriving from a different type of institution.

I would like to explore the respective roles of examining and validating bodies (EVBs), and the ideology of pre-vocationalism and institutional competition in maintaining or challenging this type of division. This dynamic between EVBs, involving local practitioners assumptions about the nature of the curriculum, can be examined in three related areas:

1 The role of validating and examination boards in the reform of curriculum and accreditation.
2 The ideology of pre-vocationalism, the segmenting of the student population and educational assumptions which have weakened the design-base of CPVE.
3 The relationship between differentiation of certification and local institutional competition in developing stratification and barriers to movement.

The varied focus of this analysis would suggest that the forces for fragmentation are not simply to be found at governmental level but are present in the various delivering agencies, both national and local, and within the practices of teachers themselves.

The role of market-led validation and examination bodies
The most seriously flawed assumptions which have underpinned decision-making about the organization of 17-plus certification are those concerned with the role of the examination and validating bodies. The DES has assumed that private organizations would voluntarily cooperate to rationalize provision. The competitiveness and entrepreneurism of all the validating bodies have, in practice, resulted in complete failure to produce a more coherent framework of certification. The idea of a voluntary relationship between competing validating bodies is in marked contrast to the more comprehensive organization of

qualifications in Scotland where SCOTVEC is responsible for a whole system of broad and vocational modules in the Scottish National Certificate.[2]

The roots of division and stratification should have been apparent from the beginning. At the outset, all the participating bodies, at least in principle, accepted the case for the rationalization of provision. The way in which the validating bodies went about their 'cooperation' soon showed that this voluntaristic relationship was untenable. The RSA very quickly withdrew from the Joint Board, both on educational and economic grounds, and has since produced its own range of pre-vocational and vocational qualifications. BTEC introduced the First Award in 1986 which in many respects competes for the same group of students who could be involved in CPVE. As the effects of the competitive relationship between the exam boards became clearer, the FEU, which had been centrally involved in promoting CPVE, criticized the entrepreneurial role of these bodies (FEU, 1985b).

The basis of the problem was both economic and educational. Those validating bodies which operate as self-financing charities depend upon maximizing their revenue from examination fees. The basic logic of economic self-interest has consistently worked to undermine any will to cooperate. But the issues which articulated the economic self-interest were in fact educational.

The concept of 'pre-vocational' at 17-plus and the design base of CPVE
It can be argued that the structural problem of competing interests was in fact crystallized by disagreements about the educational ideologies underpinning CPVE. Both in its design and implementation, an area of considerable contention has been the range of students for whom it was intended. CPVE has vacillated between being a curriculum framework for a broader cohort of students within which a range of certification could be taken (as promoted by the Joint Board itself and the FEU), and being an award for those students who had under-achieved within the school-system pre-16. Despite the aspirations to be a framework, it has never shaken off the image of a low-level course. The reasons for it being regarded predominantly as an award for under-achievers is not just to be found in DES policy or the competition between EVBs and between local institutions. The ghettoization of CPVE was aided and abetted by the curriculum decisions which underpinned its design base and the educational practices which resulted (see Chapter 13).

A central contradiction was the concept of 'pre-vocationalism' at 17-plus. Existing critiques of CPVE have emphasized its place within the New Vocationalism, the rejection of the CEE route and its appropriation by FE (Ranson, 1984). But the segmentation of the student population was also the result of its appropriation by FE lecturers committed to general education and their counterparts in school sixth forms, who argued for the need to design a curriculum for the student who was vocationally undecided. The problem was that the notion of 'undecided' became equated with 'low level'. What emerged, not surprisingly, was that 'pre-vocational' became *a type of student*, rather than *a stage of development* which all students go through.

The concept of pre-vocalisation at 17-plus directly informed major curriculum decisions and helped provide the educational space for the creation of a highly vocational BTEC First Diploma. While both awards have many curricular aspects in common, CPVE was seen as lower status not only because of its emphasis upon vocational exploration, but because it adopted a different and, in retrospect, what can be seen as a virtually unregulated approach, to assessment and course structure. It had, and still has, a profile system which is predominantly accountable to the student rather than to external standards, together with a loosely-structured approach to vocational modules (Spours, 1988a). The emphasis upon vocational exploration and core competence was not always balanced by more structured approaches to grouping vocational modules which might provide for specialization as well as breadth. The way in which CPVE was to become defined, particularly in school-based schemes, was simply not a broad enough expression of learning intentions or educational/training needs at 17-plus. Students who were vocationally-focused flocked to BTEC First Diploma, whereas CPVE had only a limited appeal to those wanting to take several GCSEs. More than any other award its image came to depend directly on its progression prospects. These have not been at all bad but good local progression patterns could not reverse the adverse characterization of its curricular design and the image of catering for low achievers.[3] These problems began to be addressed in a limited way following the evaluation of CPVE and the review of the core competences and reorganization of the vocational modules (CPVE Joint Board, 1988a). However, as far as its status in FE colleges is concerned the evaluation has come too late. CPVE invited rejection from significant groups of students who either did not associate themselves with its aims or who perceived that it would be rejected by employers or FE admissions tutors.

These curricular decisions in a competitive environment were to prove fatal. The emergence of BTEC First Diploma was the result both of BTEC entrepreneurism and a symptom of the underlying contradictions of the Joint Board relationship and of CPVE itself. Examining boards with different pre-vocational and vocational traditions were expected to agree to subsume part of their provision, and to persuade their existing clients to accept the arrangement. The problems lay in the fact that there were differing views of what was pre-vocational and what was vocational. The outcome of this voluntarist relationship was a curricular compromise, with CPVE looking like a more elaborate City and Guilds 365. At this point, BTEC, unable to persuade many business studies heads of department in FE to accept the settlement, took fright at the prospect that they might go to other examining boards.

The relationship between a market approach and problems of progression

The dependence of the reform process upon private examining bodies trying to retain their clients, and the narrow definition of the student target-group supported by a differentiated curricular design base, has produced what can be termed a 'syndrome of duplication and stratification'. The continuation of competing certification has produced a situation in which schools and colleges have had the choice of alternative awards constructed along more traditional lines. More able students have continued to be entered for academic or vocationally-specific awards. Just as important has been the market demand from the students and their parents, knowing that employers still take a relatively traditional view of certification. There are notable exceptions to this picture when innovative individuals and course teams have taken advantage of local circumstances to produce a broader recruitment pattern to CPVE, but rarely has this constituted the dominant trend, nor has it significantly altered the popular image of the award.

The process of student differentiation has also been informed by institutional self-interest. The propensity of schools to use CPVE to boost sixth-form numbers and for college departments to use BTEC First to 'own' students has been documented in details in local studies (see, for example Spours and Baron, 1988). Some schools have tried to use CPVE as a rationalizing framework by offering one year sixth-form provision in the form of CPVE core and vocational studies together with GCSEs in additional studies. Many schools, however, have simply attempted to hang on to students, justified by the assertion that they need a supportive environment, and in the process have developed separate pre-vocational provision for this 'new sixth'. In colleges on the other hand, the assertion of self-interest is based upon the relative autonomy of heads of department in determining course provision. Many are concerned either to keep up departmental numbers or to have relatively coherent provision to operate. There is virtual unanimity that BTEC First, as a vocationally-specific grouped award, has been easier to operate departmentally than CPVE, which involves a great deal of cross-institutional cooperation. The prevailing solution has therefore been that general and continuing education departments have tended to 'own' CPVE while vocational departments have concentrated upon BTEC First or RSA awards. In many cases during the last two years, CPVE in colleges has been relegated into special needs provision.

The impulses for stratification appear, therefore, to come not only from market-oriented exam boards but also from practitioners' responses at a local level and as a result of institutional competition. The analysis of exam-board competition must also be supplemented by an explanation of how curriculum ideas underpinning CPVE themselves contributed to stratification by focusing on the assumed needs of a relatively small and highly problematical group of students, rather than building a curriculum framework which had a more than even chance of embracing the majority of students at 17-plus. To achieve this would have involved reducing the educational grounds for the emergence of BTEC First Award.

NCVQ and progression

The National Council for Vocational Qualification (NCVQ) was established in 1986 with the aims, amongst others, of rationalizing and modernizing the system of vocational qualifications, and also of bridging the unhelpful divide between academic and vocational qualifications. In practice NCVQ has been approving (or 'kitemarking') existing vocational qualifications and attempting to locate them across four levels – Basic, Standard, Advanced and Higher (NCVQ, 1987). It is also now involved with a further phase, one of including professional qualifications at Level 5.

The effect upon vocational qualifications will be significant. All qualifications will have to satisfy employment-led competence defined by lead-industry bodies. There will also be a movement away from grouped awards towards more modular approaches. Learning will be recognized and accredited in different settings, particularly the workplace. Qualifications will be freed of time constraints which will enable the student to accumulate credit on a personal basis. The intention is that progression will be simplified and unnecessary barriers removed. Access to a level will be based upon accreditation of prior learning (colleges as assessment centres) and easier movement due to the development of unit credit accumulation and transfer based upon modular arrangements.

There are, however, three major problems inhibiting NCVQ from realizing these aims. NCVQ (or more precisely the lead-industry bodies whose views it articulates) have insisted that work-based competence be the sole basis of vocational qualifications. While this may meet employers' immediate training needs, it nevertheless contributes to a widening gap between vocational and academic qualifications, where the trainee's progression route is very much within vocational qualifications rather than being able to move between different types of qualifications. It remains to be seen whether or not NCVQ will adopt a broader and more flexible approach to the issue of competence in the process of bringing professional awards into the structure of vocational qualifications.

National Vocational Qualifications (NVQs) are essentially an attempt to bring employers into the centre of the validation process. But it must be questioned whether the majority of employers are interested in sponsoring trainee progression and meeting individual need. There does not seem to be a real impulse for progression within the framework since many employers may settle for basic training for most, and advancement for a few. There is also the added problem that the NVQ framework currently does not provide the broader skills or knowledge required to meet the requirements of a higher level (Tait, 1989).

In this sense, work-based competence is about 'doing the job' as opposed to 'future banking' and developing the potential for progression. It remains to be seen whether or not the development of generic units which can be seen as a movement away from purely an occupationally dominated approach will open up progression either between the levels of the framework, or across occupational sectors and across academic and vocational qualifications (NCVQ, 1989).

The NCVQ preoccupation with outcomes, and their apparent indifference to the issues of learning and delivery, have always created tensions among educationalists and EVBs. There are currently differences with BTEC whose validation process is dominanted by issues of delivery, and in particular by a whole-course integrated approach (see Jackson, 1989). There are of course other differences with academic examining boards, who themselves are interested in examining outcomes but who have a very different concept of knowledge. Here lies a real danger of further proliferation in which certain low-level and occupationally-oriented awards will be kitemarked but others, and in particular BTEC awards, could remain outside the system. We could well be faced with the situation of having both existing vocational qualifications *and* national vocational qualifications.

The real problem of the NCVQ perspective is that a radical approach to access and modularization within an occupationally-specific framework comprises an approach to progression across occupational boundaries and across different types of qualifications. It has been argued that as a result, the responsibility for development of the broader framework for modularization and progression currently lies with LEAs and institutions. (Spours, 1989, Brotherton, 1989).

Evaluation of progression strategies: the issue of personal and course progression
The problems of duplication of certification at 17-plus and the narrowness of the NCVQ approach to knowledge and skill raise the question of the type of progression strategies to be followed. Should practitioners and curriculum planners develop *personal* progression or *course* progression strategies? At present, many progression initiatives, reflected in LEA post-16 or TVE extension plans, appear to be moving towards a personalized system of progression which implicitly accepts that there is division between certification and mismatches of learning. Personal progression strategies can be seen as a way of helping individuals to find their way through the progression maze (the idea of overcoming confusion of provision) as opposed to changing the curriculum and accreditation structures which contribute to stratification.

The approach to organizing progression in academic provision has always been, and still is, a local affair, though there exists prevailing benchmarks such as five grade Cs or better at GCSE to enter three A-levels (see Goacher, 1984). In the field of vocational qualifications during the 1980s, the EVBs, and in particular the Joint Board and BTEC, have devolved responsibillity for decisions on progression to an institutional and LEA level. They have provided general guidance but have not recommended particular progression strategies. This is entirely in keeping with a market-led approach in which it is left to LEAs and institutions to produce a process of rationalization of provision and to organize local progression agreements.

Local progression strategies
Local progression strategies have arisen principally in relation to progression from CPVE, though they are now becoming more generalized to include practices such as records of achievement as a means of organizing movement between a range of provision. A key development within CPVE progression strategies has been the building of an understanding and dialogue between CPVE and receiving tutors. This relationship revolves around receiving tutors developing new processes for recognizing competence in students coming from CPVE or other pre-vocational/vocational provision.[5] The emergence of CPVE has transformed thinking about progression due to the very weaknesses of its design base and the uncertainties about standards of attainment.

Prior to the development of YTS and vocational preparation provision, progression was based upon a relationship of 'trust and tolerance' of a set of accepted and established practices and parameters in the academic and, to a lesser extent, technical/vocational qualifications. Progression was, and still is in many respects, based upon 'equivalence' between course grades. This implicit acceptance of external standards provides the link between 'sending and receiving' tutors. CPVE, however, represents a dramatic change in this kind of thinking. What has replaced equivalence of grades is a struggle to codify competence statements (by profile statements or key criteria with supporting examples) and provide an environment in which they can be evidenced by a portfolio of work and supporting statements from CPVE tutors.

These local progression agreements have produced mixed results. In some cases they have significantly improved movement to higher courses such as BTEC National Diploma, though not evenly across all subjects or vocational areas (see Spours, 1988b). Local progression agreements, however, are very time consuming and despite some positive results there is an imbalance between the amount of effort being put into this process and the prospects for permanent success. The whole process is vulnerable to the attitudes of the receiving tutor and the institution, and how they interpret the quality of CPVE provision or other basic or pre-vocational provision. These attitudes are also shaped by the impact of material and institutional factors such as supply/demand for places, particularly in prestigious courses.

In the first instance, the most positive outcome of personal progression strategies has not been a dramatic improvement in student progression across the board, but a raising of staff consciousness of progression issues and practices, and improvements in institutional collaboration. Local progression strategies can be legitimately judged by the degree to which they create more flexible attitudes towards student achievement by introducing real changes in the interview process, and in the recognition of competence by presentation of personal portfolios or any other means. But their limitation and vulnerability lies in the fact that they do not really reform provision because their main focus has been, by and large, on access and reception procedures. Local progression strategies can, in fact, be seen to be a symptom of the problem of 14–19 progression because their central purpose is to 'manage' routes through fragmented and stratified provision rather than to change the structure of accreditation itself.

Lessons from recent progression initiatives

The most obvious lesson from evaluation of progression issues in both CPVE and NVQs is the need to rethink and to design a framework which is capable of embracing different types of qualifications. Such a framework will have to promote a balance of vocational breadth and depth, relate vocational and academic learning, encourage the development of a post-16 core, and have a clear and common assessment procedure based upon both external recognition and high levels of accountability to the student.[6] The framework in fact has to be able to break down the syndrome of division based upon curricular differentiation between content, assessment and structure.

This type of accreditation framework, however, has to be able to encourage the EVBs and local institutions into more collaborative relations, with the aim of raising participation, attainment and progression levels in which they can all benefit economically. The framework should attempt to move the EVBs away from cut-throat competition which damages progression across different qualifications, to a form of 'cooperative competition' in which their modules compete with an agreed framework of interlocking accreditation. This can be seen either as a more rational arrangement of the market, or the first step towards the creation of a unitary system of qualifications embracing all certification in the 14–19 field. But a move towards a more unitary system will require high levels of government intervention, the total reform of the EVBs and a more unified concept of the academic and vocational curriculum. This is part of a future rather than a current political agenda, and in educational terms has only begun to be explored.

In the meantime, LEAs and institutions are trying to organize progression routes and learning pathways and open up new ways of thinking about recognizing competence as a basis for access. The criteria by which we judge progression strategies, however, are not simply about whether they improve personal prospects at a local level, but whether they involve making curriculum decisions about both content and structure which affects the direction of certification. The lesson of curricular reform in the 1980s is that we have to correct the imbalance between innovation in learning process and the poverty and crisis of accreditation structures.

The CBI has published its report *Towards a Skills Revolution* (CBI, 1989), which calls for the doubling of participation and attainment in A-level and NVQ Level 3 awards over the next five years. The magnitude of these targets demands that we reflect upon the 1980s and locate the factors which have depressed progression opportunities. But realizing the targets will require tackling head-on 'the low participation, low attainment, progression equilibrium' and will require more than a curricular approach. It demands a comprehensive strategy embracing post-16 reorganization, reforming A-levels within a broader accreditation framework, new financial arrangements for post-16 full-time study, broader routes of progression, and a new form of 'dual system' with increased opportunities to gain a broad range of qualifications. These changes go far beyond the kind of strategies currently being considered to facilitate progression. An agenda for the 1990s calls for an approach which does not restrict itself to 'managing' the confusion of routes and opportunities, but instead addresses more firmly these deeper issues which currently support the syndrome of low participation, attainment and progression.

Notes

1. Anne Sofer in 'Skill passports needed for the 21st century' (*The Guardian*, 11 August 1988) states that in France and the Federal Republic of Germany 70 per cent of 16- to 18-year-olds hold qualifications (both academic and vocational) based upon two or three years' provision post-16. In Britain, it is estimated that only 18 per cent have similar qualifications, with those with two or more A-levels accounting for 15 per cent, and those with BTEC National or CGLI Part 1 accounting for 3 per cent.
2. The Scottish system of post-school VET is described in David Raffe and Nils Tomes *The Organization and Content of Studies at the Post-Compulsory Level in Scotland*, (Centre for Educational Sociology, Edinburgh University and OECD, 1987).
3. Details of progression patterns can be found in the FEUs *Progression from CPVE* (1987a).
4. The CPVE Joint Board have published a discussion document *Issues of Practice: progression* (CPVE Joint Board, 1988b), which outlines a variety of progression approaches into, through and from CPVE.
5. An analysis of a range of progression strategies can be found in Ken Spours, *Politics of Progression: issues of access and continuity in the 14–19 curriculum* (Falmer Press, 1990).
6. Such a framework is being discussed as part of a joint project between the Post-16 Education Centre and the FEU on modularization at 16-plus.

Chapter 5

Comprehensive Education and Training: Possibilities and Prospects

Andy Green

The post-compulsory education and training system in this country is currently in a state of disarray. It represents the weakest point in our education system and by comparison with what is offered in many other European countries, it is seriously underdeveloped. The institutional structure of public provision is muddled, confusing and irrational and the system of qualifications borders on chaos. Traditional sixth-form education is narrow and continues to be unpopular, while new forms of training and pre-vocational education are uneven in quality and lack the social prestige and levels of opportunity which attach to more traditional courses. We have fewer young people staying on in education than in most European countries and our training is generally recognized to be below the standard achieved by our foreign competitors.

Age-participation rates provide the most graphic illustration of our long history of comparative underdevelopment in this sphere. The 1970 Donnison Report correctly observed that 'the most striking feature of the British System, when compared with those of other countries, is the heavy loss of pupils at the minimum leaving age', then 15 (Maclure, 1986, p. 344). Its data on international school participation rates for 16- and 17-year-olds showed England and Wales behind all other major European countries, except Italy. Whereas only 25 per cent of 16-year-olds were in school in England and Wales in 1965, many other countries, including Japan, Belgium, Austria, France, Sweden and the United States, had over 50 per cent in school. At 17 the picture was the same. Around 15 per cent were in school in England and Wales compared with between 40 and 75 per cent in the other leading countries (ibid, p. 345).

The post-Sputnik era of the 1960s and early 1970s was a period of massive expansion in 16–19 education in most Western countries which were anxious not to fall behind the Soviet technological advance, yet in England and Wales rates of participation did not expand at a comparable rate. By 1981, still only 18 per cent of 16–18 year olds were in school in England and Wales whereas in Japan, Sweden and the United States over 80 per cent stayed on in the upper secondary schools. If one includes other non-school, full-time education and training, the figures are still equally discouraging as Table 1 shows (DES, 1985b).

One consequence of the low rates of participation in post-compulsory education and training in this country is the comparatively low level of students gaining nationally recognized qualifications at 17-plus. Many countries now offer some form of certification for students completing upper secondary education at the age of 17 or 18, and where this is the case, most students successfully complete it. Over 70 per cent now attain the high school diploma in the United States, for instance, and similar proportions come away with a school-leaving diploma in Japan and Sweden. Britain has no equivalent aggregate qualification at this level designed for the majority of students. What we do have is the elite A-level qualification and various other post-16 vocational certificates like those from the Business and Technician Education Council (BTEC) and The Certificate of Pre-Vocational Education (CPVE), which are generally considered to be less prestigious and give no automatic right of entry into higher education. A-level is even more elite than the elite qualifications of other countries. Whilst only 10 per cent in Britain get the three A-level passes normally required for entry into university, over 20 per cent gain the equivalent Abitur in West Germany. In France 33 per cent gain a general or vocational Baccalauréat compared with about 15 per cent in Britain who achieve either three A-levels or a BTEC national diploma, and the education ministry in France aims to double their figure in the next decade (Prais and Wagner, 1983). In terms of their vocational qualifications, our students also come off badly in comparison with those in other countries with split academic/vocational qualification systems. According to Prais' research into the labour force in 1974–8, 67 per cent of German employees had recognized vocational qualifications compared with only 36 per cent in Britain (ibid, p. 1).

Table 1 Participation in full-time education and training of 16–18 year olds, 1981

Country	%
United States	79
Netherlands	71
Japan	69
France	58
Italy	47
Germany	45
United Kingdom	32

Statistical comparisons such as these are, of course, always rather inconclusive, particularly so in the case of examinations where national systems are complex and not easily given to comparison. However, there is also a considerable body of more descriptive research which bears out the conclusion that the overall quality of our post-compulsory education and training is rather poor by international comparisons. The Institute of Manpower Studies found this to be the case in their 1984 report *Competence and Competition* where they concluded that 'the UK does not attach the same order of importance to ET [Education and Training] as Germany, Japan and the United States' (Institute of

Manpower Studies, 1984, p. 50). The Coopers and Lybrand 1985 report entitled *A Challenge to Complacency*, which was prepared for the Manpower Studies Commission (MSC), showed how dismal the record of Britain's employers in training is. The recent White Paper *Employment for the 1990s*, whilst making much of the government's recent initiatives in training, could not avoid citing the findings of recent research by the National Institute of Economic Research to the effect that 'the breadth and depth of our training, its quantity and standards still show up badly by comparison with our competitors on the continent, in North America and in the Far East' (DoE, 1988, p. 29).

If the state of post-compulsory education and training represents a particular national problem, and one indeed that has been with us for a considerable time despite many attempts to rectify it, what then are its root causes? There are a number of explanations, both historical and more immediate, but for the purposes of this article I want to concentrate on just two. The first relates to the state of private sector training and the second to public sector provision.

The main problem in private sector training is simply that employers are not and have never been very committed to it. They are generally unwilling to invest much money in training their employees either because they fear they will lose them to other firms, or because they put short-term profit before longer-term considerations, or because they are simply too complacent and would prefer the state to do it for them. Countless commissions of enquiry and government reports have come to the same conclusion ever since the Samuelson Commission pointed to this syndrome at the end of the last century. The recent Coopers and Lybrand Report claimed that few employers 'think training sufficiently central to their business for it to be a main component in their corporate strategy; the great majority did not see it as an issue of major importance' (Coopers and Lybrand, 1985, p. 4). This would not have had such serious consequences were it not that governments have not wanted to do much about it either, which brings us to the question of state provision.

State intervention in technical and vocational training has always been rather limited in this country. Unlike most European states, we had no tradition of state-sponsored trade schools in the nineteenth century nor an early growth of those higher technical institutions like the grands écoles, the technische hochschulen and the polytechnics which so advantaged some continental states. Britain relied for the most part on its apprenticeship system which, for all its practical merits, had the grave disadvantage of separating the practical from the theoretical, thus embedding the idea that technical training was somehow inferior to liberal education. Training thus became cast in a form that it would never quite shake off – low in status, normatively part-time, marginalized from mainstream education and stubbornly anti-theoretical.

Vocational education and training still have many of the same characteristics today. Publicly provided training, like the Youth Training Scheme (YTS), is still separated from other forms of post-16 education; it continues to have a low status and is often unnecessarily rudimentary in character, often comprising less theoretical content than even the older apprenticeship schemes. According to the Training Agency's survey of 1988 YTS graduates, only 27 per cent gained a City and Guilds qualification while on the scheme. This means that the majority were not trained to skill- or craft-worker standard which rather belies the notion of YTS as a quality training scheme. This division between education and training is clearly one of the major problems in post-compulsory provision today. However, this is not the only way in which the system is divided.

Taken as a whole the post-16 sector in the United Kingdom must rank as one of the most disorganized and fragmented in the world. Currently, provision is spread between school sixth forms, sixth-form colleges, colleges of further education, tertiary colleges, and training schemes operating both privately and in the public sector. We have around 2,000 schools with sixth forms, 650 further education colleges, over 100 sixth-form colleges and 50 tertiary colleges, to say nothing of the vast proliferation of small training agencies. Most types of course run concurrently in most of these institutions. In many area, A-levels and prevocational courses like CPVE can be taken either in school, or in a sixth-form college where sixth forms have been so 'rationalized', or in a further education college. When one considers the types of certification available, the picture begins to look even more chaotic. In addition to the traditional academic A-level qualification and the 1,400 odd City and Guilds craft qualifications, we now have AS-levels, BTEC, CPVE, and RSA certificates and a host of home-grown profiles to boot.

In a society addicted to the notion of consumer choice, all this variety might seem like a plus were it not for its other consequences. First, such duplication is clearly costly in terms of today's scarce educational resources. Second, it is highly divisive and creates enormous barriers to access and progression in education. Many of the courses followed and certificates pursued cannot be combined with one another and do not allow for progression on to other courses. Lastly, and equally important to many young people, and indeed to teachers and parents, the system is virtually incomprehensible. Students often do not know what is on offer and institutional rivalries between schools and colleges competing for students often mean that they are not told.

There are no doubt numerous reasons for the low participation rates in post-compulsory education and some of these are probably cultural and historical. Britain's early industrial revolution for instance, with its enormous thirst for juvenile labour, helped to cement a tradition of early entry into work for working-class children which has never been quite shaken off. The attitude of the Victorian ruling elites towards limiting popular education to the basics has also died hard. When, after 50 years of struggle, the working class finally won the right to free secondary education after the last war, there was still a lingering sense that they had been allowed into a domain which was not truly theirs. The system had not been designed for mass participation, and working-class children remained largely confined to a truncated version of secondary education in the modern schools. Sixth-form education in the grammar schools remained an elite phenomena. This is still in a way true today. The sixth form is still a minority experience. Seventeen per cent of sixth-formers are in the private schools and barely more than one in three comprehensive pupils stay on into the sixth form. The sixth form has never been a popular institution, and this can hardly be surprising since it was designed as a vehicle for children taking A-level courses which are highly specialized, entirely 'academic' and, after all, designed to exclude the vast majority from participation.

Various efforts have been made in the last 15 years to create a new type of sixth-form education which would be broader, less academic, more vocational and more relevant. These courses have had some success in attracting the interest of a wider range of students but they have always suffered under the stigma of being set against the traditional academic courses and thus been deemed inferior, leading to qualifications like CPVE which gives little access to higher levels of study and training. What has been lacking is any common curricula approach to the age group as a whole. Even where attempts have been made to create general curriculum frameworks, as with the Further Education Unit's (FEU's) pioneering skills 'template' advocated first in *A Basis for Choice* (FEU, 1979), it has not led to a genuine common core curriculum because the old elite qualifications are still there to undermine it. While strenuously advocating the value of vocational education, governments have shown no inclination to dismantle the old elite educational highroad to the A-level, presumably because of the strong middle-class interests in defending it. The very moderate proposals of the 1988 Higginson Report (DES, 1988b) for broadening A-levels were turned down flat.

Despite all the new initiatives, the divisions between the academic and the vocational have not broken down at all. The National Council for Vocational Qualifications (NCVQ) has a brief to rationalize qualifications but it is doing this only within the vocational sphere, and many people fear that the effect will be to make vocational courses more narrowly job-specific. This is already happening with CPVE. (It is also, incidentally, a pretty half-baked rationalization since the levels of attainment recommended by the NCVQ do not even correspond to those in use in Europe – most European states, with their higher standards of training, seeing no need for the basic level of attainment which NCVQ has designated for Level one.) The gap between vocational and academic courses and qualifications thus remains as sharp as ever.

The main problem with our post-compulsory provision is simply that it has not been designed for majority participation. It has become a would-be mass provision not by design but by accident, or rather because of the effects of youth unemployment which has forced young people to stay in education when they would otherwise have gone to work. Short-term reactive policies have thus allowed the accretion of various new bits to the old elite system without there having been the thoroughgoing recasting of institutions and curricula which would have created a more appropriate mass provision. In the absence of any comprehensive planning or consistent policies by governments, we now have a hotch-potch of policies and different initiatives aimed at different segments of the age group and a very muddled institutional framework to deliver them. The system has no centre and the policy no vital core. There have been no normative social expectations about what young people between the ages of 16 and 19 should be doing, and government policies have not sought to shape any. Consequently, there is no clearly-defined set of educational objectives for the age group and no focal institution which might provide it. Young people reaching the school-leaving age cross a threshold into a kind of limbo-land where there are no clear expectations or certain identities. They are either pupils or students, or workers or trainees, but nothing for certain. To policy-makers, they are simply in transition from school to work.

The arguments for redesigning post-compulsory provision along more rational and comprehensive lines are now overwhelming from both economic and educational points of view. Economically, it makes no sense in a period of financial retrenchment in education to perpetuate a system with so many overlaps and duplications and thus so much wastage of resources. Demographic changes make this a particularly urgent consideration. The 16–19 age cohort will continue dropping until 1994, by which time it will be a mere 66 per cent of its peak 1983 level (DoE, 1988, p. 7). The rationalization of school sixth forms, no longer able to recruit sufficient students to justify a broad provision, is thus inevitable. Educationally, some form of comprehensive restructuring is essential not only to increase participation rates and thus to give all young people the broad education they deserve, but also to equip them for the economic changes now occurring which will require higher levels of skills from a much larger segment of the work force.

If some kind of rationalization of post-compulsory education and training is thus essential, what form should it take? There are a number of models worth considering which have been developed in this country and abroad. Local authorities in this country have been experimenting with sixth-form and tertiary colleges since the early 1970s. The sixth-form college is traditionally an amalgamated or centralized sixth form catering mainly for 16- to 18-year-olds taking A-levels and run under the DES schools regulations. They tend to offer a wide range of academic subjects, get good exam results, are generally popular with the students who attend them, and receive a good deal of support from middle-class parents in particular. However they do not offer a comprehensive solution to the problem of 16–19 provision since they are basically geared only towards A-level students. Only around 20 per cent of sixth-form college students are engaged in non-A-level work (Watkins, 1982). The sixth-form college must therefore run alongside the college of further education which provides the more vocational work. This has the considerable disadvantage of perpetuating the old split between academic and vocational learning.

The tertiary college model is the only solution to have been tried in this country which can claim to adhere to comprehensive principles. Advocates of tertiary colleges point to a number of advantages. As a rationalized, all-in form of provision, they are financially efficient in that they avoid costly duplication of facilities and can achieve economies of scale. They can offer a very wide range of vocational courses and a full complement of academic subjects without unduly small class sizes. While most existing sixth forms can offer only around 10 or 15 A-level subjects and some considerably fewer, tertiary colleges on average offer around 25. They can do this and still maintain class sizes of 10–15 students, while many schools can achieve a decent range of subjects only by reducing class sizes to as low as 5, thus forcing lower staff–student ratios lower down the school (Janes et al, 1985). Not only can the tertiary college offer a wide choice of subjects to students, but because it combines both academic and technical provision, it can help to reduce those damaging divisions which currently separate these arbitrarily distinct categories. Tertiary colleges have also proved to be popular, no doubt partly because they offer a more adult environment to young people keen to escape the confines of school, and because they can provide a wide choice of courses. Where tertiary colleges have been set up, as in Richmond in London and Halesowen in Birmingham, they have generally improved the age-participation rates in the locality. Although it is rather too early for them to be very conclusive, statistical surveys have suggested that tertiary colleges get pass rates at A-level which are rather better than the national average (Janes et al, 1985).

The tertiary college could provide the institutional basis for a more comprehensive system of post-compulsory provision, avoiding the wastefulness and divisiveness of our present fragmentary arrangements. However, there is more to comprehensive education than providing unitary or common institutional structures, as we found out to our cost with comprehensive schools. Equally important are the questions of curriculum and assessment. Here we can learn something from overseas models. The North American community college cannot provide an *institutional* model for us since it is designed to follow on from high school rather than to take students from the age of 16 which is the issue here. However, the course and assessment structures of the community college do provide a good example of how increased access can be facilitated through open structures. All assessment in the community college is in the hands of teachers, and operates on a continuous accumulating credit model. Students enrolling at the college are assessed and placed at the appropriate stage on the courses they wish to follow. There are a wide range of courses on offer and combinations of subjects are very flexible, but most vocational pathways require the accumulation of credits by successfully completing various units where some of these are compulsory and others optional. The inclusion of compulsory units avoids over-specialization and ensures that all students get a balanced vocational and general education. All courses can be retaken and progression routes are built into the system so that all courses can lead on to further courses.

A number of factors thus contributes towards the relative openness of the system. Courses do not have minimum entry requirements: they merely have different entry points. (The distinction is not entirely semantic; whereas in an English college a student failing to reach a course entry requirement might be sent to another department to try something else – that is, to set out on a different educational track – in the North American community college they are simply told 'you start here and work your way up'.) There are no major examination hurdles to put students off and all courses offer progression, even if this means retaking certain units. The scheduling of courses is highly flexible to suit the needs of part-time students: colleges often run courses from eight in the morning until ten at night. Courses are not bound to institutions since credits can be transferred from one institution to another. Whatever the drawbacks of the North American college system, and there are a number, it does at least provide an example of how relatively open and flexible course and assessment structures can increase access. In some states in North America up to 50 per cent of the age group attend college at some point.

Sweden provides another example of an integrated system of post-compulsory education and training and arguably comes closer to a comprehensive model than many others in Europe. The Gymnasieskola system was first developed in 1971 through the amalgamation of existing Gymnasia and vocational schools, and since 1980 has become the main provider of post-16 education and training. Although not all institutions yet provide the full range of courses, the full Gymnasieskola offers 23 different lines of study lasting between two and four years. Each requires a broad combination of subjects and points in a general vocational direction, and some involve periods of work experience. Around 40 per cent of applicants choose the more academic courses, 45 per cent the vocational courses, and 15 per cent the more theoretical–vocational courses. The majority of cases, excepting the shorter vocational courses, allow entry into university on successful completion. Manpower planning authorities stipulate the number of places available in each line and so although recruitment on to the majority of study lines is non-selective, in a few of the most popular areas, students are selected on the basis of final school grades. In 1979 19 per cent of applicants failed to get places and 24 per cent did not get on the course they wanted. More recent statistics suggest that now over 90 per cent of the age group go into the Gymnasieskola for at least two years (*The Economist*, 12–18 November 1988, p. 27). Sweden's upper secondary schools still involve a degree of selection, and although there are still visible distinctions between the academic and vocational lines of study, they have thus gone a considerable way towards integrating areas which are wholly distinct in most other national systems. This factor, together with the wide choice of courses, the accessible continuous assessment system, and the mandatory provision of grants to students, have all contributed towards the achievement of the highest staying-on rates in Europe (Boucher, 1982).

Sweden and North America offer two examples of how an integrated form of provision can be developed with positive outcomes. Of course no educational institution can be simply cloned by another country even if that were desirable. However, the experience of institutions such as these, together with our own experience of tertiary colleges, does give some indication of what kind of changes might improve our own system. Four things would seem to be axiomatic for the comprehensive post-16 system. First, education and training would need to be combined in a new network of unitary, focal institutions specifically designed to cater for the needs of the entire age group. Second, a range of courses or study lines would need to be developed which would combine a high degree of choice and flexibility in subject combinations and modes of attendance, while maintaining compulsory core elements to guard against over-specialized or unbalanced programmes. Third, there needs to be an entirely new system of certification based on principles of continuous assessment and credit accumulation which would allow a greater degree of access for students. Lastly, some form of financial inducement might be necessary to attract larger numbers of pupils to stay on. We have not yet developed a culture of extended education as some other countries have. The various stop-gap measures adopted to deal with youth unemployment over the last 20 years have not, despite marginally increased staying-on rates, really changed attitudes towards early entry into work and the increased availability of jobs for young people at the end of the 1980s threatened to undercut YTS and re-establish the old status quo as far as this is concerned. To encourage continued participation, 16- to 18-year-olds should be entitled to mandatory paid study leave from their employers or to grants if they are on full-time courses. If the latter appears to be prohibitively expensive, it should be means-tested like the existing grants for higher education. It is regrettable that the Labour Party appears to have abandoned the latter policy in the course of its recent policy review.

Thoroughgoing changes such as these imply would not be easy and nor, of course, would they be universally popular. Many of those involved in youth training might argue against incorporation into an integrated system of education and training and many teachers in schools understandably would resist the loss of their sixth forms, although falling rolls mean that in many cases this will happen anyway. However, it would not be impossible. Current experiments with tertiary colleges have been very successful and often very popular with students and parents. Where tertiary systems are developed from scratch, drawing on the expertise and staff of existing colleges and schools equally rather than being simply on extension of the college, there has been less resistance to them. Parallel improvements in the conditions for teachers in schools are equally necessary and would be a precondition for successful reform in the post-compulsory sector.

The arguments for a comprehensive restructuring of this sector have always been powerful and perhaps now more than ever. Yet the prospects of such changes occurring, at least under the present Conservative Government, look somewhat less likely than they did at the beginning of the 1980s, principally because of the effects of the 1988 Education Act and the recently announced plans for the further privatization of training.

The Education Act has explicitly aimed to reduce the powers of local education authorities (LEAs) and give a higher degree of self-management to schools and colleges. One of the results of this will be to make it very difficult for LEAs to engage in the kind of planning necessary to bring about the changes envisaged here. The right of schools to opt out of local authority control has already generated several hundred applications from schools threatened with closure or the loss of their sixth forms due to reorganization plans. The Act also gives college governing bodies, soon to have a majority representation of 'employment interest' members, control over staffing and the spending of the college budget under the new schemes of financial delegation. This will make it difficult for LEAs to effect the redeployment of staff and may weaken their ability to plan the distribution of courses between different institutions. Anticipating such problems, a number of authorities like Nottinghamshire have already dropped their plans for 16–19 reorganization. The Government has not yet rejected the tertiary model outright but Kenneth Baker, during his tenure at the DES, made it clear that he would not want to see 'good' sixth forms disappear. It remains to be seen what will happen to future applications for tertiary reorganization but it seems clear that the Act will create a degree of planning blight which will make such plans hard to carry out. Furthermore, successful reorganization on a 'clean slate' basis would require a level of funding which is hardly likely to be available to hard-pressed local authorities, whatever happens to the poll tax.

The new government plans for training look even less auspicious. Far from suggesting a movement toward the integration of education and training, the proposals put forward in the recent White Paper *Employment for the 1990s* (DoE, 1988), recommend further doses of privatization in training and thus its further segregation from mainstream education. The main proposal is to invite local groups, led by employers, to submit plans for setting up Training and Enterprise Councils (TECs). These new councils, which in the first instance will probably grow out of existing chambers of commerce, will have two-thirds of their members drawn from leading local employers and will have the responsibility for assessing local skills requirements, promoting private training and supporting small business enterprises. It is envisaged that within two or three years there will be a national network of 100 or so TECs which will become the bodies mainly responsible for providing youth training. They will receive £15–50 million each to spend on training, the greater part of which represents what the Training Agency currently spends on YTS, and will have the power to spend this money on training which can be commissioned from private training agencies or colleges. Meanwhile the existing 60 Skills Centres providing adult training will be prepared for privatization and the remaining 7 Industrial Training Boards will be turned into independent non-statutory bodies.

What is truly remarkable about these proposals is that they fly in the face of all the lessons of our past experiences with training. Countless government reports have shown the reluctance of British employers to take sufficient responsibility for training and yet now they are to be given control over it to a degree not seen since the days before the 1964 Industrial Training Act. Employers are now to take the leading role on college governing bodies, on the Polytechnics and College Funding Council, on the Universities Funding Council, in the development of City Technology Colleges and now it seems in the local management of training. One cannot help wondering where all these civic-minded business leaders with time on their hands are going to come from. If they can be spirited into existence, and we know from the early experience of YTS that the Government has ways of conjuring them up, what influence are they going to bring to bear on a system of education and training meekly delivered into their hands? Will they use their new-found influence to promote education and training which is relevant to today's economic needs but also broad enough and imaginative enough to serve the whole range of community needs for the coming decades? Or will they merely act as self-serving cliques bent on securing a provision which serves only their own short-term economic interests? The Association of British Chambers of Commerce was not alone in its fears when it warned ministers of the dangers of the new TECs falling into unrepresentative and narrowly-interested hands (*The Times Educational Supplement*, 9 December 1988).

Market-led systems are by their nature fragmented, unplanned and non-integrated. If the argument of this article is correct, and we do badly need a more coherent, unitary and integrated public system of 16–19 education and training, then at present we are clearly moving in the opposite direction. Privatizing large chunks of education and training will make it harder to plan, harder to integrate and rationalize, and harder to make education and training responsive to the whole range of society's needs. The addition of a new tier of elite City Technology Colleges and grant-maintained schools will only add to the byzantine complexity and confusion of existing institutions, courses and certificates, and will multiply the social divisions which they embody. With a disoriented and demoralized teaching force, an emasculated and insolvent array of public planning authorities, and a government which abdicates its public responsibilities to the market, the system will have no unifying core or focus. It will be easy prey for manipulation by unrepresentative interest groups and subject to the vagaries and inequalities of the rampant market. Such a system cannot serve the public interest and probably cannot last. 'Things fall apart; the centre cannot hold' (Yeats).

Chapter 6

Towards New Definitions of Vocationalism

Clyde Chitty

When politicians and industrialists talk glibly about the need to provide courses of a *vocational* nature for specified groups of young people, they are using a term which is capable of many different interpretations. For one thing, it is clearly not to be confused with the noun from which it comes. *The Collins English Dictionary*, for example, defines the term 'vocation' as both a specified occupation, profession or grade and a special urge, inclination, or predisposition to a particular calling or career, especially a religious one. Deriving from the Latin words 'vocatio' (a calling) or 'vocare' (to call), it is the second nobler, perhaps even bourgeois, meaning which is in use when one talks of someone having a vocation to become a priest or nurse or teacher. It has little to do with the cruder notion of simply preparing young people for 'the world of work', the sense in which so-called vocational courses are currently being advocated.

The philosophy of successive recent governments has been variously described as 'vocationalism', 'the new vocationalism' and 'narrow vocationalism', though Andy Green has argued (Green, 1986, p. 102) that all these terms are inadequate and misleading. If the new training philosophy in both schools and further education (FE) establishments has been concerned with preparation for work in general, with its roots in market economics, then it is neither 'narrow' nor strictly 'vocationalist':

> Vocational education has normally meant preparation for a particular job and its connotations of 'calling' are clearly tied up with a protestant work ethic and the middle-class preoccupation with choosing a career. Youth training schemes, however, are explicitly concerned with training for work in general and not preparation for a particular job, and there is precious little real choice for most young people involved. Furthermore, one of the defining characteristics of youth training is that it does involve broad-based skills training and specifically eschews skill specialization. Although it may be narrow in other, and especially, educational senses, the use of the term would be confusing in the training context. Perhaps the best designation is simply 'the new training philosophy'. (Ibid)

The characteristics peculiar to this 'new training philosophy' tell us much about the educational outlook of the Thatcher Governments in general, and of the second administration (1983–7) in particular, and deserve to be considered in some detail later in this chapter.

The historical context

The debate about the vocationalization of education has assumed a special significance in Britain over the past 15 years, with the nation's economic problems being blamed on the failure of schools and colleges to relate their curriculum to the requirements of industry. Indeed, it has been common practice to view the actual starting-point of the debate as the speech delivered by James Callaghan at Ruskin College, Oxford in October 1976. This was clearly a significant initiative demonstrating that the Labour Prime Minister was well aware of employers' critique both of secondary schools and of other institutions providing education and training beyond the age of 16. Yet it is also important to take account of Reeder's argument (Reeder, 1979, p. 115), that recent complaints about teacher indifference to industrial development and the quality and attitudes of the labour force represent only 'the most recent phase of a long-standing controversy about the role of schooling in a modern industrial society'.

The support for technical and scientific education in the late-Victorian period had much to do with developing anxieties about Britain's capacity to sustain an Imperial role and to carry on a war with Germany. It was, in fact, the First World War that highlighted the state's need for efficient and trained manpower. As Lloyd George argued at Manchester in 1918:

> The most formidable institution we had to fight in Germany was not the arsenals of Krupp or the yards in which they turned out submarines, but the schools of Germany. They were our most formidable competitors in business and our most terrible opponents in war. An educated man is a better worker, a more formidable warrior, and a better citizen. This was only half comprehended here before the war. (Quoted in Bernbaum, 1979, p. 6)

The emphasis placed upon national efficiency was influenced by intimations of internal disorganization, particularly fears about the role of youth in a society where traditional moral and social values had been undermined by the erosion of apprenticeship and the advance of machine processes. Once victory over Germany had been secured, a concept of 'industrial citizenship' was advanced, both as a way of solving youth problems and as a means of creating greater social harmony in the post-war world. For example, H.A.L. Fisher, the author of the 1918 Education Act, told a group of 'paternalistic' employers whose interest in 'works schools' had led them to form the Association for Education in Industry in 1911:

> I have always felt the great problem for the next years is to bring the world of business and the world of education into clear connection. We have the same interests, and I believe that the solution of all the difficulties between

capital and labour will ultimately lie, not in the sphere of wages at all, not in any material sphere, but in the kind of improvement in the general condition which is due to the spread of knowledge and intelligence amongst the people and amongst the employers. (Inaugural address to the Association, *Proceedings*, 1 May 1919, in the archives of the British Association for Commercial and Industrial Education; quoted in Reeder, 1979, p. 122)

A few years later in a speech at an advertising convention at Olympia, Lord Eustace Percy, President of the Board of Education in 1924–9, urged businessmen to put pressure on schools to teach subjects relevant to commercial and industrial needs. The Board, he said, was currently working out standards for the new forms of post-primary education, but 'our success . . . must depend . . . upon the advice and assistance . . . from organized Commerce and Industry and upon the standards which organized Commerce and Industry can set for these schools'. (Percy's speech at the advertising convention at Olympia, 20 July 1927; quoted in White, 1975, p. 32.)

It can be argued that Eustace Percy was one of a small group of people in the inter-war period to see in the separated development of technical education after the Education Act of 1902 a potential for genuine educational and social innovation – an alternative route as well as an alternative curriculum. For too long, in Percy's view, the liberal professions had exerted an undue influence on the secondary-school curriculum. The time had now come for the industrial and commercial professions to become more highly organized and insist on the need for more practical and realistic curricula in schools. In the event, Percy's views did not prevail. As Reeder points out (Reeder, 1979, p. 124), the consensus is that the effect of the settlement of 1902 was 'to remove the practical–technical curricula from the mainstream of English schooling'. Older ideals and traditions were drawn back into the system; and the vocational educationalists who shared Percy's perspective made little headway in the inter-war years.[1]

Developments since 1945

Moving on to the period after 1945, it is important to distinguish between the various evolving concepts of vocational education and training that have been a feature of the past 45 years.

The 'old vocationalism', if it is possible to use the term, was intimately associated with the apprenticeship system operating in a number of industries after the Second World War, which saw it as being the main task of training to equip a privileged minority of working-class youngsters to practise their crafts. The typical craft apprentice in the post-war period was white and male. The 23 Industrial Training Boards (ITBs), set up by the Industrial Training Act of 1964, had an important role to play in the production of a skilled workforce (see Cantor and Roberts, 1986, pp. 53–4); and the provision of off-the-job training helped to account for the steady expansion of the FE sector in the 1960s.

The crisis in the domestic economy in the 1970s exacerbated by the quadrupling of oil prices in 1973, had important consequences for the stability of the labour market. As Shilling has observed (Shilling, 1989, p. 52), 'the 1970s was a period of sharply rising unemployment and a dramatic decline in the apprenticeship system'. Job opportunities became scarce in key areas of the economy, and this began to affect skilled manual occupations. The decline in the apprenticeship system meant that the opportunities for such a career route were substantially reduced. For example: in the 1960s, 40 per cent of boys leaving school at 16 or earlier got apprenticeships; by the early 1980s this proportion had been halved. In the manufacturing sector, the number of school-leavers obtaining apprenticeships declined from a peak of 236,000 in 1968 to under 150,000 in 1980 and around 100,000 in 1982. The number of other trainees in manufacturing fell from some 210,000 in 1968 to 90,000 in 1980 (Manpower Services Commission (MSC), 1982, paragraph 2.2). In engineering and shipbuilding the number of apprenticeships almost halved between 1964 and 1974; and in the same period the number in construction fell by well over a quarter (National Youth Employment Council (NYEC), 1974, p. 20). These developments affected young people disproportionately, and fundamentally altered the context for education–industry relations. To quote Shilling again:

> . . . the effects of a declining apprenticeship system and economic recession led to large increases in youth unemployment and the emergence of a distinct labour market for young people concentrated within a secondary sector characterized by poor working conditions and low wages. (Ibid, p. 44)

The new vocationalism

The cosy post-war world of male-dominated craft apprenticeships could not survive the acute economic crisis of the early 1970s, which highlighted the uncomfortable fact that Britain had been in relative economic decline since the end of the Second World War (see Gamble, 1985). With the steady growth in youth employment and the virtual collapse of the apprenticeship system, the old vocationalism gave way to the new: a philosophy of training where 'the deskilling of manual work has its corollary in the deskilling of youth training' (Green, 1986, p. 104). And the central body concerned with both the formulation and the implementation of the 'new training philosophy' was the MSC, set up in 1974 under the terms of the Employment and Training Act of 1973 and answerable directly to the Secretary of State for Employment. The largest programme that the MSC was involved in during the late 1970s was the Youth Opportunities Programme (YOP) which began life in 1978 at the request of the TUC (see Benn and Fairley, 1986, p. 265). And the traditional system of apprenticeship – so heartily disliked by the Thatcher Government returned in May 1979 – was further undermined by the abolition in 1982 of all but 7 of the

23 ITBs which had at least 'imposed some coherence on patterns of training' (Finn, 1985, p. 117).[2]

Implicit within the concept of the 'old vocationalism' had been an assumption that vocational education and training involved the acquisition of occupation – specific knowledge combined with experience in the appropriate workplace. If training was characterized by anything in the policy-making literature, it was, as Slater has pointed out (Slater, 1985, p. 186), 'an emphasis on the skills required to do a job, rather than the personal development of the individual'. Expressive notions of personal development, as represented by General Studies, found survival difficult in the instrumental curriculum of FE colleges, whose main task was to produce product skills in their students for particular industries.

The virtual abandonment of the apprenticeship system in the 1970s facilitated the development of a new concept of vocational preparation which emphasized *process* rather than *product* skills and was couched in the language of personal development. The irony of the situation, together with the difficulties involved in changing attitudes, was commented on in the influential 1984 report *Competence and Competition*, prepared by the Institute of Manpower Studies for the National Economic Development Council (NEDC) and the MSC:

> Paradoxically, the sharp decline in apprenticeship opens the door to less tradition-bound ways of recognizing, assessing and accrediting competence. The new emphasis on competence, and not only knowledge and skills, will not, however, be easy to achieve. (NEDC/MSC, 1984, p. 6)

The new concept of vocational preparation actually owed much to the work of the Further Education Review and Development Unit (FEU), set up in 1977 as an advisory, intelligence and development unit for further education within the Department of Education and Science (DES). FEU ideas were borrowed by the MSC which needed a way of producing a flexible workforce with process skills, such as planning and diagnostic skills, that could easily be transferred as the context of work changed in the economy. In the process, 'general (or liberal) education' was to be replaced by 'basic skills' and 'personal effectiveness'. To quote Slater:

> Paradoxically, the expressive has now also become the instrumental: the notion of personal development has been transformed, through the medium of vocational preparation, into that of personal skills. (Slater, 1985, p. 188)[3]

It is usually argued that the twin objectives of 'the new training philosophy' were to keep youngsters off the streets and to cultivate the sort of attitudes previously acquired in work. But it is also important to emphasize that the 'new vocationalism' was an all-embracing philosophy which saw schools, colleges and mass youth training programmes as all having a role to play in the moral and economic regeneration of the nation.[4] There was perceived to be a need for *all* youngsters to understand the basic facts of economic life,[5] alongside the requirement that those of 'limited ability' should be *socialized* into acceptance of unskilled, routine work. Some even argued that to vocationalize the curriculum would serve as a useful means of motivating secondary-school pupils – and particularly those at the lower end of the ability range. For example, in an article published shortly before the 1979 election, Mark Carlisle, the future Conservative Education Secretary, advised that:

> . . . schools should concentrate more closely on relating the last years at school to the world of work to retain the interest of those who find the school atmosphere stifling. (*Education*, 20 April 1979)

Economic arguments, however, remained predominant. The 'new training philosophy' saw a direct correspondence between youth training and economic need. According to the 1982 MSC *Youth Task Group Report* which recommended the introduction of a new training programme to be called the Youth Training Scheme (YTS), the main objective of the new arrangements was:

> . . . to develop and maintain a more versatile, readily adaptable, highly motivated and productive workforce which will assist Britain to compete successfully in the 1980s and beyond. (MSC, 1982, paragraph 4.3c)

In the 1984 report *Competence and Competition*, vocational education and training (VET) was defined as, 'learning activities which contribute to successful economic performance' (ibid).

At the same time, the new training programmes devised by the MSC, principally YOP and YTS, were prompted by the fear on the part of both government and employers that unemployed youth could no longer be *socialized* into work through their first jobs. Indeed, long periods of unemployment could, it was felt, actually serve to undermine the motivation for work and create severe social problems, particularly in the inner cities. The collapse of the youth labour market had important implications for social control.

The training programmes themselves were concerned primarily with the development of lower order skills and were based on the assumption that when work did become available, it would take the form of unskilled manual work or junior white-collar jobs in the service and manufacturing sectors. Training would also be geared towards locally available work rather than towards work meeting national needs. The 1984 Department of Employment (DoE) White Paper *Training for Jobs* argued that training should be 'to agreed standards of skill appropriate to the jobs available', and announced that the MSC would 'relate the supply of skill training of unemployed people more closely to identified local employment needs' (DoE, 1984, pp. 4, 12).

It was also accepted that training schemes must be flexible enough to cope with the needs of a rapidly changing economy. According to *Training for Jobs*:

> It does not make sense . . . for either industry or Government to train people

who will have no foreseeable opportunity to practise their skills. Instead, the system of training must be able to respond quickly and flexibly to changing needs. (Ibid, p. 10)

At the same time, young people had to be taught that for most of them, their working life would consist of frequent job changes and intermittent periods of extended unemployment. In the words of the 1982 *Youth Task Group Report*, trainees should:

> . . . receive an introductory programme of training and skills related to a broad group or family of related occupations and . . . be able, at completion of the [training] programme, to transfer his or her acquired skills, knowledge and experience to other employment contexts. (MSC, 1982, paragraphs 4.10c and i)

And in an article published in 1987, Parry Rogers, at that time Chairman of the Institute of Directors and newly-appointed Chairman of BTEC, argued that:

> . . . all young people should be prepared for a working life in which they will change skills and occupations several times . . . This is as much a matter of attitude and outlook as of knowledge, and both parents and teachers have the highest responsibilities in this. (Rogers, 1987, p. 18)

Training youngsters to fit certain low-status jobs was only *one* aspect of the 'new vocationalism'; just as, if not more, important was the inculcation of the 'right' attitudes, beliefs and behaviour patterns. As the Industrial Training Research Unit reported in 1981, 'job skills hardly merit consideration in young people's jobs'. What really mattered in youth training was the cultivation of adaptability and a set of attitudes conducive to the execution of unskilled, routine tasks. Reports confirmed that for the majority of jobs, the most important qualities for employers were not specific qualifications, but rather such characteristics as punctuality, attendance, timekeeping and discipline (see Shilling, 1989, p. 45). And there were those who argued that the work ethic should be promulgated in schools. For example, in an article published in *The Times Educational Supplement* in October 1976, the late Sir John Methven, at that time Director General of the CBI, argued that secondary schools should be seeking to encourage certain 'positive' attitudes in their pupils – attitudes calculated to turn school-leavers into efficient and reliable workers when they made the transition into 'the world of work'. In his view, employers were looking more closely for:

> . . . evidence of such personal qualities as self-discipline and self-reliance, loyalty and enthusiasm, the right attitudes to work [and] . . . willingness to accept change. (Methven, 1976)[6]

Such examplary qualities were also expected in those completing the YTS.

According to Employment Minister Peter Morrison, speaking in a Commons debate in July 1983:

> The Scheme is not a social service. Its purpose is to teach youngsters what the real world of work is all about. That means arriving on time, giving of their best during the working day, and perhaps staying on a little longer to complete an unfinished task. (Quoted in Finn, 1984, p. 7)

Important features of the new curriculum and pedagogy associated with the 'new vocationalism' have been found in courses in social and life skills (SLS). Here we have a clear illustration of the shift from knowledge to competence and from concept to practice. The main objective of SLS has been to promote social and communicative skills for 'coping' in the worlds of work and employment. As Green has pointed out:

> Even where the emphasis is on 'personal effectiveness', implying assertiveness rather than passivity, the primary objective is to *adapt* to given situations, not to analyse or change them. Preferred, or dominant, methods of teaching in these vocational areas reflect these objectives and their distance from traditional education.
>
> Where the latter stresses 'transmission' and 'instruction', SLS emphasizes 'participation' and 'self-discovery'. Where traditional education is seen to be knowledge- and paper-based, SLS attempts to be experience-based and skills-based, thus stressing the 'active' as against the 'reflexive' aspects of learning. (Green, 1986, p. 109)

Given the low-level nature of much SLS work, it might at first sight appear rather strange that this new form of compensatory education should have been so enthusiastically adopted by teachers and lecturers; but it may be, as Cohen has suggested (Cohen, 1984, p. 124), that 'the paradigm was all too easily recast in terms of demands for, a "relevant" curriculum for early leavers'. It is certainly true that a remarkable number of different practices have been subsumed under the SLS umbrella. Cohen goes on to say that:

> Elements from various models of self-improvement (personal growth, behaviour modification and straight Samuel Smiles) are being selected and combined in numerous ways. Assertion training and psychodrama may be in vogue in one programme; training in good interview manners, lectures on personal hygiene and life-style enhancement mixed together in another. The choice of approach often seems determined by the context and the personal outlook of the teacher, and the fact that this very diversity allows some measure of control over what is taught should not be overlooked. Yet this also has its dangers. It has enabled SLS to invade 'soft' areas of the school curriculum, liberal studiers, careers teaching and even pastoral care. In these contexts, SLS tends to be narrowly confined to the rehearsal of interview

techniques, filling in job application forms, signing on and the like. This is clearly no substitute for social education or even personal counselling. (Ibid, pp. 124–5)

The widespread adoption of SLS in the 1980s has clearly shown how the concept of preparing young people for 'life' as well as 'work' can secure ready adherents to an otherwise crude utilitarian philosophy.

The technical and vocational education initiative (TVEI)

Without apparently consulting either the DES or the MSC commissioners, the Thatcher Government launched its Technical and Vocational Education Initiative (TVEI) in November 1982 (see Dale, 1985; Chitty and Worgan, 1987; Chitty, 1989). It was designed, in the words of the accompanying DoE press release, 'to stimulate technical and vocational education for 14–18-year-olds as part of a drive to improve our performance in the development of new skills and technology' (DoE, 1982, p. 1); and in the course of the next few years, TVEI approaches were to be generalized to all schools but without the same level of funding. The fact that the TVEI is often cited as an example of the 'new vocationalism' in education is a clear indication that the term is capable of many different interpretations. TVEI courses were designed to provide 'a variety of skills ranging from manual trades to computer science' and 'leading to recognized qualifications', and could therefore be said to represent a rather eccentric strand in the new philosophy of education and training. But the eccentricity is not restricted to the types of subjects on offer. As I have argued elsewhere (Chitty, 1989, p. 174), the TVEI fits uneasily into any account of the 'new vocationalism' largely because the term 'vocational' in the title was never clearly defined while, at the same time, there was considerable vagueness about the Initiative's intended 'target group'.

The question of the exact nature of the target group is a particularly important one since, as we have seen, vocationalizing strategies are now normally associated with pupils and students in the lower half of the ability range. Indeed Sir Keith (now Lord) Joseph, Education Secretary in 1982, was one of those who saw the initiative as having special significance for this group. In discussing the TVEI in a BBC TV *Panorama* programme 'Good enough for your child?', broadcast on 28 February 1983, he talked about:

. . . the very large proportion of children who are not getting a benefit from school. They're certainly not getting a parity of esteem. They're either dropping out, or they're emerging from school without what they themselves, their parents or their potential employers would expect them to have got at school . . . These are the children who will benefit from the Government's new plans.

David (now Lord) Young, on the other hand, who as the then Chairman of the

MSC had played a leading role in devising the TVEI, clearly did not see it as being intended for either the *most* or the *least* able pupils but rather for those occupying the *middle* of the ability range. Shortly after the official launch of the scheme, he said courses would be aimed at 'the 15 to 85 percentiles of the ability range in schools' (quoted in *Education*, 19 November 1982, p. 386). Later, he again conceded that the TVEI was not designed for pupils who at that time were heading for 'good' O- and A-level results:

> They are not going to join the Scheme. My chief concern is for those who are bright and able – and haven't been attracted by academic subjects. (Reported in *Education*, 24 December 1982, p. 490).

Upon his later appointment as Secretary of State for Employment in the Cabinet reshuffle of September 1985, Lord Young outlined a clear vision of the future:

> My idea is that, at the end of the decade, there is a world in which 15 per cent of our young go into higher education . . . roughly the same proportion as now. Another 30 to 35 per cent will stay on doing the TVEI, along with other courses, ending up with a mixture of vocational and academic qualifications and skills. The remainder, about half, will go on to two-year YTS. (Reported in *The Times*, 4 September 1985)

This would seem to be a definitive statement of the role of TVEI in Lord Young's concept of secondary and tertiary tripartism.

The Young approach outlined above tells us a good deal about the Thatcher Government's flexible approach to vocationalism in education and training. The Conservatives took over the concept of the 'new vocationalism' and imbued it with a much higher degree of targeting and selection. In so doing, they could be said to be responding to a widespread view among employers that there was little point in students receiving the same kind of vocational experience when they were likely to end up doing different jobs (Shilling, 1989, p. 47).

Ken Jones has shown how this important aspect of modern Conservatism, which could roughly be described as 'a modernizing tendency' and which was particularly powerful in the first half of the 1980s, entailed radically different experiences for different social groups. It was simply not true that modernization necessitated higher skills and thus an improved education for all. According to Jones:

> The areas of employment growth are, on the one hand, among 'managers, administrators, engineers, scientists and technicians'; and, on the other, in part-time, temporary or casual employment – low-paid work for which women are thought particularly suitable. These latter jobs could be in private services, in the public sector, or on the sub-contracting periphery of manufacturing, where workers can be hired or laid off according to the week-by-week requirements of the market. The demands of employers thus take

two major forms. There is both a chronic, unsatisfied need for 'skilled, technical and craft workers' and a demand for casual and part-time employees who can spend the rest of their time on the fringes of the social security state. All sections of the workforce, however, will face a more volatile labour market, in which there is an increased possibility that they will be required to change jobs, develop flexibility, or, and especially if they do not belong to the core of the workforce, adapt themselves to periods of unemployment. (Jones, 1989, pp. 106–7)

It was against this background – of a process of modernization and vocationalization that was selective in its effects even though it was frequently presented as a democratizing initiative – that the MSC was encouraged to develop both TVEI programmes in schools, and training schemes for the unemployed. Programmes of work preparing selected pupils for a small number of jobs requiring specialized training and high qualifications could co-exist with large-scale training schemes preparing increasing numbers of youngsters for low-skilled, insecure employment.

The future of vocationalism

We have heard fewer demands recently for the vocationalization of the school curriculum. Diminishing concern about the levels of youth unemployment, and the 'triumph' of New Right pressure groups so evident in the preparation of the 1988 Education Act, could be said to represent something of a defeat for the 'new training philosophy' endorsed by the now-defunct MSC.[7]

Yet there would certainly seem to be justification for the 11–16 curriculum to contain a genuine vocational dimension, and here we are not using the term to denote a narrowed concentration on practical tasks. As I have argued elsewhere:

> If vocational education is to exist, there is no reason for it . . . to involve the separate preparation of one set of pupils for university entrance and the professions, while another set is being trained for the butcher's shop or the building site. Vocational education in comprehensive schooling must be about the world of work *as a whole* and about all the jobs that people do. It must be education *about* work, not the socialization of specific groups into specific lower levels of work. It must be about the wide variety of workplaces – and about why they differ and how conditions have changed (or not) over the years. It must be about the growth of trade unions and workers' rights as well as the way employers and governments spend and distribute the wealth all have created. It must be about the need for full and active and wholly equal participation in local, national and international life. (Chitty, 1986, pp. 89–90)

This would fit in well with the view of vocationalism put forward by the great American educationalist John Dewey. When Dewey argued for the development of vocational education, he defined it as an activity which

... acknowledges the full intellectual and social meaning of a vocation, including: instruction in the historic background of present conditions; training in science to give intelligence and initiative in dealing with material and agencies of production; and study of economics, civics and politics to bring the future worker into touch with the problems of the day and the various methods proposed for their improvement. (Dewey, 1916, p. 372)

For Dewey, vocational education could exist alongside, and sometimes even subsume, all manner of academic activities.

It is equally true that there is a real place for the vocational in post-16 education, but not in terms of a structure which divides students up into two categories: 'academic sheep' and 'vocational goats'. Andy Green has argued in a recently-published article (Green, 1990 and in this volume) that in the matter of post-16 provision we have much to learn from Continental countries – and particularly Sweden with its comprehensive system of post-compulsory education and training. Eighty per cent of school leavers in Sweden go on to the Gymnasieskola where they can choose from some 23 different lines of study, each combining general education with a vocational area. There is a modular course structure and a credit accumulation assessment system which encourages students to combine general and vocational subjects. With colleges providing a broad-based general and vocational education, employers are left to provide the job-specific training thereafter.

Such a concept accords well with the idea that Britain should have a nation-wide structure of comprehensive post-16 centres, offering a range of study routes based on a common core of general education and vocational studies. The ideal of a system of tertiary colleges as the most effective and efficient way of delivering an integrated education and training provision is also the long-term aim of the IPPR Report *A British Baccalauréat*, published in July 1990 (see Green, 1991 and in this volume). In the meantime, the Certificate of Pre-Vocational Education (CPVE) should be replaced by courses of a higher intellectual content. Access and progression through the system should be made easier. And we might then begin to catch up with our leading foreign competitors in the matter of participation rates in higher education.

Notes

1. Further details of the debates of this period can be found in Lord Eustace Percy's *Education at the Crossroads* (c. 1930), and in Brian Simon's *The Politics of Educational Reform 1920–1940* (1974), especially pp. 84–115.
2. The seven ITBs that were retained were: clothing, construction, engineering, hotel and catering, road transport, rubber and plastic processing, and petroleum. Industry had complained that the majority of the ITBs were unnecessary and expensive and that the training schemes which they had stimulated and supervised could be properly monitored by the employers themselves (Cantor and Roberts, 1986, p. 54).

3. It is fair to point out that although the MSC and the FEU sought to present a united front on the curriculum implications of the 'new training philosophy', their approaches did, in fact, differ. The result, according to Green (1986, p. 107), was 'a practice that owed something to each: the raw objectives of the MSC garnished and modified by the FEU; the sophisticated pedagogy of the FEU tramelled and constrained by the structural limitations of YTS courses'. See also Seale, 1984, pp. 3–10.

4. In the context of a declining apprenticeship system, employers at a CBI workshop were concerned that *the schools themselves* should prepare young people to 'work effectively within the constraints and disciplines of an industrial or commercial environment' (*CBI Work-Experience Workshop*, 14 October 1985; quoted in Shilling, 1989, p. 45).

5. For example former Education Secretary Sir Keith Joseph, in a speech at the annual convention of the Institute of Directors in March 1982, declared that, 'I welcome the efforts of businessmen in all sorts of ways to open the eyes of schoolchildren and schoolteachers to the realities of business life [and] I believe it has to be done in a campaign to come within a moral education' (printed in full in a supplement to *The Director*, May 1982, pp. 3–5).

6. Entitled 'What industry needs', this TES article by Sir John Methven was based on a talk he had given on 'Secondary education and employment' at a DES course held in Oxford in September 1976 on the secondary curriculum and the needs of society. For further details, see Chitty, 1989, pp. 62–63.

7. It is not necessarily true that high rates of youth unemployment are a thing of the past. A report published by the CBI at the beginning of April 1990 forecast persistent inflation, high interest rates and rising levels of unemployment. The 'new training philosophy' may yet make a comeback!

Part II

Specific Issues and Case Studies

Chapter 7

The Role of the Further Education Sector in Post-16 Education

Jack Mansell

Definitions, origins and scope

Throughout this book and elsewhere, 'technical colleges', 'further education colleges', 'colleges of technology', non-advanced further education (NAFE) colleges, and other similar titles are often used synonymously. This is only one indication of the complexity of the further education (FE) sector. FE is a diverse and dynamic sector, often under-appreciated and generally perceived to be of low status in academic terms. The few writers who attempt to monitor and describe its development, such as Cantor and Roberts (1986), are often forced to produce successive editions to reflect the changes that are taking place.

The origins of 'technical colleges' in Britain are usually related to events in the nineteenth century such as: our competitive deficiency exposed by the 1851 Great Exhibition; the existence of the Mechanics Institutes; the establishment of technical institutions and examining boards; a windfall of customs and excise 'whisky money'; and a growth of educational provision at all levels. A closer study, however, shows that these developments were crisis-led, uncoordinated and patchy. Nevertheless, the establishment of local education authorities (LEAs), a national system of elementary education, and two world wars accelerated the growth of post-school education, and a further significant landmark was the 1944 Education Act. This Act set up a Ministry of Education, and defined education as comprising three sectors – primary, secondary and further – and put specific responsibilities on the LEAs to provide education in all three sectors. 'Further education' was supposed, by definition, to cover all LEA-provided post-compulsory education. It thus included adult education, but not explicitly.

Although the main focus of attention of the 1988 Education Reform Act has been on the schools sector, it has had a significant effect on the FE sector in England and Wales. 'Further education' is therein defined as:

. . . full-time and part-time education (including vocational, social, physical and recreational training) for persons over compulsory school age; and organized leisure-time occupation provided in connection with the above.

The Act has further education including adult (or continuing) education, but again not explicitly. 'Higher education' under the Act, includes 'advanced' further education (AFE) and roughly equates to courses above A-level.

Under the 1944 Education Act, LEAs were required to submit their plans for FE to the then Ministry of Education, but not many actually did. The extent to which LEAs have planned and controlled their FE provision over the last 45 years has varied considerably between LEAs, and their vulnerability in this area was exposed in 1985, when the Manpower Services Commission (MSC), with the backing of the Government, intervened with its work-related NAFE initiative. This enabled the MSC to hold back 25 per cent (about £100 million) of LEA FE funding in order to purchase more relevant 'work related' further education. Up to that point, most of the planning of FE was on a regional basis through the Regional Advisory Council (RAC) structure, and the mechanism was the approval, or otherwise, to run specific courses. The effectiveness of this varied between the regions; this in turn depended on the relationships between colleges and their LEAs, and on the Department of Education and Science (DES) through the Regional Staff Inspector.

Under the 1988 Education Act, LEAs remain responsible for the overall planning, coordination and *provision* of adequate school and further education for its area. However, greater school and college autonomy, with the possibility of some opting out of LEA control, now exists. The RAC-based mechanism of course approval no longer appears to exist. The delivery of an LEA's FE has now to be prescribed in some detail, and (once again) LEAs have to submit their schemes for FE to the DES for Secretary of State approval.

Until recently there were some 700 FE institutions, and approximately 1500 adult education centres. However, over the years the status of the sector has been reduced by the progressive removal of its more advanced courses and its higher level institutions. The Robbins Report (1963) resulted in the LEA-maintained Colleges of Advanced Technology (CATs) becoming technological universities. In 1967, 30 major FE colleges became polytechnics, creating a 'binary' system of higher education. More recently, the 1988 Act, as forewarned in the White Paper *Higher Education – meeting the challenge* (DES, 1987a), has removed from the LEA sector more advanced further education (AFE) colleges which were providing a substantial amount of higher education. There are now about 400 LEA-maintained FE colleges in England and Wales. Some of the AFE colleges will continue to do non-advanced work and some FE colleges will continue to provide advanced courses, but inevitably these will come under greater scrutiny as central control of higher education increases, through the Polytechnics and Funding Council (PCFC).

FE colleges themselves are relatively complex organizations, dealing with anything from 2000 to 20,000 students. An HMI survey (1987) describes a 'typical' FE college as having approximately 1000 full-time and 2500 part-time students, a full-time teaching staff of about 150, and an annual budget of over £2 million. The same HMI survey indicates that over 80,000 teachers are employed full-time in FE colleges in England and Wales; only about half are graduates – another contributory factor to the relatively low status of the sector – although almost without exception the remainder possess one or more vocational qualifications. A significant number of part-time teachers are employed in further education and the range of courses offered by colleges is extremely wide, matching both local and national needs.

Approximately 1.7 million students attend FE colleges on a full-time or part-time basis (with about the same number in adult education institutions). The HMI survey estimated that some 1400 different qualifications exist in FE. Although FE is non-compulsory, about 40 per cent of college students are in the 16–18 age group.

Notwithstanding the changes described above, and the occasional questioning as to its legal status, the FE sector continues to survive and is identifying itself with a widening clientele. FE colleges, in ideology and operation, are between secondary schools and industry. They contribute directly to training as well as to education, although we shall see that this is not without its tensions. Like the schools and the higher education sector, FE numbers are heavily dependent on the demography of the adolescent population. The 16–18 population will have decreased by some 30 per cent over the decade 1984–94, from about 2.35 million to 1.75 million, and DES projections (1988) forecast a general downturn in students during the mid-1990s, with a partial recovery around 2000.

The FE sector is also particularly sensitive to changes in industry and the structure of the workforce. For example, the decline in engineering drastically reduced the number of traditional craft apprenticeships; and the volatility of the construction industry has made many courses non-viable. Over the period 1974 to 1982, day-release enrolments decreased from almost half a million to about 330,000. Not surprisingly, these changes have sharpened the quest for new types of students, which, in turn, has demanded more than normal curriculum change. Youth unemployment increased the number of school-leavers entering full-time courses, both in the schools and colleges, and the Youth Training Scheme (YTS) introduced around 90,000 students into the colleges, many of whom would not normally have attended.

Educational provision and curriculum change

About 95 per cent of FE students are studying for some kind of qualification, and while the traditional image of FE is one dominated by male apprentices and other trainees, the HMI survey showed that in 1985 over 40 per cent of the enrolled students were women and girls, and the largest single area of study in FE colleges was associated with O-level and A-level GCEs. It is possible that the rationalization of CSE and O-level into GCSE will increase this study area, as CSE subjects were not available in colleges. Of course, the majority of students study for qualifications in a wide range of vocational areas, with business and professional studies, and engineering in its various forms dominating the field.

The vocational qualifications are in the main associated with either the City and Guilds of London Institute (CGLI), the Business and Technician Education Council (BTEC), or the Royal Society of Arts (RSA). These, and the other examining bodies, are highly entrepreneurial. And while they each have their main areas of specialization, they are often in competition and overlap with each other, particularly in new and developing areas of study such as pre-vocational education, information technology, supervisory studies, retailing, etc. All these awarding bodies provide a service to the FE sector, but they also make considerable demands on it. Curriculum development, validation, in-course assessment, and moderating and examining, have for many years involved FE teachers in tasks that are now becoming more familiar in schools through GCSE and the national curriculum. The 1400 or so different qualifications on offer make available to those who are willing and able to study a range of courses associated with most areas of vocational activity; and where the qualification does not exist, examining boards such as CGLI, will (for a modest fee) provide one! FE colleges also provide courses related to the many professional bodies that offer specialist qualifications. Some colleges may also provide their own certification, but these are normally associated with short-courses.

Thus FE provides, usually below degree level, a wide range of educational opportunities. However, Beryl Pratley (FEU, 1985), has described this as a 'jungle'. Also a national review of vocational qualifications (1986), while acknowledging the essential role of FE colleges alongside the 250 or so professional bodies in providing a diverse system of qualifications, concluded that there was a need for a more coherent and easily understood system of vocational qualifications. Following this review, the National Council for Vocational Qualifications (NCVQ) was set up, and this body which reports to the Department of Employment (DoE) is heavily influenced by the Training Agency. It is intended to have an impact on post-school education and training, and its initial strategy is to bring together, under a simplified structure of National Vocational Qualifications (NVQs), qualifications associated with practical competences and the associated FE vocational qualifications.

Not surprisingly, the FE sector, in attempting to relate to education and training as well as to local and national needs, has perhaps seen more than its fair share of curriculum change. The post-war decade saw a considerable expansion, due mainly to the implementation of the 1944 Education Act and to the provision of courses for returning ex-service personnel. Four training colleges were opened to provide professional education training for 'technical' teachers. And although their services have now been augmented or taken over by other institutions, neither the DES nor the FE system itself has come to terms with the problem of training the profession, and today only about half the FE full-time teachers have teaching qualifications: another indicator of its low status.

The 1956 White Paper *Technical Education* (Ministry of Education, 1956), apart from upgrading 10 regional FE colleges into CATs, announced a five-year plan for the development of technical education, set targets for increasing day-release, and brought about significant increases in resources for FE. This, and the Carr Report *Training for Skill* (Ministry of Education, 1958), were reactions to a new awareness that we were lagging behind our industrial competitors in terms of skilled manpower and technological expertise.

Ministry of Education Circular 323 *Liberal Education in Technical Colleges* (1957), sought to widen the scope and quality of vocational education in colleges. It primarily suggested that this could be done by the existing vocational teachers adopting a liberal approach to the teaching of their technical subjects. Not surprisingly, in view of the already overcrowded syllabuses and the inadequate training of FE teachers, this proved to be largely impractical. But it eventually led to the creation of separate liberal/general studies subjects and departments, and new types of FE teachers began to appear on the scheme. The Crowther Report (Ministry of Education, 1959), which was virtually rejected out of hand, recommended among other things that all young people should have the right to some form of further education. Thus the role of the technical colleges was being widened, at least conceptually: broader technical education, the possibility of offering general education to a wider range of ability, and stronger links with higher education.

Another White Paper *Better Opportunities in Technical Education* (Ministry of Education, 1961) set up an hierarchic structure (dominated by an engineering model) of FE courses comprising operative, craft and technician qualifications. It assumed that technicians would generally enter courses with four O-levels. This proved to be a miscalculation, adding to the credibility gap that was being generated. Over the next few years this policy led to a rapid decline in Ordinary National Certificate (ONC) students and a corresponding increase in the more practical CGLI technician courses which allowed entry to those with CSE qualifications. The Henniker Heaton Report *Day Release* (DES, 1964), recommended that the number of employees released for day classes should be doubled by 1969–70, with priority being given to those in occupations requiring knowledge and skills such as associated with FE courses. This report was virtually ignored: its recommendations were based on voluntary action; it was considered too expensive by employers; and its priority targeting was not liked by those who wished to see some form of (compulsory) day-release for *all* young people.

This persistent lack of vocational education and training could no longer be tolerated, and in 1964 the Industrial Training Act was passed. Over the period 1964–7, over 20 Industry Training Boards (ITBs) were established, covering over half the work force. The ITBs had power to levy their respective industries (generally as a percentage of the pay roll). This put money at risk and the aim was to penalize those employers who 'poached' skilled labour from those who did train. There was an emphasis on better formal training for craft workers, technicians, supervisors, etc, and the training rhetoric was for 'integrated' off-the-job training. Many FE courses became more closely aligned with training requirements, and many colleges with ITB funding set up new training workshops.

The 1973 Employment and Training Act set up the MSC to create a more coherent and proactive manpower policy. It reflected an impending recession, with structural changes in industry and unemployment, and a growing dissatisfaction with the ITBs and the levy/grant system. There had been improvements in formal training but there was no significant change in the proportion of the workforce being trained. Indeed as far as the colleges were concerned, the recession was beginning to reduce the numbers on part-time day-release.

'Vocational preparation' entered into the vocabulary of education and training; and it became mainly associated with less qualified young people and unemployed adults. FE colleges began to get involved in providing MSC-funded courses associated with job creation and work-experience, and skill training for unemployed adults. In 1976 the government produced its plan for unified vocational preparation (UVP), which were courses aimed at enriching the skills of employed young people in jobs but without formal training. FE college lecturers, in conjunction with their training counterparts, ran courses often on company premises. It was a popular and exciting curricular concept, but statistically it was a failure and its clientele never approached its potential target of 200,000. It was poorly resourced and out-of-date as far as employers were concerned and, as usual, only the larger employers supported it. It was a scheme designed to extend the spectrum of day-release, but was too little and too late and was overtaken by the MSC's more immediately relevant and generously funded Youth Opportunities Programme (YOP).

Alongside YOP, many LEAs, schools and colleges attempted to provide for the increasing number of 16-plus school-leavers who were staying on in full-time education. In 1980, the long-standing debate on the future of the (experimental) Certificate of Extended Education (CEE) was officially terminated when a Government paper *Examinations 16–18* (DES, 1980a) rejected the proposals of the Keohane Report (DES, 1979) in favour of the FEU report *A Basis for Choice* (1979). The FEU report recommended the adoption of an integrated general and vocational curriculum framework, with a common core and assessment through profiling. After its development as an interim City and Guilds course, it was eventually launched in 1985 as a Certificate of Pre-Vocational Education (CPVE) by a DES-appointed Joint Board.

As youth unemployment increased, YOP schemes became increasingly criticized as a means of getting young school leavers into employment. They were poorly monitored and in 1983 the one-year YTS scheme was launched, with the objective of providing (government funded) employer-based training rather than job placements. This subsumed the UVP scheme, losing much of its FE input. In 1986, without much evaluation, this was transformed into a two-year YTS scheme of (higher quality) training, with the opportunity to obtain 'relevant' vocational qualifications.

By 1987 the total number of 16–18-year-olds in YTS was about 400,000 and although this is now declining due to the demographic downturn and recent fluctuation in youth employment, it remains the single largest activity for 16-year-old school-leavers. This new scheme aimed to provide 'a foundation of broad-based vocational education and training', and its training rhetoric emphasized more relevant (and presumably less expensive) on-the-job training and experience, providing opportunities to do a 'real job in a real world'. As with ITB courses in the previous decade, those representing FE on the national working parties associated with YTS found it extremely difficult to maintain any kind of educational ideology in the face of a more instrumental approach from employers and trainers, and in recent years the vocabulary of 'education and training' has been virtually conflated into 'training'.

At the time of writing, the effects of the December 1988 White Paper *Employment for the 1990s* (DoE, 1988) and of the December 1989 Employment Act are still working their way through the system. The most obvious manifestation involves the transfer of much of the executive power and money (about £3 billion) from the Training Agency to a network of employer-dominated Training and Enterprise Councils (TECs). These Councils began to come into operation in April 1990, amid some controversial cuts in their finance, and are responsible for planning and delivering training and supporting enterprise. They assume responsibility for YTS (now changed to Youth Training) and for the adult Employment Training (ET) schemes. Some TECs and their Scottish counterparts will also be responsible for the pilot Training Credits Scheme for Young People, announced in March 1990 and due to start in April 1991.

The philosophy both of the White Paper and of the Employment Act is about giving employers increased responsibility and as much freedom as possible in the formulation and fulfilment of their local training needs. The rhetoric of training (and education) has now been extended to include 'enterprise'. The few remaining ITBs are now non-statutory, restrictions on the hours of work for young people and some safety regulations have been relaxed, and there is some evidence that the national criteria for YTS and ET schemes are also being relaxed. Bearing in mind the difficulties that the FE sector has had in negotiating an element of education into these schemes, there is some apprehension about the long term outcome of this legislation.

By removing the remaining statutory requirements and handing over large sums of money to employers for training, the government is signalling its confidence that there has been a fundamental change in the corporate attitude of British industry towards training, and that the long-standing problem of 'poaching' has disappeared. Many would regard this apparent optimism as misplaced, and this shift in responsibility a huge gamble, with little chance of success.

Opportunities and access

From the above analysis, it could be claimed that the FE sector occupies a pole position in post-school 'non-compulsory' education. It provides for over three million students per annum, over half of whom are in mainstream FE colleges. But although it has demonstrated an ability to respond to change, its vocational education remains narrow and regarded as low-status. Apart from in a few LEAs, FE colleges remain isolated from the school system, and initiatives such as TVEI have done little to radically increase the number of 16-year-olds going into FE vocational courses.

Notwithstanding the continued narrowness and isolation of vocational education, FE colleges are widely regarded by many adults as 'second chance' open-access institutions. About half the students in FE colleges are over 21, but in the above review limited space has resulted in more emphasis being given to the younger age group. FE colleges, however, have been involved in pioneering access (to higher education (HE)) courses since 1978. Further and adult education institutions provide introductory courses for those with non-traditional qualifications who aspire to HE. They are increasingly using techniques such as the assessment of prior (experiential) learning, and individual portfolios tailor-made to suit a 'parent' HE institution. Not all LEAs and institutions of HE yet have specific policies with respect to access. Indeed, various studies, such as those of Evans (1988) and Fulton (1989), have indicated that many HE institutions do not use effectively the powers of discretion that they already have.

For well over a decade, FE colleges have also been major providers of the various government-funded schemes for unemployed adults. Schemes such as TOPS, REPLAN, JTS and ET have not generally provided recognized vocational qualifications because of their relatively short duration and the imperative of obtaining employment. The image, procedures, techniques and curricula of FE do not apparently attract the majority of unemployed adults. Those who do study for qualifications tend to have some previous experience of FE. It is interesting to note that the DES has designated teacher training as a national priority area, 'to develop competence in the teaching of adult literacy, and related, basic skills'. As with youth training, the 'initiatives' in the training of unemployed adults are contentious, subject to political and economic pressures, and follow on each from other with a rapidity which does little to generate confidence in their stability.

In the more conventionally defined area of equal opportunities, i.e. race, gender and ability, FE colleges are playing an increasing role, although the FEU (1989) has pointed out that blacks do not get on some FE courses mainly because they are employer-oriented. Certainly, there is no lack of evidence of inequality at all levels with respect to race, and one of the newer DES national staff development priorities for the LEA Training Grants Scheme is 'the teaching and planning of the FE curriculum in a multi-ethnic society'. Some LEAs and their colleges have developed anti-racist policies and strategies, but whatever the dialectic, the emerging recommendations are all concerned with developing appropriate policies, consulting with the community, increasing the recruitment of black staff, appraising the suitability of curricula and materials, and with staff training and ethnic monitoring.

Much the same applies to woman in FE. Indeed, gender equality in education and training is a popular issue. There is some query, however, as to whether the increased proportional female participation in FE is due more to a decline in traditional male occupational training than to permanent changes in attitudes. The recommendations for effective action, however, are similar to those related to race: adequate policy, monitoring, staffing, management support, facilities, staff development, appropriate curricula and marketing.

Another dimension of equal opportunities, and thus of access, is that of ability. There is a small percentage of the population who are severely handicapped and for whom coping with day-to-day life is very difficult. Special units and institutions exist, but integration into the wider community is now encouraged, and FE institutions certainly have a role to play.

Statistically however, it is those with 'moderate' learning difficulties that comprise the main problem. The 1978 *Warnock Report* (Des, 1978) indicated that about one in five of the population had special learning difficulties, and it identified school-leavers as an area of neglect, deserving some priority. Those with moderate learning difficulties are often designed as ESN(M) or simply 'slow learners', and in many respects it is difficult to distinguish them from others who are disadvantaged. A lack of mastery of basic skills, of confidence in learning ability, and of transferable work experience, are characteristics common not only to those designated as having 'moderate learning difficulties' but also to many adults who have been unemployed for some time; they too could be a legacy of the Warnock statistic.

The 1981 Education Act required LEAs to take particular account of the need for special education, but this was under-resourced. This is an expensive area of provision: by definition it is a slow business, it requires small student–staff ratios, and special teacher training. Consequentially, it does not show up well in the battery of efficiency indicators that are now being pressed on colleges by the DES (1987a). 'Training to meet the needs of FE students with learning difficulties' is another DES national staff development priority for LEAs. But as with all DES-supported staff training priorities, it requires some investment and support from local authorities and for many, special needs is not a priority area.

Finally, however, in assessing the role of the FE sector in the context of post-school education, the extent to which the 16–19 school-leaving population is attracted to FE colleges must be considered a key issue. The participation rate remains one of the lowest in Europe, and FE provision for this group remains as crisis-led as it was a century ago. The 'popularity' of post-school education is as dependent as ever on crises associated with demography, productivity and competitiveness. The concepts of some form of curriculum continuity including vocational education for all adolescents, and of further education providing a community service, are regarded as the products of pressure groups rather than as a natural part of a national education system. The DES appears to have no unified concept of curriculum continuity across the 16-plus divide; the only 14–18 curriculum initiative has been the MSC's Technical and Vocational Education Initiative (TVEI) programme and this is now being undermined by the national curriculum. Neither is it possible to identify a DES 16–19 educational policy that could in any way be called comprehensive.

Our post-16 educational culture is class-ridden and this is exploited by those who wish it to remain divisive. In general, the middle-class financially support their children in 16–18 education and prefer the school-based examination route. The working class generally require income support for their 16-plus school-leavers, and immediate employment is the preferred option. The motivation to accept paid part-time study at college varies with the job-culture; and the pressures for (relevant) on-the-job training rather than for (less relevant) off-the-job education does little to encourage rigorous study.

Full-time post-16 education is too often regarded as an emergency alternative to employment, and LEA discretionary grants for NAFE appear to have lost out to income support schemes related to youth training and being unemployed. Thus choice is distorted and the class divisions are perpetuated. Vocational qualifications in FE are being increasingly determined by the DoE through NCVQ; and the FE sector is expected to compete with private training organizations. With a few, socially committed exceptions, these organizations generally cream off the easy, cost-effective, popular programmes, leaving the colleges to deal with the disadvantaged and community needs.

There are a few signs that FE is attracting more attention from the policy makers. The DoE maintains its pressure on its agency NCVQ to negotiate an increased use of vocational qualifications for entry into higher education. This means that some form of relationship must exist between the NVQ structure, GCSEs and higher qualifications, and hopefully an assured role for FE colleges. Not to be outdone, the DES published (1989) a speech by Kenneth Baker, the then Secretary of State for Education and Science, in which he identified FE as a sector in its own right, and suggested a 'coherent strategy' on three fronts comprising: action on the FE curriculum; action on the image and marketing of FE; and action on the organization of FE colleges. There is little that is new in such a strategy. However, the concept of a core curriculum for the 16–19 group was followed up in November 1989 by Secretary of State John Macgregor. He instructed the DES agencies, the Schools Examination and Assessment Council (SEAC) and the National Curriculum Council (NCC) to take the lead in constructing a form of core curriculum for 16–19-year-olds. These 'initiatives' are to be welcomed, but they could be educationally flawed if they remain separate from one other and the role of FE is left merely to market forces.

Perhaps the greatest test of the government's intention as to the role of mainstream FE colleges in post-16 education, is whether the demographic downturn in this age group will be used as an opportunity to increase the participation rate and quality of vocational education, or simply as an opportunity to reduce the size of the FE teaching force.

Chapter 8

The Education Reform Act and the Future of the Tertiary College

Paul Barrow

It is clear that the Education Reform Act of 1988 is already having a significant impact on all sectors of education in England and Wales. The Act has a cohesiveness which is bound together by a general political framework borne not out of consensus but out of a determined political, economic and ideological conviction. An aspect of state education which has received little attention in this respect, and indeed which is largely ignored by the Act itself, is the tertiary college.

The establishment of tertiary colleges as new institutions of post-compulsory education has been potentially one of the most significant educational developments of recent years. It has provided an opportunity for post-16 education to develop a clearer, less fragmented, more cohesive identity: an opportunity at local level to establish a planned educational provision within the plethora of certifying bodies and qualifications, across a wide range of needs and experiences in local communities.

The aim of this paper is to identify the unique nature of tertiary colleges and to examine how the provisions of the 1988 Act will affect this. Let us first outline those provisions of the Act which will most significantly affect tertiary colleges.

The two major issues which lie at the heart of the reform of further education (FE) are the delegation of powers from local authorities to individual colleges, and the changing composition of governing bodies. The former includes significant managerial and financial control given over to the governing bodies of these institutions. The make-up of governing bodies will also radically change in that their composition will reflect the Government's keenness to give a greater degree of involvement within the institutions to the business and industrial sectors. In addition, other reforms will affect colleges. Schools will have the right to opt out of local education authority (LEA) control, and to be funded directly by the Department of Education and Science (DES). The implementation of the national curriculum will have an impact on the academic and vocational curriculum of colleges. Finally, the current review of vocational qualifications by the National Council for Vocational Qualifications (NCVQ) will affect the way in which the vocational curriculum is developed and delivered.

It is the contention of this chapter that because of the particular nature of tertiary colleges, as opposed to sixth-form colleges or colleges of FE, the Act will have a significant effect on their future development.

There are five basic but interrelated considerations which help to define a tertiary college: its students; its curriculum offer; its ethos; its structure; and its place within the overall state education provision within the locality. Let us consider each of these in turn.

Students

Students themselves reflect the wide range of academic, vocational, pre-vocational and recreational opportunities that a local education provision will need to offer (see Terry, 1987, p. 32). Within the 16–19 age range, this provision will encompass a wide variety of educational outcomes from university matriculation to the requirements of students with special educational needs.

In addition, two other groups of students might be identified. The first are those students from colleges' 'partner schools' (ibid, p. 64), who may be using colleges' specialist facilities or who may be on a 'link' course to further enhance the educational continuity between the compulsory and post-compulsory sectors in the area. The second group consists of the students who are undertaking academic, vocational or recreational studies, normally associated with FE or adult education colleges, on a part-time day or evening basis (ibid, p. 62).

It can thus be seen that a tertiary college might seek to provide for a student population which encompasses the whole community, from pre-16 to the grave, a population with wide needs and vastly differing individual aspirations and expectations.

The 1988 Act will have an impact on the range of clientele for which tertiary colleges seem to provide. In terms of the 16–19 age group, the provisions of the Act which enable schools to opt out of LEA control will further divide the educational provision within localities as schools seek to maintain their sixth forms. The thrust of tertiary reorganization is designed, in part, to create a planned education provision, and with the increased competition between schools and colleges, such planning is made more difficult. There is the distinct possibility that some schools will attempt to 'cream off' the most able students for their sixth forms, encouraging a bipartite provision of academic and vocational curricula within the locality, one associated with schools the other with colleges. Tertiary colleges will then be forced back into the position of colleges of FE and technical colleges, competing for clientele rather than being part of a planned continuum.

Financial delegation to schools will further encourage a sense of insularity, leaving the position of the LEA, in terms of strategic planning, rather obscure:

> The overlap in the work of secondary schools and further education in relation to the 16–19 age group, and the blurring of demarcation lines which

comprehensive education has brought about, means that tertiary planning must be undertaken across all sectors. The proposals apparently require LEAs to accept this responsibility without the power to deliver. Once schools and colleges become semi-autonomous in their separate sectors through financial delegation, the scope for future tertiary schemes will be effectively precluded. (Forum Editorial Board, 1988, p. 59)

As has been noted in *Education*, the creation of a bipartite policy for 16–19 education would clearly be inconsistent with the philosophy of tertiary institutions, but extremely consistent with the views of education ministers:

They [Kenneth Baker and Angela Rumbold] saw FE as being mainly responsive to industry's needs, not as providing a second road to higher education through general academic courses such as A levels. (*Education*, 18 March 1988, p. 222)

Curriculum

The impact of the Act on student intake into tertiary colleges is interrelated, as can be seen by the quotation above, with the curriculum offer of tertiary colleges. Not only does a tertiary college attempt to provide courses for a wide clientele – from finding a job to retiring from one, from university entrance to basic literacy and numeracy – it also seeks to offer a curriculum which might cross the traditional curricula boundaries: the academic and the vocational. The common dilemma, which tertiary colleges seek to obviate, is defined by Holt:

A fundamental decision we have to make about education is whether it should transform the mind to equip us for independent judgement and rational action, or whether it should be directed towards practical skills for particular ends. This is the distinction between liberal education – education for freedom, for tackling problems as yet unknown – and schooling as training for instrumental tasks as they are currently perceived. (Holt, 1983, p. 84)

The potential for the admixture or combination of such curricula forms is often seen as a tertiary college's defining feature.

Such a definition of tertiary colleges, through curriculum offer, is common to all writers on the subject, though as with the general definition as outlined in Terry's book, differences of emphasis exist. In advocating a tertiary model, Dean et al have argued (Dean et al, 1979), that the sixth-form college cannot provide the breadth of curriculum needed by students in the 1980s. Taylor has written of 'the integration of the best features of the earlier and separate traditions of the secondary school and the further education college' (Taylor, 1985, p. 51). Clegg illustrated such integration by describing the 'mixed economy' curriculum model for tertiary colleges based on a modular system (Clegge, 1985, pp. 57–60).

Ballard has argued that there is a 'current curricula dichotomy' in post-16 education, and also advocates a modular system which 'synthesizes' the two curricula pressures (Ballard, 1985, pp. 60–61).

However, such a tertiary curriculum is not favoured by all. Others would temper it with a more prescriptive, though still integrated, curriculum plan. Terry argues for 'a programme of lilberal studies covering all [the college's] full-time, 16–19 year old students and crossing the academic–vocational divide' (Terry, 1987, p. 71). The need for course structure rather than one based on modularity is argued by Austin, though as with other writers, he makes the case for the 'exploitation of the full range of expertise in a tertiary college [as found in a] General or Liberal Studies programme'. (Austin, 1982, p. 25.)

These examples of the curriculum debate within tertiary colleges illustrate a similar approach to attain a common end. Tertiary colleges can, therefore, be defined in part through the development of a curriculum which is both widespread in terms of its outcomes, and one which seeks a means of generating a complementary rather than divisive curriculum offer.

Aspects of the Act threaten this development. The financial delegation of colleges will result in increased pressure on college managers to provide courses which are cost-effective. However, an element of subsidy needs to be considered if a tertiary college can be said to fully provide for the community's needs. The Act may increase the preponderance of full-cost courses at the expense of the less financially attractive, with management perhaps concentrating their energies on the development of full-cost courses rather than seeking to meet minority needs within the community (Field, 1988, p. 17). This is further emphasized by the means by which college efficiency will be measured:

Less noticed is that the Act also introduces formalised and mechanistic performance measurement into further education. As foreshadowed in the Joint Efficiency Study conducted by the DES and the local authority associations, college performance will be largely judged – and rewarded – on two principal indicators of 'efficiency': student staff ratios and unit costs (or total cost per successful students outcome). Schedule 7 lays down recommended full-time equivalents which mean that 156 evening class students will count for the 12 that you need for the recommended SSR! A crude and simple rule of success for the ambitious college principal would be thus to run down part-time provision in unpopular subjects where costs, failure and drop-out rates are high . . .

Potentially the impact might be crippling for LEAs . . . where moves towards a tertiary system have been accompanied by community involvement in curriculum development and programme design. (Ibid, p. 18)

There is thus the prospect of marginalization of community education, which forms an important part of the nature of tertiary colleges, as perspectives of management shift from the wider community need to financial efficiency based on imbalanced performance measurement.

This will be compounded by the composition of governing bodies. The intention of the Act in this respect is clear: the influx of 'industrial, commercial and professional' interest on to governing bodies is intended to make the FE curriculum more accountable and relevant to these sectors of society. However, this is at the expense of accountability to the general local community, LEA representation, and at the expense of a professional education input into decisions affecting the running of the college, a major part of which is the curriculum content.

A more optimistic view is taken by Pratley, who argues that because the FE curriculum is largely consumer-led anyway, nothing much will change in terms of curriculum maps; that it is the responsibility of LEAs in their strategic role to give funding for specific curriculum provision, such as social and general education programmes (Pratley, 1988, pp. 67–8).

As a result of the opting-out provisions in the Act, the popularized model of the curriculum, separating out academic from vocational curricula, might be encouraged. Schools whose sixth forms are under threat, have been handed the opportunity to argue for their retention over the head of the LEA (which, under the Act, ironically retains a strategic planning role) directly to the Secretary of State. The curriculum implications are that the two competing sectors of education in a locality will either duplicate course provision (often inefficiently), or divide the curriculum in a traditional manner.

A further implication is the difficulty of retaining the 14–18 continuum, as developed through the Technical and Vocational Education Initiative (TVEI):

> The tertiary college, with its mix of academic, technological and vocational courses is ideally suited to deliver the last half of the 14–18 programme. The traditional sixth form is much less so, and the sixth form college has limitations without collaborative arrangements with a local FE college. (*Education*, 18 March 1988, p. 222)

A tertiary system implies planning and cooperation between the various educational sectors. The opting-out provisions of the Act undermines this, and therefore can be said to undermine the tertiary concept.

Ethos

In describing tertiary colleges by means of their students and curriculum offer, a framework upon which an ethos may be developed is constructed. As with all educational institutions, individual tertiary colleges will have individual characteristics. However, it is possible to draw some useful generalizations about the nature of the tertiary ethos, generalizations which spring from its student population and the curricula provision it seeks to service.

Perhaps the most useful starting-point on ethos is the comprehensive concept. In seeking to provide for the whole community, and in seeking to cross traditional curricula boundaries, tertiary colleges have been described as post-16 comprehensives:

> The tertiary college is . . . organised on comprehensive lines and, just as a comprehensive rejects a division of its pupils into two artificial categories – grammar and modern – so a tertiary college should reject a similar classification into academic and vocational. In its place is the concept that each student is an individual and the aim of the college is to organise its resources as far as possible to provide for each student an individual programme of studies suited to his [sic] own level of attainment, ability, interests and career aspirations. (Janes et al, 1985, p. 6)

This is a useful definition of the nature of tertiary colleges since it also makes the point that such institutions, consistent with the pedagogic developments of the 1980s, are student-centred.

The concept of comprehensiveness, which became pre-eminent in compulsory education in the 1960s, suffices as a general guideline. Another keyword at the heart of tertiary institutions is 'openness' – openness of access, management and relationships (within the institution and beyond to the partner schools and the community at large).

Local context

Local context is an important consideration for a tertiary college, which though identified as a third, separate tier of education within a locality, can exist within its philosophical framework only in the context of the wider educational provision of a community. What matters in the context of a college's place within the local educational provision are the principles of structure, since these help to define tertiary education. Two major principles need to be mentioned here: the break at 16 and the need for a planned provision.

The break at 16 is a contentious issue. Advocates of the tertiary college have argued that rather than basing its identification on age, the major distinction is the difference between compulsory and post-compulsory students. It is, in fact, ironic that the creation of distinct tertiary colleges has led LEAs and colleges to consider in greater depth the need to see education as a continuum. One of the main tasks of any new tertiary institution is to forge curricula, pedagogic and managerial links between itself and the partner schools. The high level of unemployment in the 1980s and the subsequent need to cater for the needs of the 'new sixth', has made it increasingly clear that the break at 16 is becoming less necessary in curriculum terms. The implementation of TVEI as an educational framework in the 1980s has emphasized this view since it is an initiative based on the 14–18 continuum, not recognizing a significant break at 16.

Advocates of the tertiary college, therefore, do not see significance in the break at 16, but rather in the break between compulsive and voluntary attendance. They argue that each set of students is best served in institutions of different characters. The 1988 Act, in encouraging schools to maintain sixth forms through the opting-out procedure, is facilitating the maintenance of what has been the status quo, but which is under threat from tertiary reorganization planning.

The fragmentation of the secondary sector, through the financial delegation provisions of the Act, and the opportunity to attain grant-maintained status through the opting-out procedure, must result in the greater difficulty of planning the local provision across all sectors. The LEA's strategic role does not lie comfortably with the idea of autonomous schools and colleges, each undertaking larger amounts of financial, managerial and administrative duties. It has been said that:

> ... collaborative initiatives will be jeopardised by the new proposals to delegate college budgets to the governing body whose focus of interest must necessarily be that of the college alone. Moreover, taken with the proposals of financial delegation of school budgets, the coordinating role of the LEA would be severely weakened and its ability to deploy resources restricted. (Forum Editiorial Board, 1988, p. 58)

There is a sense in which the Act is extremely regressive in that the tensions of competition which will arise from the opting-out provision, and the insularity which will accompany the greater powers of internal institutional control through delegation, will 'uncouple the existing mechanisms for ensuring coherence, access and progression throughout a range of local opportunities' (Field, 1988, p. 17).

Structures

Principles of planning and cooperation have been reflected in the development of managerial structures within tertiary institutions. Indeed, there has been an attempt to develop structures which mirror the fundamental concepts of post-16 comprehensive education:

> Structure determines the attitudes of those who work within its confines. The competitive structure of sixth-forms and colleges of further education determines that they will compete for fifth-formers rather than cooperate in meeting their needs. The structure of a new tertiary college is a major factor affecting the attitudes of its staff. (Janes et al, 1985, p. 43)

In the initial stages of the development of tertiary colleges there occurred a movement away from traditional departmental structures to matrix structures. This can be seen as an attempt to break down the worse effects of intra-college divisiveness and competitiveness, enabling staff to devote their energies and loyalties to the whole college rather than to one part of it. This is certainly consistent with the cross-curricular theme of tertiary education, promoting both cross-college servicing (of staff and resources) and dissipating the hierarchical conventions enshrined in the Burnham Agreement on Pay and Conditions. It also encourages cross-college roles for senior management personnel to supplement the work of the principal and vice-principals.

There is by no means a universal model for a tertiary structure. Indeed, Austin has expressed doubt concerning the effectiveness of one system as opposed to another:

> Many tertiary colleges have introduced a matrix pattern of management (in which teaching and pastoral work are organised on two different systems, and the student's programme is negotiated with the teaching staff by the student and his personal tutor) as an attempt to overcome the rigidities of the Burnham structure. Inevitably, such an arrangement argues for a college perspective on resources, staffing and consumables, rather than a students-hour, points related basis for calculation. Other tertiary colleges have placed faith in the more traditional FE departmental structure and in the willingness of managers or heads of department to work together because of a shared philosophy rather than because of a particular organisational pattern. There seems to be no clear evidence that either model is of itself more likely to deliver the goods. (Austin, 1987, p. 196)

What is, perhaps, more important is the function of senior management personnel in tertiary colleges; the potential for cross-college responsibility functions can exist in both the matrix and departmental patterns. It is possible that these cross-college functions might entrench the curricula divide rather than dissipate it, if, for example, the vocational and academic curricula responsibilities are separated. What is crucial to the success of tertiary institutions is the concept of 'shared philosophy' of tertiary managers, based upon cooperation rather than competitiveness, on whole college perspectives rather than narrow spans of control, marking them out from their FE predecessors. Such a philosophy filters through the managerial hierarchy rather than being limited to the apex.

Within the discussion of structure above, educational values are very much to the fore. However, a part of every principal's duties revolves around the financial management of the college. A major concern regarding the 1988 Act is that financial delegation will make this aspect of the principal's management duties unremitting. The kind of college which the Act foresees is of an 'entrepreneurial' kind in which the senior manager must decide the kind of role he or she must take:

> Should principals and directors concentrate on leadership, on establishing the

key values or culture of the organisation while delegating the actual management to others?

The single most important task facing top management may well be finding a balance between educational objectives and the new, higher profile and potentially overwhelming pressure of 'management' which, at worst, could be sterile managerialism which takes little account of the purposes of the particular institution. (Crisp and Melling, 1988, pp. 37–3)

Changes in managerial function will inevitably affect the structure of colleges as responsibilities for the running of the college filter down through the hierarchy. Equally as important, the encouraging of full-cost courses will focus attention on curriculum areas which can sustain such courses. This may be at the cost of creating curriculum ghettos within highly competitive institutions.

The economic imperative

Finally, in defining the nature of tertiary colleges we must look at one of the major reasons why LEAs have found them so appealing: the economic imperative.

LEAs have been examining their provision for a number of reasons in recent years:

> . . . not only because of falling rolls, but also, [because] of other changes resulting from the new perspectives being placed upon education and training by central government, developing professional opinion, altered economic climates and the views of parents, industry and – not least – the young people themselves. (Janes, 1988, p. 1)

The declining numbers of 16–19-year-olds has brought pressure to bear on local authorities to reappraise post-16 provision in traditional institutions. The provision of a broad curriculum within sixth forms of decreasing numbers of pupils has proved to be less and less attractive to LEAs. However, one must view this demographic trend in a broader economic context. Indeed, it can be argued that this economic imperative has been the major factor in the increasing number of post-16 reorganizations based upon the tertiary model.

LEAs have been compelled to apply economic strategies within the market place of education. This is by no means a new view. In his original proposals in 1970, Mumford stressed the economic sense of tertiary colleges:

> It is more cost-effective than any other system. Numbers can often be large enough to ensure that staff are used economically and waste arising from the duplication of provision for the 16–19 age group in schools and further education is eliminated. (Mumford, 1970, p. 21)

Mumford was writing at a time of relative prosperity in education. The urgency of prudent economic planning has been extreme in the 1980s. However compelling the social and educational arguments for tertiary colleges have been, one might suspect it is merely coincidental that they are, happily, complementary to the consequences of falling rolls and the economic factors which have led to the deterioration of the infrastructure of education in England and Wales.

Thus, falling rolls must be seen in a broader context. It is easy to imagine why a local authority, faced not only with falling rolls but also crumbling buildings, should seek to target economic activity in a single institution. The initial thrust towards tertiary colleges in the 1970s can be seen as a belated development of the comprehensive concept posited in the 1960s and before. The expansion in the number of tertiary institutions in the 1980s is very much a product of the economics of the age.

This is the fundamental contradiction of the Act. At a time when tertiary reorganization is a mechanism for making education more cost-effective, the Act appears to be a means by which active discouragement of tertiary reorganization is taking place.

Conclusion

To return to my opening assertion, the Act is an ideological document designed to facilitate a 'shift from a producer- to consumer-led system', giving choice to individuals within society by means of competitive market forces (see Chitty, 1987b). Tertiary colleges function properly within a system of local, cross-sector planning and this is at variance with the theological thrust of the Act. This will undermine the educational and social reasons for the very existence of tertiary colleges, and, as has been said earlier, will reduce the amount of tertiary reorganization taking place in the future.

In terms of the curriculum, the 1988 Act is a centralizing Act – at odds with the *laissez-faire* nature of financial delegation and opting-out. It is also a reassertion of narrow, subject-based models of the type which have prevailed in English education since the last century. This will have a constraining influence on the general education curriculum offer of tertiary colleges, and, in conjunction with the work of NCVQ, will reassert a bipartite model of the curriculum. Once again, this undermines the philosophy which informs the curriculum offer of tertiary colleges.

It is difficult to see, in the face of such changing priorities within the education service, how tertiary colleges can maintain the educational and social philosophies which have motivated many professionals and managers to opt for this model of post-16 education. The forces of instrumentalism within the curriculum, the fundamentally competitive (as opposed to planned) nature of local educational structures, the bipartite model encouraged by the national curriculum, the necessarily inward-looking demands of financial efficiency, and the shift of balance towards employment interests on the more powerful governing bodies, will all mitigate against the development of the tertiary model of post-compulsory education.

Chapter 9

The Politics of Pedagogy: Problems of Access in Higher Education

Shane Blackman

The working class and higher education

In order to understand the present relationship of the working-class adult population to higher education, it is constructive to examine the history of that relationship. What are today's improved opportunities built upon? If we begin with the era when secondary schooling was not 'free', before the 1944 Butler Act, what chances did the working-class student then have of access to higher education? Glass and Gray (1938) state:

> Students beginning their education in fee-paying schools enjoyed opportunities of proceeding to these Universities (Cambridge and Oxford) ninety times greater than ex-Elementary schoolboys. [One hundred and ten times, if we compare them only with secondary school free-places]. (p. 468)

The key to social class privilege in education was the ability to pay. Here we see that both secondary and higher education were in large measure the preserve of the middle class, as a result of working-class lack of cultural and economic capital. Further evidence of discrimination in the social structure, in favour of wealth rather than ability to obtain an education, comes from Gray and Moshinsky (1938a) who state:

> Taking children of equally high ability, seven feepaying pupils will receive a higher education for every one free pupil. Conversely, if we consider children who fall below the selected level of ability, for every one free pupil who is offered the opportunity of higher education, there are one hundred and sixty-two fee-paying pupils who enjoy the same advantage. (p. 375)

Students educated in elementary schools at the expense of the state were in large majority the offspring of manual workers, whereas students who were educated at the expense of their parents in fee-paying secondary or public schools were from the professional and business classes. Was there, then, a relationship between social class privilege and academic ability? Gray and Moshinsky (1938b) discovered that:

> In spite of the higher average ability of the children of larger business owners and professional workers, their numerical contribution to the total of able

children is relatively small. For example, manual workers contribute one half of all children attaining the level of ability represented by the achievement of the top 50 per cent of fee-paying pupils, while children of larger business owners and professional workers together contribute less than 10 per cent. (p. 416)

The conclusion Gray and Moshinsky arrive at is that if we take the upper or lower limit of high ability, an able, privately educated pupil had a six or seven times greater chance of receiving a higher education than an equally able state-schooled pupil. They suggest 'this is a conservative estimate and that the extent of social inequality may well be greater than that here recorded' (p. 372). In other words, a place in higher education was gained by the parents' possession of either financial or cultural capital (Bourdieu and Passeron, 1977). The bulk of working-class children entered the labour market between the ages of 12 and 14, and only middle-class parents could afford to keep their children at school until 16 or over, and later at university (Banks, 1955).

The central thrust of work by Tawney, and later Hogben and his colleagues (at the Department of Social Biology under the direction of Beveridge), was an examination of social inequality in terms of opportunity (capital) and ability. The core issue identified was a loss of talent detrimental to the national interest. Owing to the discrimination built into the principles and operation of the social structure, formal equality in education was not available. Therefore, as a nation we lost generations of skilled and intelligent working-class women and men who were denied the chance of (higher) education (Lindsay, 1926). When the Butler Act became law in 1944, 'ability to pay' was no longer the sole determinant of whether a student received secondary or higher education. But the system established after 1944 still did little to enhance opportunities for working-class children.

The measuring device popularly known as the 'eleven plus', psychologists such as Burt (1909, 1921) assured us, could measure abilities in children which had been inherited in 'a fixed and unchanging amount at birth', and which were impervious to influence by subsequent education. The two central ideas were the unitary nature of ability and its transmission by heredity. Thus at the age of 11 or 12, children could not only be put into separate classes but into separate types of school. This method provided three 'occupational levels' and three corresponding 'types of ability'. For Burt, general intelligence became an ideology. As Sharp (1984) reveals:

It determined the stratum of society to which an individual would rise and even had an indentifiable relationship with income; that the distribution of intelligence over different social classes was stable and provided confirming evidence for their existence; and that the mechanism by which intelligence was passed from one generation to another could be traced to the natural workings of the genetic mechanism as elucidated by the science of genetics and applied to height and other human variables. (p. 45)

What was previously selection by elimination or ability to pay, became selection by differentiation – by the establishment of three specific types of school designed to cater for pupils with three different 'kinds of ability' and with a more or less specialized relation to three occupational sectors: manual, technical and professional (Halsey, Floud and Anderson, 1961). Put simply, grammar schools fed the middle-class professions and modern schools fed the manual working-class jobs. There was free access to secondary schooling but not within *sectors* of secondary schooling. The tripartite divisions were rigidly maintained and supported by pseudo-scientific IQ tests which were culturally biased towards middle-class males.

What evidence is available about the post-war take-up of university places by working-class students? Floud (1962) found that from 1937 to 1946 only 1.7 per cent of working-class boys entered the universities, compared with 8.5 per cent from the other social classes. Ottaway (1962) suggests that 'the percentage of working class entrants was unchanged by 1957, while for boys from other families it had more than doubled . . . This offers evidence that the chances of getting to a university are still weighted against even the highly intelligent working-class boy'. (p. 120)

The question of the relationship between ability and opportunity was again studied in 1980 by Halsey, Heath and Ridge. The study revealed that when the universities expanded during the 1960s, this meritocratic expansion kept pace with the growth in the middle classes; although the fastest rates of growth in entrants almost always accrued to the working class, the greatest absolute increment of opportunity went to the middle class. A significant finding was that the crucial cut-off point in working-class lack of representation in universities derived not at the entry stage, but earlier, at the *end of compulsory schooling*. They conclude:

The boy from a privileged school or from a privileged social background had a much higher chance than his unprivileged contemporary of gaining a place at university. These inequalities, however, were very largely a consequence of earlier decisions in the educational process: seventy per cent of service class boys who stayed on at school until 18 went on to university; sixty per cent of those from the intermediate and working classes did so. For those who survived in school as far as 18, therefore, the chance of going to university were very similar. It is the earlier inequalities of access to selective schools and to the sixth form that are crucial. (p. 193)

To summarize, working-class students have historically been under-represented in the various institutes of higher education. At the beginning of the century, this imbalance could be explained as the discrimination of social class built into the social structure of society. The wealthy possessed the freedom to buy education. Ability to pay determined firstly the type of schooling received, and secondly the length of education pursued. The poor possessed no such capital and therefore were unable to participate in these rights.

During the 1930s the focus upon the extent of social inequality showed that opportunity provided by wealth did not necessarily mean an equal amount of ability (Lindsay, 1926). The pre-war goal of educationalists became the provision of secondary schooling for all which might turn a waste of talent into a net gain in the national interest. Unfortunately, the structure of the new 'free' secondary system barely changed the proportion of working-class students in higher education. More recently, Reid's (1986) analysis of university entrants has shown:

> A clear over-representation of the middle classes – who are only 35 per cent of the population, but 80 per cent of university undergraduates – and under-representation of working classes – 65 per cent of the population, only 19 per cent of undergraduates. (p. 183)

Some questions about access to education

For some pupils, the experience of education is a challenge not to succeed, but in terms of how you can avoid its effect. Has the function of education in any society been other than to maintain an elite culture at arms length from the majority? How can we understand the role of the British system of education?

In a school, a central problem teachers encounter is that to obtain social status the subordinate groups require training in the dominant culture. During the 1950s, both Becker (in America) and Bernstein (in Britain) examined how pupils fail within the terms of the educational institutions' stated objectives. Both observed that where teaching proceeds within the cultural and linguistic framework of the dominant group, working-class students, who have not had preparation in the daily experiences presupposed by formal education, do not do well. Explanations of this phenomenon from educational psychologists pointed to inadequate socialization in the home/family (Bowlby, 1953). Advocates of compensatory education programmes mushroomed (see Giles and Woolfe, 1977). The working-class student was seen as being 'without culture', and lacking the necessary tools to learn. Deprivations in the home pointed to deprivation in the mind.

It was not until Bernstein (1962, 1970) and Labov (1969) revealed the complex nature of social language and social learning that such shallow interpretations became apparent. School knowledge is not delivered in neutral terms. Transmission and reception within the classroom are neither neutral nor context-free. Qualitative studies on secondary schooling from Hargreaves (1967) to Lees (1986) show that young working-class girls and boys normally wish to leave school early. This evidence supports the assessment of Halsey et al

(1980), that working-class under-representation at the level of higher education is crucially related to selective secondary school experience, and that the end of compulsory schooling is the important cut-off point.

It is not adequate simply to examine the range of working-class responses to school. It is also necessary to examine the dominant values in society, and how they operate in school. The organization of the education system reflects the organization of society. Merton (1957) looked at the action of norms in American society in an attempt to analyse the function of social inspiration. For him, the dominant principles of that society were to aspire to wealth, power and success. He tried to measure the degree to which an individual rejects or refuses these values as the proper goals and the legitimate means by which these might be achieved.

Although, in British society there may not be an exact equivalent of the American Dream, there does exist a meritocratic ideology and a need to 'get on'. So why do working-class students leave school at the earliest opportunity, when this greatly reduces their chance of achieving success? We need to look again at the dominant values in society and the working-class response to them in general. Brown (1987) looks at working-class pupils' responses to school in terms of *getting in* to the working-class labour market, *getting out* of that social class location, and *getting on* with the practical struggle of life. What needs to be fleshed out are the sociological and cultural pressures which make up female and male working-class responses. This must include the way in which stereotypical sexual and occupational identities place boundaries on class aspirations (Blackman, 1987; Holland, 1988). Working-class students can see education as an alien influence because it separates them from friends, parents, family or local community. The response to school is not a straightforward rejection or acceptance. To reject school is not a rejection of social aspiration. What is achieved by leaving school is a refusal to accept a certain kind of knowledge and learning (Willis, 1982).

Given this the question still remains: Why do working-class pupils leave school with such urgency? The thrust to become an adult and have access to adult commodities and pleasures drives many pupils to assess further education as too prolonged. These values also dominate and structure available options for the working class, who, without capital ('the ability to pay' for education), see the likelihood of success as *outside* education.

This may go some way to explaining popular support for the recent spread of the New Vocationalism in the higher and further education sectors (Benn and Fairley, 1986), which affects the provision of courses available to the access student. Green (1986) and Robinson (1986) identify problems of divisions, barriers and predestined outcomes for adults who enter college: thresholds remain with respect to access to the privileged academic curriculum. But hurdles are reduced for specifically vocational courses which direct individuals into restricted occupational sectors relevant to their social origins (Finn, 1987;

Cockburn, 1987). Thus we have *further* access to a curriculum of transferable skills and low aspirations rather than *newfound* access to a curriculum of high aspiration and self-development (see Brown 1989; Chitty 1989).

Teaching access

Why then do working-class adult students present themselves before an education system that has already classified them as ineducable? Unlike undergraduates straight from school, access students have to shake off the routine developed to cope with repetitive work or the daily round of bringing up children, and often both (Mee and Wiltshire, 1978).

Traditionally, a place in higher education has been available only after meeting numerous thresholds. College courses are high status because they are part of an elite culture. Access to this status knowledge is kept out of sight of the 'uncertificated'. These qualification barriers create and foster a powerful imagery which is a key element to the introspective way in which access students view higher education. Entrance to college evokes personal memories of school and its social and symbolic order. Whether positive or negative, this past experience may be their only reference point for understanding their new educational environment. These feelings of unfamiliarity and strong attitudes of mistrust are real, and ones which the college lecturer needs to be sensitive towards (Thompson, 1980).

Access students possess an immense range of different expectations. At the outset many are convinced that they do not deserve to be in the building. These assumptions require unravelling in a manner which allows the students to respect themselves, their aspirations, other students' differing aims, and the new relationship with a teacher.

A difficult issue for the teacher is how to accommodate the students' willingness to learn; the desire to understand something new. While the teacher will try to use and build upon the experience of the adult student, the student may find it difficult to examine those experiences in an objective way. Students possess relevant first-hand experience and practical knowledge which can be brought to the lesson and discussed, and such experience does not present a problem which must be either extracted or replaced with something new and better. For example, a student's experience of attending an elementary school before the Butler Act 1944, is valuable in a lesson assessing the historical context and development of state schooling. Or an individual who has had direct experience of sexual abuse as a child can bring a more sensitive understanding to a discussion on problems within the modern family and welfare services.

However, students may consider that their experience is unworthy or not relevant in the classroom because it is not 'objective' or academic. They may have been taught that lived experience is unsuitable as a matter for discussion. These expectations can make the student unwilling and unprepared to speak.

Feminist studies and theory have been a major source of validation here, with respect to challenging what is a legitimate subject for learning (Oakley, 1981; Harding, 1987). This approach insists that female experience of a social phenomenon is a valid subject for discussion. Can we imagine men having to insist upon the legitimacy of their experience?

Access students face the additional problem that they have entered college to be taken *beyond* their experience. They may demand that the teacher bring forth the 'new knowledge' and not dwell upon their subjectivity, which may be seen as irrelevant to learning. Adult students are suspicious of the new learning environment because their past socialization into school-based routines still resides in them. It takes time to voluntarily put pen to paper or fingers on a keyboard without the thought that they could be totally humiliated.

The access class will necessarily be of mixed ability since selection does not occur. The teacher is obliged to operate a variety of different techniques to encourage learning from formal lecture through to project work, the use of audio visual resources and games. There is considerable flexibility in the context of open learning which is not determined by examination or a specified syllabus. However, this flexibility can be dangerous because the students often expect the teacher simply to 'open the door' of knowledge.

When given individual help and support, access students may feel that they are either receiving undue special attention or that this amounts to soft treatment, which reinforces the feeling that they are unworthy. In this way, students can be made to feel culturally deprived. Here, access education raises an old issue – the problem of 'compensatory education'. The central ideological thesis of the compensatory approach reveals pupils to be 'inadequate' because they 'lacked something'. Within this model, students blame themselves for their failures and so the issues are personalized. This internationalization in turn causes the student to reject personal experience. From the access teacher's perspective, realization of the potential within this problem can provide re-routing strategies, to show adult students the necessity of an adequate educational environment and the power of social assumptions underlying what counts as valid knowledge (Bernstein 1970) in the learning environment. Although the student may perceive problems on returning to education, it is incorrect for the teacher to use such perceptions as a starting-point. This would be to direct attention away from the context and transmisssion of knowledge which previously failed to give the student an adequate educational context for reception.

The university lecturer does not usually face the problem of the undergrad-uate who has not written an essay for five or ten years. New students fresh from A-level studies and those who have simply taken a year or two out before going on to university still possess a structured pedagogic practice. In contrast, access teachers encounter students who not only suffer from 'writer's block' but who are unable even to put a word on a page. In general, access courses supply students with 'user friendly' booklets on how to write essays. However in the early stages, whether a piece of work is a short story, interpretation of an article in a newspaper or an essay, students approach the task with an expectation that they themselves rather than the work are being examined. The experience of essay writing becomes an evaluation of their capacity.

The teacher must allow space for the students so that their lived experience can nestle alongside the academic approach. It should not be the priority of the teacher to demand that the student switch from an everyday common-sense mode to an academic mode as though one approach is at the expense of the other. Many students are not just unfamiliar with a more analytical style, but are positively fearful of such conceptual understanding because it can appear value-laden or abstracted from real life. Furthermore, a classroom setting which offers a competitive arena may leave little room for students who need encouragement rather than league tables of merit.

How, then, can one assess access students' academic work? It is surely preferable to return students' essays without a grade: to give a mark is too restrictive. To grade a piece of work from a student returning to education reinserts the old competitive system which previously excluded them. However, it does not follow from this that the student's work goes without rigorous examination. Grading as a system of hierarchial award represents the tip of an iceberg underneath which should be the teacher's evaluation of the student's whole effort. In this context, a grade is irrelevant whether D+ or A−. More important to students are constructive comments which will help them to improve their style, clarity and depth in writing an essay. To give a grade with little comment leaves the student alone in a world of academic mythology: 'How did I get such a high (or low) grade?' An additional reason for not using grades is due to their unsuitability within a mixed ability classroom; certain students are very capable and could quite easily move on to a degree course, whereas other students may have equal capacity but need to develop their confidence.

Access students require a base of confidence, and signposts from which to work until they can develop their own independence. When I see each student, I write a page of notes and sometimes more. First, this is to explain what good features are within the work; second, to provide a commentary on the areas covered and their relation to wider points or examples which may not have been mentioned; third, to suggest points for improvement, dealing with language, style, structure, elaboration of central arguments, depth of understanding and coherence. Such an approach to marking essays provides the students with a holistic understanding of their work. Finally, I end on an encouraging note with reference to the next piece of work.

The challenge that access students bring to higher education needs to be received by the academic community − not pushed outside its boundary. It is because the adult student enters college without the correct 'pass cards' that they can be seen as dangerous; the culture and knowledge traditionally enshrined through specification is no longer confined to special, well-chosen persons.

Without the pedagogic discipline of A-levels, the access student still has a tendency to question both the knowledge within the subject and the means of explanation. These students return to education with a more critical eye. The access student does not enter college on a 'pedagogic high': her or his perceptions bear more relation to how education failed or excluded them in the past. Furthermore, the age grading within education gives the impression that if you are an adult student at college, your presence is due to an earlier failure. The predominance of young people within higher education encourages the assumption that this is not your second chance but your last chance. However, all this does not mean that the access student enters college on a 'pedagogic low'; the attitude is rather one of: 'Is this really for me?' or 'I think I can pick up the pieces'.

Conclusion

This chapter has dealt with the historical and sociological factors relating to working-class under-representation in higher education. It has also focused upon the new emergence of adult access students into this selective education site.

Formal equality before the law to receive free secondary education as laid down in the Butler Act, gave the appearance of 'parity of esteem' by generalizing educational opportunity. Instead, a divisive tripartite system of selective schooling was set up, which did, and does, not fulfil these optimistic hopes. The story of under-representation has continued through to the 1990s like some tragic soap opera. To fuel this pessimism, the most up-to-date statistics from the DES about school-leaver qualifications reveal that for the first time since the war, all measures of educational improvement are at a standstill; indeed there has been no improvement in standards since 1983 (Sofer, 1988). This serves to reinforce the conclusion by Halsey at al (1980), that the crucial cut-off point in working-class lack of representation is at the end of compulsory schooling, owing to inequalities of access to selective schools and to the sixth form. Educational outcomes are notoriously slow to show their effects, but the length of the Conservative administration to date suggests that this stagnation is at least partly attributable to current policies.

The history of British state education has been the history of working-class under-achievement. Early explanations of this failure were pathological, with respect to inadequacies in the individual, family and local community. This deficit model was exposed in the early 1970s for its gross inaccuracies and misleading assumptions. Attention then moved towards the internal organization of the school, examining the social assumptions underlying what counts as valid knowledge.

The arrival of access students in polytechnics or universities has been seen as a problem because they do not possess the correct 'entrance cards'. This lack of legitimacy can have disastrous consequences for all concerned if the college fails to examine its transmission, evaluation and reception of knowledge. It would be all too easy to replay the old problem of working-class unfamiliarity with the middle-class context of education as a means to validate exclusion from status knowledge.

Current changes to the education system can be seen as a movement away from the principles of equality to the new principles of acquisition. Thresholds and barriers are being reintroduced within the secondary and higher education sectors to ensure that any choice a student may make will still have a predestined, class-based outcome. It is the purpose of access teaching to try to limit the effects of such inequalities.

Chapter 10

Gender and Access

Mavis Green and Pamela Percy

It is widely accepted that there is a need to increase participation in higher education. Statements from the Council for Industry and Higher Education (1987), Foundation for Science and Technology (1987), Industry Matters Forum (1988), the Engineering Council and Society of Education Officers (1988), the Equal Opportunities Group of the National Advisory Body (1988), the Committee of Vice-Chancellors and Principals and Standing Conference on University Entrance (1988) all argue for wider access. After a period of cutting university places, it is even government policy. (Alan Smithers and Pamela Robinson, *Increasing Participation in Higher Education*, 1989)

Flavour of the month, the notion of access to higher education thus appears on influential agendas. Sponsored by BP, the largest blue-chip company in the land, the report quoted above provides further evidence of the emphasis currently accorded to 'access'. But, as Smithers and Robinson acknowledge (p. 26), access is not a simple or unambiguous term. For some, promoting access to higher education means simply encouraging *more* students, while for others, access implies opening up higher education to *different* students, to groups not traditionally granted easy entry to higher education. Such groups may be defined by reference to age, class, gender, and ethnicity.

Yet even the 'different student' camp has its own tensions, between those whose focus is on facilitating access to a specific subject area – computing, for example, or law or teacher education – and those whose focus is more on the subjective, on empowering members of 'non-traditional' groups to value themselves as eligible and appropriate candidates for study at an advanced level. This latter, multi-exit approach to access offers a more generalized preparation for higher education. Not all doors are opened by this empowering approach: science and engineering departments commonly place more emphasis on the subject than on the learner and demand high levels of knowledge in maths and physics. In practice, multi-exit access students largely enter courses such as social science, humanities, teacher education and social work.

This paper is particularly concerned with these multi-exit forms of access provision; such courses are characterized by their return to study, confidence-raising, and experiential elements, as well as having more specific components which prepare students for particular degree routes. Their titles reinforce the renaissance spirit of their project; with such names as Threshold, Fresh Horizons, New Horizons, Open Routes, Gateway, Fresh Start, Making Experience Count, they appeal to optimism, social advancement and personal progress.

Multi-exit access provision has grown substantially during the past 10 to 15 years. Courses may take place in adult, further, or higher education contexts. They share a common purpose: to encourage non-traditional students into formal learning by realizing their own potential; to offer a relatively informal pedagogy which is participative, and which draws on, and seeks to affirm, students' own experience. While early subject-focused forms of access provision aimed at encouraging more Asian and Afro-Caribbean men and women to become teachers and social workers, the vast majority of multi-exit access provision is designed to meet the needs of women students. Thus multi-exit access provision is largely part-time day provision, chiefly for women who have had no previous post-school formal education.

This paper attempts to explore some of the ways in which multi-exit access relates to gender divisions. This is not a straightforward task since both 'gender' and 'access' are complex notions, each operating on a number of levels. Access arrangements have had a remarkably good press over the last three to four years. Access is a 'good thing' in policy documents; it is a 'good thing' for important committees to investigate and champion. But there is more to access than public triumphalism. Access is more than policy; it is also a set of institutional and pedagogic practices, and a cluster of experiences for adult students. Whilst *historically* these dimensions interrelate in a mesh of specific and local events, *analytically*, sharp divisions are drawn between policy, practice, and personal experience. Social analysis in general offers no easy ways to reconcile public provision and private experience. Indeed one of the challenges to sociology from feminist analysis has been the task of bringing together broad social movements, and personal and local experience.

While access arrangements may be viewed from both policy and experiential perspectives, so too may gender divisions be explored in economic, familial and subjective terms. Both access arrangements and gender divisions intersect the public and private, and both are many faceted. We have tried to indicate this by the form of the discussion presented here as well as by its content. So far as form is concerned, the two authors of this piece have for some years been closely involved in counselling or teaching capacities in multi-exit access provision in a London polytechnic. Over the decade we have made personal contact with about 1,000 access students, the vast majority of whom have been women. The discussion draws largely on this shared experience. We have sought to illustrate the cross-cutting public and private aspects of gender divisions and access provision by presenting instances of this personal experience alongside more discursive material. Thus direct reportage from counselling and teaching perspectives is included along with more specific 'pictures' – box-ruled accounts of incidents and individual students. We do this as a reminder of the many mediations which take place between policy and practice and personal experience – a reminder that the actual lives and educational careers of women students are constructed in the interstices of often conflicting forces: the climate of opinion and possibility shaped by policy pronouncements; the local and specific character of access provision; and familial relations which substantially frame educational opportunities, aspirations, and self-doubts.

So far as content is concerned, the discussion moves from the broader social context of women students to focus specifically on issues of teaching and learning. Our central argument is that access to higher education courses has been constructed around an idealized version of women students which, in some important respects, works against the explicit purpose of democratizing access to higher education. We present the view that the ideal-type student inscribed in access courses is built around a limiting stereotype which confirms and reproduces gender divisions, serving to constrain rather than to empower women students.

The discussion proceeds as follows: a first section considers the wider context of access provision at the personal costs of educational participation, and briefly looks at the particular hurdles – economic, familial, subjective – which confront women students. The second section discusses a central dilemma of access pedagogy – the difficulty of providing a supportive, flexible and non-threatening learning environment, while at the same time inducting students into modes of teaching and learning to be found in higher education, modes which have markedly masculine characteristics. Multi-exit access shares many of the pedagogic assumptions of other liberal arts and social science provision. This second section, then, considers the adequacy of liberal pedagogy for women students.

Personal costs of access participation

Economic costs
Financing full- or part-time study is difficult for any student, since many factors contribute to the worsening climate of economic support for study – changes in the grants system, the introduction of student loans, sharply rising fee levels, and the increasingly severe application of the '21-hour rule' which allows unemployed people to study part-time.

> Jack spent 2 years preparing for his return to education. A 43-year-old nurse on a mental ward, he managed to save enough to pay his rent and all household bills for one year in advance, to give up his employment and concentrate on education. After access, he realized an ambition of many years by completing a social work course.

Adult students, with their already existing domestic, familial and financial commitments, face a high economic barrier to study. For women students on part-time access courses, this impediment takes on a gender-specific character. Women may be waged, unemployed on benefit, or supported by a family wage. While waged women may be able to meet fees, many unemployed women on benefit usually have young children. They may be able to find concessionary fees but cannot cope with child-care costs associated with study. The high costs of nursery provision in education (where this is available) have done nothing to ease this financial burden. For women who are dependent on a family wage, there are more subtle difficulties in getting access fees recognized – by their partners *and* by themselves – as a legitimate expense. Often the family wage barely covers household expenses as far as women are concerned; even wives of high-wage husbands cannot necessarily afford the costs of study. And frequently we have met women who, although poor and in reality unemployed, have been held back from claiming a concessionary fee because their self-employed husbands were already claiming for them as 'secretaries' in order to reduce tax liabilities.

Fees, travel and other costs associated with even part-time study create a high threshold to entry for women, especially as they are unlikely to be used to justifying expenditure on themselves and their own advancement, rather than on their role as wife and mother.

Familial costs
The financial costs become intimately bound up with the *time* cost: time spent attending classes is time not spent at home.

> Counsellor: 'Once women get on the course they get possessive about that time each week. It becomes precious. They make great efforts to hold on to that space in the week which is for them.'

> Counsellor: 'I hear from a lot of women that time is a problem. Obviously women have to spend some time at home doing their college work. Husbands and children do not like it. They begrudge every minute of it.'

> Counsellor: 'For some women, even taking two hours a week is difficult. There are many women who say "I'd love to come, but is it all right if I get here five minutes late?" Or they have to go ten minutes early to pick up children.'

The division of time through the week is one influence on women returners, another is the years which pass while children are growing up.

> Counsellor: 'Many women come to talk with me when their children have started at school. They say "I want to go back to work, but I don't want to go back to the same kind of work I did before I got married.' Women who wait until their children are teenagers often seem a bit regretful of not doing something sooner.'

Many women students have reported resistance from partners.

Jill, a 31-year-old mother of two children, cried when she couldn't afford the access course in 1985. She returned in 1986 after spending 12 months doing cleaning jobs to save the fees. She is about to complete the Sociology BA despite violent objections throughout; from a husband who flushed essays down the toilet, who turned the TV up to full volume to disrupt her homework, and who actively encouraged their children to do the same.

One woman described how her partner had solemnly warned the children that they would have to have casserole every Wednesday from now on, since she studied on Wednesday afternoon and prepared the evening meal before coming to college. Other women have reported the disbelief and incredulity with which their family – husbands, children, and wider-family network – have greeted the news that they are starting a course of study. Even partners and children who do not initially object, do so when they find some aspect of their servicing disturbed. Other women report dramatically changed relationships with grown-up children, with neighbours, and with close friends, coming as a result of even a small amount of educational achievement.

When Liz started the access course she had 9- or 10-year-old twin boys, with a husband who although he did nothing actively to stop her, definitely did absolutely nothing to support her (he is a teacher), and hated her studying. She progressed to a degree. During the first year he suddenly decided they should have another child. Liz thought he would take an equal share in bringing up the baby, as she had the baby largely to please him. She had a daughter in her second year, working on until the last possible minute and returned when the baby was 4 weeks old! She took the baby to lectures because she was breast feeding. The husband refused to share in the child rearing. When the baby was about 9 months old, Liz was in bed for a month with a slipped disc and her husband had no choice but to do the work. She was then in the third year of her degree. The chid is now two, and Liz was nearly prevented from doing the PGCE because her husband wouldn't take the child to nursery. She gave him an ultimatum, and now he does. The twin boys are 14 and very supportive.

Ann started the access course last year, but due to family commitments – children and a sick mother-in-law living with her and her husband – she couldn't go on to degree. She has returned to the access course for a second year and hopes to start a degree shortly. This isn't the first time a woman has done two years of the access course, but where family commitments have made a degree difficult after the first year.

> A woman in her early forties with nine children started the access course. Half-way through the access course her husband walked out on her leaving her with several of the children still at home, so she dropped out.

Risking herself

Counsellor: 'Many women do not begin this course as an access to anything. They would have a fit if they thought it necessarily led on to a degree. Most of the working-class women that I see don't have an idea to go on initially. The course is an end in itself.'

> Emily originally re-entered education in 1984 as an attempt to help her overcome agorophobia. She then realized she had the potential to embark on a degree course and has just completed her BA in Sociology at 45 years of age. (During her study, Emily began to see that her relationship with her husband was the key to her undermined self-confidence and associated agorophobia).

For women who have been at home for some time, coming to college is a daunting step.

> Since I've been at home I've lost all my confidence.

Housework, child care and casual part-time work – the lot of many working-class women – offer neither status nor a sense of worth. Wives and mothers are not encouraged to take their own intellectual abilities seriously. Signing on for a course makes demands – it confers an identity separate from husband and children; and being a student requires a woman to take herself seriously. This is exciting, even dangerous, and is invariably tinged with guilt about taking time for oneself. Going to college, even making use of part-time, multi-exit, liberally-defined access provision is an individual act, but one of great ambivalence. For many women, study represents an assertion of identity: something which is not-wife, not-mother. By the same token, it is unmotherly and unwifely and thus laden with guilt. For women, study involves risk to relationships and thus risk to self. Once a woman has enrolled, the course can mark out and confirm a self she hardly dares to remember or to acknowledge. Yet there are powerful factors pulling against striving for success. Being 'clever' is associated with masculinity or with being an unfeminine woman: being feminine is often associated with a learned helplessness, an uncleverness.

Counsellor: 'It's not just having confidence, it's having a particular kind of confidence. You see what appears to be the most confident women almost crumple as they come through my door. After they have been coming for a bit, many women say "You don't know what an effort it was just to come and see you."'

In this first section we have briefly sketched some of the contextual constraints which confront women access students. We have done so with some hesitation. While there are very many injustices surrounding women's access to study, we are wary of the dangers of simply painting a gloomy picture. That inhibitions, hurdles, even downright barriers to women's study exist needs to be acknowledged (and corrected). However, we would want to make a distinction – between the grim restrictions on women students and the strengths, talents, and rich experience which women students can and do bring to bear in their studies. Adult women are a force for positive change in education. We want to recognize the constraints on women students without pathologizing the women themselves. Too often, it seems, access commentary has focused on multiple layers of disadvantage experienced by non-traditional students, and not on the challenge which such students bring to formal education. (An opposing but related danger found in access commentary is to focus solely on educational rags to riches success stories. There is a tendency to celebrate individual mobility to the neglect of the more significant structural barriers to educational advancement for non-traditional students.)

Teaching and learning on access courses

It seems fair to say that, by and large, the cloth of higher education in the United Kingdom is cut to suit the needs of a white male 18-year-old student with A-level qualifications. Students who, for reasons of class, age, ethnicity and gender, are non-traditional have a harder time. The task of access provision is to prepare adult students successfully to undertake degree or diploma-level courses. That is, preparation which is concerned with increasing the confidence of the learner in the form of study skills, literacy, numeracy, oracy, and other aspects of critical thought and expression.

Multi-exit access courses, then, are generally designed: to raise aspirations; to broaden personal and educational horizons; and to strive to make progression to higher education a *thinkable* option for students who traditionally undervalue themselves. This poses a thorny problem for access providers: on the one hand they want to make entry and progression through the access course a series of attainable steps; on the other, they want to initiate adults into the ways of being a successful student in higher education. The tensions are those of transition, of rites of passage – specifically of wanting to start with the realities of students' lives, yet wanting to end up meeting the demands of higher education and thereby equipping access students to profit from advanced-level study. This bifurcation, between a concern to be supportive, to cater for students' lack of confidence, and a concern to be tough, to introduce students to the skills, knowledge, and cultural practices of a relatively exclusive social organization, places great demands on tutors – it structures the form of access provision in important ways.

Course design for women students

Post-school education is not compulsory, it is voluntary. You have to *attract* students: they are not compelled to attend. So it has become very fashionable in adult, further, and higher education to appoint marketing managers. Appointees are concerned with advertising and promotion and with finding buyers for college products – short and long courses, training opportunities, conference facilities, research and consultancy, and so on. Whilst these developments are largely driven by a concern to earn income and to recruit students, to a limited extent these appointments signal a growing awareness in education that markets are diverse and embody significant differences in their desire for educational products. In commercial contexts it is taken for granted that product design follows from a close knowledge of markets, of specific consumer groups; that assumption is not so widespread in education. While adult education is most closely in touch with local markets, higher education (with the notable exception of the Open University) has continued to build provision around a presumed 18-year-old market. The marketing task for multi-exit access courses is to develop a close knowledge of their target group – to understand the fears, doubts, aspirations, and the *desires* of women in part-time or unwaged work. This entails not only recognizing the economic and familial constraints (keeping fees to a minimum, fighting to provide child care), but also taking account of women's subjective orientations to formal learning. Marketing in this sense is a specific kind of cultural studies. The design of part-time access courses has been built around the perceived needs of women students.

One example of this is a recognition that many women have unhappy memories of school (as do many men, although they may have different reasons for their sense of failure or frustration – even unhappiness can be gender-specific). Access tutors try to impute into their courses the strong message 'We Are Not Like School'. They do this through their methods of promotion and reception, and through the timing, pacing, and placing of courses. They also do this by stressing the informality and negotiability of classes. Anxious to demonstrate their understanding of domestic circumstances, tutors are prepared to negotiate attendance, time-keeping, homework. Mainly women themselves, access course tutors recognize the many difficulties facing women students. Yet that very recognition may be counter-productive.

Counsellor: 'Men on access courses seem able to change things in their life so that they can study. Women students try to do it without a ripple in domestic routines; women try to accommodate their study around all the things in their life.'

Linda was a 40-year-old mother and housewife when she returned to education in 1985. Modular access was the only provision that could be fitted into the limited 'spare-time' she had, without disrupting her domestic routine. Her husband objected but is now proud that she got her degree and is on a PGCE course.

However, by being flexible, access tutors may be colluding in that process of accommodation, contributing to the expectation of complex coping which forms such a central part of women's socialization.

Classroom interaction

Tutor: 'The first few meetings are crucial: if you get that wrong, the women vote with their feet and don't come back. Everyone is apprehensive on the first day. They all think that everyone else is confident and they alone are shaking in their shoes. I try to name that fear early on – it does produce smiles of relief and recognition.'

Counsellor: 'Many women who come to make enquiries think they have got to battle through the course on their own, without support. This may be an indication of how they see their lives generally.'

Tutor: 'It's important to get everyone talking to each other and feeling that they have a right to be there – but to go around and ask women to introduce themselves individually to the group is a very tall order indeed. Some women would never come back if we tried that straightaway. When we do build it in, women often describe themselves in terms of how many children they have – they rarely say anything personal about themselves.'

Within the first few months of an access course, many women students undergo a transformation – they metamorphose from hesitancy into an enthusiasm for learning and for academic work. The challenge for tutors is then how to channel that thoughtful and critical enthusiasm into disciplined enquiry.

Tutor: 'After the end of the first session I often ask students to write a letter, perhaps to their mother or best friend, describing their first day on the course. A letter is a fairly familiar form – it is light years away from the immobilizing concept 'essay'. Students can write as much or as little as they choose in the letter, but a piece of writing, even a pretend letter, is a personal product – giving it in feels like revealing part of your soul. Some women are reluctant to give in their work at first. One student submitted her letter homework about a month into the course. She wrote about how she had used the toilets in a nearby shop for three weeks as she couldn't locate them in the Poly. She didn't have the nerve to ask.'

Even on a practical level, women students need to establish some ownership of the learning environment. But more than this, they need to gain some ownership of the learning process, some sense that the ideas and concepts studied will relate their own experience to the public world of formal knowledge. It is not only the form and content of academic knowledge which is alien and alienating to uninitiated women students; the very institutions of higher education can be as forbidding as other powerful organizations – hospitals, town halls, and courts of law.

> Counsellor: 'The tutors changed the days of one of the courses. One student was furious: 'I can understand that they are trying to be informal and flexible – but why can't they understand that most women who do this course lead quite structured lives in terms of time?' She thought it would be helpful if they laid down the lines of the study programme a bit more firmly. I do think women on the course would find time structure and discipline supportive rather than oppressive.'

> 'Tutors don't make allowances for the fact that we are grown women. I feel we are being treated like schoolgirls.' Woman student.

The danger is that in their attempts to be friendly and non-threatening and not-like-school, tutors risk undervaluing the very skills that women do have. They negate the one skill that women *can* recognize in themselves, that of organizing, coping, and running a home. Domestic skills are transferable skills. They are reduced or denied in pedagogic relations which are endlessly accommodating.

> Counsellor: 'The women seem to be asking for a model of teaching, that is structured more like work – so they know where they are.'

> Counsellor: 'A woman told me that although she could see that the tutors were trying to be caring and helpful, their attitude could also be seen as patronizing and condescending.'

The irony is that the kindliness of liberal relations of teaching and learning does not have many familiar referents outside education.

> Counsellor: 'Tutors need to be supportive, but only in certain ways. It's not good enough just to be kind. Women students tell me that they don't mind a few rules and regulations, otherwise they feel it is not serious. I think that tutors can only get away with a touch–feely approach because most of the students are women. Perhaps the women tutors feel they are being sisterly: "I'm a woman too, when I go home I have to cook a dinner as well". But that's the wrong sort of equality, that's equal oppression.'

Building on experience

Multi-exit access courses try to build on student experience. There are precedents for this in progressive education and from the importance accorded to personal experience in feminist writing and practice. The processes of reviewing, re-evaluating, and formally re-presenting experience can be mightily empowering. Students can realize their own strengths and affirm one another. The danger is that this affirmation may have currency only within the group. The task for the access tutor is to bring that experience into a public domain, to link up experience to legitimated and organized bodies of formal knowledge. By contact with formal knowledge, students can learn rigour and academic discipline. They can be introduced to the creativity of working within a formal framework. This is not to suggest that academic knowledge is the *sole* gateway to creative and critical thought. But it is one way; it can be exciting and it does provide some tools for survival in higher education. Experience and formal knowledge are not readily brought together. Some tutors seem to veer in the direction of affirming experience. Others seem to emphasize the demands of organized knowledge. The skills which women have acquired are likely to be those of organizing, managing, integrating; of making things happen smoothly for other people. These are not skills which have important names: they are integrative skills which have not been elaborated into distinct bodies of theory.

> Tutor: 'A woman student gave an impressively detailed account of how she had designed and constructed her garden from scratch. She had to take into account colour, height, seasons and contrasts. She had to do the physical work as well. Another student told how she had contributed to the planning of Crisis at Christmas, the charity for homeless people. She had to collect clothes throughout the year, buy hundredweights of flea powder, and organize a wide range of other things. I was knocked out by their creativity, problem-solving skills and persistence, but I was at a loss to make a clear connection between those accounts and a body of literature.'

To some extent, access provision for women has been built on a recognition of the difficulties which confront women students, of the relative neglect of the strengths which women do have, and of the strengths which they have acquired confronting those very difficulties; strengths which women bring to academic interaction. By their flexible accommodation, access tutors may unwittingly reconfirm gendered divisions of labour and emphasize the apparent deficiencies in women as students.

> Counsellor: 'The women say that they like allowances being made for the difficulties and constraints that they have, but they do not want allowances to be made for themselves, as people; that reproduces how they are treated in other parts of their lives.'

By adopting a highly flexible, understanding, and supportive posture to students, access tutors may do a disservice to women in two respects: firstly, a flexible pedagogy may also be a non-demanding pedagogy. If 'it doesn't matter if you give the homework in next week', then perhaps it does not matter if you give it in at all. Making few demands on students may suggest that their work is not valued or is not important – precisely the evaluations which unconfident women students tend to place on their own work. Secondly, an understanding, kindly and hand-holding pedagogy fosters dependency. It suggests that students cannot cope and makes the transition to the tough world of higher education much more difficult to make.

Throughout this paper we have tried to convey some of the substantial inhibitions to study faced by women, and the superhuman persistence which many of them have displayed. That persistence comes, in part we believe, from the very circumstances which inhibit study – from women's role in the family. We see the denial of identity and self-hood, which many women experience in their domestic role, as a strong motivating factor for adult women students. The tension, then, is between familial constraint and individual opportunity. Returning to education may provide an opportunity to reflect on these tensions. Education offers affirmation – different, but perhaps equal in personal value, to the economic independence which paid work can bring. But there is more to it than that. We have also hinted at the limiting ways in which access provision caters not for *women* but for wives and mothers. We have tried to suggest that access tutors need to recognize not only those forces antagonistic to women's study, but also to work with the strong personal quest for learning, for knowledge, for the elements of personal control which adult women students bring with them. They deserve an exacting pedagogy.

Chapter 11

Access Courses (1978–88): Challenge and Change in the Education of Adults

Peter Mangan

Living traditions, just because they contain a not-yet-completed narrative, confront a future whose determinate and determinable character, so far as it possesses any, derives from the past. (MacIntyre, 1981, p. 207)

One important starting-point in attempting to understand 'access' provision as an alternative educational route, into the higher education (HE) sector for adults lacking formal qualifications, is to acknowledge its position as a product of the mainstream tradition of adult education in Britain. This may not be immediately apparent for two reasons: access courses are run mainly within colleges of further education not adult education institutes, and both sectors have now come to display an increasing number of points of dissimilarity to the other, particularly in their respective capacities to benefit from central and local government funding. This current picture of separate sectors with weakening links ought not to displace the valuable insights to be gained by an historical perspective and the assistance this gives towards a better understanding of access today. A short historical survey ought to assist, therefore, in drawing out some of the features of a developing adult education tradition which have been significant in enabling access to evolve. It is also important to grasp that this tradition 'lives', in MacIntyre's sense, through being an historically extended, socially embodied argument about the nature of educational provision for adults.

This chapter begins by looking at some features of the structure of English education as it emerged from the flux of nineteenth-century society, and attempts to relate these to the developing adult education tradition. Present within this tradition was a current of resistance as exemplified through the growth of an alternative working-class voice. The tension between what is mainstream and what is alternative in adult education is a hidden freight which has continued to weigh heavily on the movement of adult education tradition up to the present day. With access, the challenge posed to the tradition from which it springs can be seen as essentially political: the movement enables people who have, in the main, been alienated from the formal structures of education to re-enter the system as mature adults with a wealth of experience upon which to draw. Collectively these adults present a profile of active learning rather than passive recipiency, with all the implications this has for those individuals and institutions engaged in the teaching of such students. As the authority which offered the most extensive spread of access provision, the Inner London Education Authority (ILEA) is briefly considered as an illustration of how access emerged from existing policies on disadvantage and became, in turn, a powerful expression of those policies. The chapter concludes with a look at the status of the closer further-higher education links which are a consequence of access development.

In the half-century from 1821 to 1871 the population on the British mainland almost doubled from 14 million to 26 million. In tandem with the desire to reorganize education which this increase produced went opposition to the idea of universal education. The system was rigidly class-based. By the 1830s, the inter-dependence of public schools and universities had been established, with access into the university sector restricted to entrants from a narrow social class (Williams, 1961). As the century progressed, the need for change began to be felt within other levels of the system and in ways which challenged blanket opposition to universal education. Entrenched opinion could not withstand the sheer impact of social and economic change which was taking place in the nineteenth century and was forced to engage in the restructuring of the education system, albeit reluctantly.

Wars and national conflicts from Napoleonic times onwards acted as stimuli for educational development. It would be fair to say that such responses to crises were characterized by the attempted unification of different classes against a common enemy. At the height of the Revolutionary and Napoleonic Wars, the introduction of the monitorial schools was seen as a means of insulating the poor from the 'pernicious' doctrines of the Revolution. Education was recognized as the hidden weapon in the armouries of the European Powers; witness the French reorganization under Napoleon, and Prussian national recovery being powered by a new educational system after their defeat by the French in 1806. In England, blunders during the Crimean War of 1854–6 could have, in some measure, prompted contemporary commissions of enquiry at Oxford and Cambridge and the establishment of the Clarendon Commission to examine the public school system (Wardle, 1976). Perhaps a better system of secondary-level education would produce a more efficient fighting man, led by a more professional officer? The British nation had, in the words of W.E. Forster introducing the 1870 Education Bill, to hold its position among the nations of the world: 'Upon this speedy provision of education depends . . . our national power' (quoted in Wardle, 1976). However, while the appearance of nation states posed a military threat to national power and indirectly prompted educational development, it was through servicing the needs of economic expansion that education was most directly affected. In a clear parallel with the emphasis on vocationalism in British education provision of the late 1970s and early 1980s (seminally influenced by active comparisons between Britain and its main economic 'rivals' – Japan, Germany and the United States – as delineated in reports such as *Competence and*

Competition produced by the Institute of Manpower Studies in 1984), the imperative for nineteenth-century British education was to become winning the peace.

The huge surge in economic growth was mainly felt by the ruling classes across Europe in the challenges presented by a new middle class and an urban proletariat which was capable of self-organization (Reid and Filby, 1982; Williams, 1961). The century saw the growth of democracy in England prompting responses from figures such as Mill, Ruskin, Matthew Arnold and Carlyle, which coalesced around the notion of education being the means by which democracy might cease to be a threat to order. The notion was most clearly defined by Arnold and, as his views resonate so clearly through the history of British education, it is worth mentioning briefly the centrality of education to Arnold's work.

The Reform Bill of 1867 gave suffrage to the urban proletariat, and although its passage was marked by public disorder, this was not the 'anarchy' Arnold feared. While many of his contemporaries and writers earlier in the century wrote in the shadow of the French Revolution, Arnold's liberalism allowed him to recognize 'the inevitability of the transition to democracy, and [he] saw the problem of his generation as that of helping it to occur, without the destruction of the whole social fabric' (Jump, 1982). 'Anarchy' meant the absence of any principle in political life, above the claims of Party, to which all might turn – the new middle classes and urban working classes alike. The principle to which people could turn was that of 'the state', and the process which would enable this to occur would be 'culture' in the Arnoldian sense of bringing the power of intelligence and of imaginative reason to bear upon social and political life. It was a bold manifesto at a time of great social and political flux: the Act of 1867 had almost doubled the electorate. What was its significance for education?

The passing of Forster's Education Act in 1870 acknowledged dramatic extension of the franchise in providing a framework for a national system of elementary education. There was a palpable sense of urgency about development as indicated by this celebrated observation: 'we must compel our future masters to learn their letters'. It is in this context that Arnold's work can be seen to take on its enduring form which determined much subsequent educational thought in Britain. This form accepted that the development of education in Britain was to be conducted along fundamentally sectarian lines, and it is in this division, in all its modern manifestations, which has so deeply affected access work.

Arnold can be profitably compared with the Irish revolutionary Padraic Pearse, in that both men were teachers speaking directly to society and with a notion of civilization as their subject. Pearse's railing against mean-spiritedness, pusillanimity, cowardice and commercial wisdom before Easter 1916 'is precisely the old Victorian-Romantic crusade against the spiritual atrophy of middle-class rule':

. . . both Arnold and Pearse believed in the link between education and the recovery of an old nobility of the spirit which had been stifled by the development of modern social, economic and political institutions . . . [they] had the creation of a regenerated society as their aim. (Deane, 1985, p. 65)

In Britain this *risorgimento* was to be located within the ranks of the bourgeoisie through the system of schooling which would inculcate the best in national culture. In such a way would the 'future masters' (now that the power of the aristocracy was visibly waning) 'learn their letters'. But what of the swelling numbers of the urban proletariat? – 'The true beauty of this manoeuvre, however, lies in the effect it will have in controlling and incorporating the working class' (Eagleton, 1983).

The huge mass of working-class children would be catered for by the consolidation and spread of the elementary school system, but what the social history of Britain in the nineteenth century illustrated was the unquestioned manner in which there was a clear differentiation at work in the approach to the task of education, and how this separate development was dictated by a refined perception of the class system. The determining effects of this were felt all through the evolution of adult education in Britain. The response of working-class people was to become more self-reliant. This was an essential component of the developing adult education tradition. It is fruitful to examine how real was working-class perception of an alternative to their being educated for the economic and political good of the country.

Parkinson (1976) states that there has always been an alternative voice clearly audible in demanding education for the working class:

> The formation of an alternative education policy has always been uppermost in the minds of working-class leaders, scorning an education they saw as just one more way of enforcing social and political control. Thomas Hodgskin (in *Mechanic's Magazine* of 11 October 1823): 'Men had better be without education, than be educated by their rulers; for their education is but the mere breaking-in of the steer to the yoke'. (quoted in Parkinson, 1976, p. 153)

The desire to dictate the nature of their education was also noted by Williams (1961) in the reaction of workers to the beginnings of technical instruction in the Mechanics' Institutes. They found the proposed isolation of science and technical instruction 'largely unacceptable' because 'it was precisely in the interaction between techniques and their general living that this class was coming to its new consciousness'. Politics was excluded from these institutes.

In Manchester in the 1840s, workers were said to have avoided the Mechanics' Institutes which had come under middle-class influence in favour of 'Socialist institutes dispensing an alternative syllabus in science, economics and aesthetics. This was a typical observation of those participating:

> I have often heard working-men, whose fustian jackets scarcely held together,

speak upon geological, astronomical and other subjects with more knowledge than most 'cultivated' bourgeois in Germany possess. (Engels, 1969, p. 265)

Despite Engels' partiality, the significance of this image is important to acknowledge within the developing strand of English adult education. It implies the innate intelligence of the working class which is somehow at variance with 'bourgeois' education. An image of the independent learner is at work here; materially less well-off but, despite evident disadvantage, still capable of study and learning. Clearly (so the reasoning might go) such a learner, who is constrained within class limits and incapable of advancement through social mobility, must be engaging in the activity of learning for intrinsic reasons, for the 'joy' of learning itself. Such a line can be traced through the history of adult education even to the present time. Was the refusal to acknowledge this 'joy of knowledge' the reason for the failure of attempts to make instruction for adults acceptable?

> . . . it must be admitted that there were grave weaknesses in the approach of the middle classes to adult education . . . [they were] too patronising, too dogmatic, too conservative in their social and economic outlook, too austere and utilitarian . . . They forgot about the joy of education. (Kelly, 1970, pp. 181–2)

As mentioned earlier, there was clear evidence that one requirement – that of access to power – was denied within the capitalist enterprise and, irrespective of the education received, still a controlled unit of production. It is at this point that the strand of adult education history needs to be unravelled.

In the history of adult education initiatives, as they impinge upon and prepare the way for access course development, the perception of education as intrinsically worthwhile, as providing personal fulfilment rather than political effectiveness, has been (despite the sincere desires of many proponents) a disabling rather than enabling notion. For this reason alone, much of the history of adult education can appear 'static' in its depiction of a refusal by successive adult educators to engage with the notion of 'empowerment'. The history of nineteenth-century liberal reformism shows most clearly the benefits, as well as the inadequacies, of a gradualist approach to the problems of adult education. People were receiving an education in increasing numbers but what they learned, how much they were free to learn and what would occur with that learning were all questions subject to paternalistic control. Arnold disliked the abstraction of 'freedom'; it was not just a question of being free to speak out but 'of a kind of national life in which people knew enough to have something to say' (Williams, 1980). The guideline being laid down here is one which has become the hidden impulse behind much adult education development – the adult learner must be educated into the forms of communication to which those in power will listen. This reveals one of the great deficiencies of gradualism: its capacity to apparently control development through inertia, to assimilate and contain: whereas the system may, in fact, lose the control is seeks through denying a satisfactory and comprehensive voicing of the problems encountered. If the only voices governments listen to must sound like their own, with problems defined in 'acceptable' terms, then difficulties are only compounded; groups become alienated and disengage from the political process. For these reasons the spread of access courses answers and has answered in a positive, proactive manner the needs of non-traditional entrants to HE, facilitating entry as much as possible on *their* terms as on those laid down by the HE sector. Access provision attempts to amplify the voices of its beneficiaries – such as women, ethnic minorities, the working class learner and the other adults it attracts – rather than muffle them which has been a danger of the tradition stemming from Arnold.

Political, social and economic change in the late 1970s created a questioning of the quality of flexibility within the system of education for adults and of its capacity to respond to need. Groups and individuals wanted to know the level of 'readiness of governmental and academic institutions to respond' to their needs. At the time there was a 'growing uneasiness' detectable 'about the repercussions, if that readiness and that response grow too far apart' (Millins, 1984). Though Millins was writing about the 1979–83 period, the apprehensions noted here echo those in the Department of Education and Science (DES) August 1978 press-release and Letter of Invitation where the DES encouraged the development of Special Courses in Preparation for Entry to Higher Education (later, 'Access Courses'). This 1978 initiative took place against a background of anxieties about race relations and recession. As a response to fears of disaffection preceding social upheaval, this step revealed the kind of unease experienced by the Victorians. The degree to which this late twentieth-century change accords with a gradualist tradition already laid down within British adult education, or the extent to which it marks a departure or re-definition of that tradition, is a question which must be fully analysed elsewhere.

However, even in this analysis, as such a brief historical survey implies, it is difficult to ignore the contention that 'the dynamic for educational change is politically controlled' (Salter and Tapper, 1981). The complexity of the inter-relationships involved is worth registering:

> Education has always been shaped by ambivalent purposes seeking to fulfil the complex needs of individuals as well as striving to fulfil social functions of control and reproduction – shaping the skills and dispositions which the system requires. (Ranson, 1980, p. 19)

This ambivalence is reflected in the position of access provision: is it properly to be conceived as part of or separate from adult education in Britain? In 1978, it seems access represented in its establishment precisely that effective flexibility which the existing system of adult education lacked. The determining feature was that its engagement with higher education was active rather than passive in collaborating to ensure that course provision accurately met the needs of the HE entrant without a typical A-level profile (Parry, 1976). To more completely understand the significance of the challenge posed to HE, certainly in the early spread of access provision, it is worth concentrating briefly on the position within the ILEA. This can also be seen to have formed the backdrop for developments which were affecting the universities nationally during this period. The ILEA was one of the original recipients of the DES Letter of Invitation in 1978. (The other LEAs were Avon, Bedfordshire, Birmingham, Haringey, Leicestershire and Manchester, with Bradford being added later.)

The early years of the 1970s marked a period of self-examination within the ILEA. There is much evidence to suggest that the reviews which took place were often conducted with a sense that the Authority could more fairly and equitably distribute resources. Most importantly, it was believed that the ILEA could take decisions about curriculum which would have a direct impact on not only the users of education in London, but on those who were outside the system or under-achieving within it. The ILEA evidence to the Russell Committee of Enquiry into Adult Education in England and Wales (ILEA, 1970), pinpointed those who were not being served by the ILEA. The evidence included a survey of students in London which posed a central question: 'How far are we providing for all classes and types?' The perception of educational disadvantage was expressed as it applied to 'illiterate men and women' but the concept was present in the minds of policy-makers in its broadest interpretation, embracing social deprivation as well. Broadly, the feeling in this period was that new and existing provision ought to have an 'outreach' capability, taking in groups and individuals hitherto neglected or marginalized. This approach was also recognized as being capable of extension to ethnic minorities.

For a satisfactory explanation of how this attitude evolved, it is perhaps more convincing to consider a level of meaning deeper than that of a political rationale. Some concept of natural justice would appear to have been at work which accords with this contemporary view:

> The inability to take advantage of one's rights and opportunities as a result of poverty and ignorance, and a lack of means generally, is sometimes counted among the constraints definitive of liberty. (Rawls, 1971, p. 204)

Rawls goes on to state that the limiting presence in society of 'poverty' and 'ignorance' can cause us to question the very worth of 'liberty' itself. This finds its echo in the 1973 report *An Education Service for the Whole Community* (ILEA, 1973a), in which the ILEA noted the cylical nature of deprivation and accepted the inextricable association between educational and social disadvantage (Devereux, 1982). It is from this period, therefore, that a concerted strategy to tackle disadvantage can be dated and it is into this context that the 1978 DES initiative must be placed.

Dr Briault, the Education Officer of the ILEA who took over in 1971 and was author of the above report, also produced the very influential *Review of Vocational Further and Higher Education* (ILEA, 1973b). This was of immense importance in determining the future of the further education sector within London and was crucial in providing a supportive framework for the development of access courses. Although the report was primarily involved with the rationaization of provision, it was concerned that the third principle of the review should be:

> . . . that the special concern for the needs of the younger, less able and less advanced students should be preserved in any re-organisation. (ILEA, 1973b, 2.1c)

Evidently there was approval of the experimental and flexible response to need which many colleges of further education had developed under the 'general education' heading. It is clearly indicated that the Authority, through its director, could see the value of the existing general education provision in terms of its curricular flexibility and teacher expertise. The challenges presented by the 'raising of the School Leaving Age, immigration and the employment situation' could be confidently encountered, given that general education could be developed. It was within this framework of positive encouragement of initiative that access innovation, *before* 1978, was able to take place in London.

Millins (1984) notes a major development within London to have been the Polytechnic of North London and the City and East London College setting up a foundation year of study at the college which would lead on to a two-year Diploma of Social Work at the Polytechnic. The planning for this arrangement occurred in 1974 and a key feature of the course was its 'targeting' of black people. The same targeting procedure was used with a preparatory BEd course for black prospective teachers. This course ran from 1978, just as the DES initiative was announced. As Millins goes on to point out, the 1970s saw reports from the Select Committee on Race Relations and Immigration highlighting the under-achievement of black British children and stating the need for more black teachers. The July 1977 Green Paper *Education in School* (DES, 1977), restated the case for attracting more members of ethnic minority groups into the teaching profession. From this London experience we can note certain features which have been present throughout the spread of access in the last ten years: its reliance on staff with a flexible approach to curriculum change; the use of the initiative as a positive strategy for implementing equal opportunities policies: and the developing further and higher education collaboration. It is necessary to briefly consider this last feature.

As a consequence of expansion during the 1950s, the University Grants Committee embarked upon the foundation of new universities not only to cater for increased numbers but also to create a new pattern of university education (Locke and Pratt, 1979). This latter point is significant in that it captures the impression of a change being sought actively within the university sector. This was confirmed not only by the report of the Robbins Committee in 1963, with its recommendations for a great expansion of university places, but by the Government's declaration of the 'binary' policy whereby 'public sector higher education' came into being. This sector, comprising the polytechnics, further education and, later, the reorganized colleges of education, was to be developed as an equal partner to the autonomous (university) sector. It was from within the HE institutions, which were part of this new sector, that access work received its greatest assistance, the universities, on the whole, preferring to remain aloof from this development. If strategies for the development of access courses within and into the university sector were to prove largely ineffectual in producing concrete results during the 1978–88 period, this was essentially due to universities' reluctance to move from traditional positions on the curriculum, entry criteria and control over sixth-form provision: 'Universities felt themselves under no pressure to work for change. They were evidently successful' (Reid and Filby, 1982). In a position of apparently unassailable power and able to ignore Robbins' recommendations such as those designed to develop a smoother school–university relationship, the passage of time, until now, has revealed one significant area where, from the access perspective, the university sector has been vulnerable: demographic trends. Universities which were aloof from the access initiative in 1978 are now interested in access as a mechanism by which, as they enter a period of severe decline in the numbers of traditional A-level entrants, they can fill up empty places on course with well-trained and motivated mature entrants. Apparently, by now, the misgivings aired about access courses in terms of their presumed effects on the quality of HE have disappeared. On one reading of the last ten years, therefore, it could be said that as determinants of change within higher education, arguments predicated on issues of quantity (ie student numbers) will always supersede those based on concerns about quality (ie the curriculum).

In April 1985, the Lindop Committee's Report (DES, 1985c) spelt out its fears on the issue of ensuring quality:

> Institutions should bear in mind the possible dangers involved in themselves organising, or helping to organise, such courses with a view to admitting students from them to their own degree courses . . . Arrangements of this kind can result in the formation of relationships and understandings which lead to students from the access courses being accepted for degree courses even if they lack the ability to reach degree standard. (DES, 1985c, p. 70)

Sentiments such as these have prompted many, including Millins (1986), into accusing Lindop of 'unsupported assumptions, prescriptive observations and ill-founded judgements'. The implication that access courses were a covert means of permitting sub-standard undergraduate material to enter HE revealed fundamental incomprehension about the nature of further-higher education collaboration, since its major preoccupation is with *guaranteeing* the quality of student learning. Studies subsequent to the Lindop Report showed the concerns put forward therein to be unjustified, with Bourner and Hamed's (1987) comparative study of traditional and non-traditional higher education entrants' degree performance showing that the former did not out-perform the latter, as Lindop may have assumed.

This brief survey ends with access entering a new phase of development which must be viewed in the context of changes within HE funding, the growth of the accreditation movement, and the recent participation of the Government's Training Commission. What ought to be remembered is the potential of this provision to affect centrally those at the periphery of established education, even though, until recently:

> . . . the development of such provision has been piece-meal and rather slow, hindered in some local authority areas by the lack of a central policy. What are needed are more courses [and] further changes in curriculum and methodology. (Cantor and Roberts, 1986)

The point reached by the access movement at the beginning of the 1990s is one where it has been recognized by the DES as an established route into HE (DES, 1987a). The focus has now shifted towards the university sector which is being encouraged to change its attitude towards the access entrant. The indications are that the willingness to change and ability to shift from traditional positions vary greatly with, of course, attendant implications for access providers in the hinterland of a given institution. Experience of institutional responses ranges from the university which sees widening access as an opportunity to be grasped and actively engages in staff development and structural reorganization, to the university where staff are pressurized by their vice chancellor into adopting CVCP policy on re-examination of present provision with a view to radical change and the acceptance of this new type of learner. Just as 1978 revealed a sense of urgency about access development, so too does 1991 since the future form and spread of access in Britain will depend (whether access practitioners like it or not) to a large extent on how successfully the university sector as a whole can cope with these imminent changes.

Chapter 12

The Role of the National Council for Vocational Qualifications

Martin Cross

In discussing the role of the National Council for Vocational Qualifications (NCVQ), one must be aware that the Council is still very much in a formative stage, finding out what works and what is acceptable to those with whom it deals.

The NCVQ had its origin in recommendations made by the Working Group to Review Vocational Qualifications (RVQ) which the Government set up in April 1985 and which reported in April 1986 (NCVQ, 1986). The group's Chairman was Oscar De Ville, who subsequently became the founder Chairman of NCVQ. The group was a classic example of the British 'Commission', containing leading figures from education authorities, professions, examining and validating bodies, higher education, the TUC, the CBI and training boards, plus observers from several government departments. It was clear that the Chairman placed considerable importance upon securing unanimity on the final report, which he did well to achieve. Inevitably, however, this meant that some of the key issues were avoided or mentioned merely as issues which needed to be considered and resolved by the body (the NCVQ) which the Group was recommending be established. It was clear that on these issues there was no consensus of unanimity, and that deferring their resolution might lead to considerable early problems for the NCVQ.

The RVQ report placed its recommendations firmly in the context of the national and international economy: a coherent national system of vocational qualifications, it maintained, would promote greater competence in the British workforce, more competitiveness in British industry and improved quality of services. Wider opportunities for personal development and self-fulfilment for individuals were also seen as benefits of such a system. The report emphasized that its recommendations should address five concerns:

- the nation needs a greater number of better qualified people;
- action must be taken to reduce the confusion of present provision;
- the unhelpful divide between so-called academic and so-called vocational qualifications should be bridged;
- vocational qualifications should relate more directly and clearly to competence required in work;

• we should try to build on what is good in present practice.

The focus for action in relation to these issues was to be a new National Council for Vocational Qualifications which should ensure the development of a clear, coherent and comprehensive system of vocational qualifications, based on the assessment of competence directly relevant to the needs of employment and the individual. More specifically, the system should be comprehensible, relevant, credible, accessible and cost-effective. A number of other activities were also proposed for NCVQ: to define criteria for National Vocational Qualifications (NVQs); to accredit approved bodies to offer NVQs; to enter discussions with the Secondary Examinations Council at an early date to establish linkages between the new framework, the new GCSE and A-levels; to undertake a major promotional campaign to generate awareness of the NVQ; to secure the implementation of a substantial extension of skills testing; from the outset, to seek the full cooperation and commitment of appropriate bodies for full recognition of the NVQ in entry procedures and regulations for degree courses; and to establish a national database of vocational qualifications.

Implementation

In the White Paper *Working Together – Education and Training* (DoE/DES, 1986), the Government endorsed the RVQ recommendations and announced that it would establish the NCVQ. The Council was set nine specific tasks, namely to:

• identify and bring about the changes necessary to achieve the specification and implementation of standards of occupational competence to meet the needs of the full range of employment, including the needs of the self-employed;
• design, monitor and adapt as necessary the new NVQ framework;
• secure the implementation of that framework by accrediting the provision of approved certifying bodies;
• secure comprehensive provision of vocational qualifications by the certifying bodies;
• secure arrangements for quality assurance;
• maintain effective liaison with those bodies having responsibilities for qualfications which give entry to, and progression within and from, the system of vocational qualifications into higher education and the higher levels of professional qualifications;
• collect, analyse and make available information on vocational qualifications and secure the operation of an effective, comprehensive and dependable data base;
• undertake, or arrange to be undertaken, research and development where necessary to discharge these functions;

- promote the interests of vocational education and training and, in particular, of vocational qualifications and to disseminate good practice.

The National Council itself has stated that through the provision of NVQs it aims to:

- improve the value of vocational qualifications to employers and individuals alike;
- encourage individuals to develop their vocational competence by improving access to vocational qualifications and by clearly defining progression routes;
- encourage the provision of more and better vocational education and training through vocational qualifications which meet the real needs of employment and prepare individuals for changes in technology, markets and employment patterns, thus contributing towards improved national economic performance.

The major theme running through all the various formulations is the argument that the country's economic performance would be improved if vocational qualifications met the 'real needs' of employment. At this stage of course it is not possible to test the hypothesis itself. Indeed, the hypothesis seems to be advanced as a result of various reports on the performance of overseas economies, as in the 1984 document *Competence and Competition* (Institute of Manpower Studies 1984). Study of these, however, shows no proven causative link of the kind being suggested: the factors contributing to economic success may be many and varied. Thus there can be strong correlation between economic performance and general broad-based education, between economic performance and particular working/leisure cultures, and between economic performance and the level of capital investment.

The needs of employment

Be that as it may, a principal role for NCVQ is to ensure that vocational qualifications relate directly to the needs of employment. What are these, and how should they be determined? The RVQ report, the White Paper and the NCVQ itself felt that the key to answering these questions lay with the concept of 'competence'. A NVQ is now defined as 'a statement of competence clearly relevant to work and intended to facilitate entry or progression into employment and further learning, issued to an individual by a recognized awarding body'. This statement should incorporate specified standards in the ability to perform in a range of work-related activities, and the underpinning skills, knowledge and understanding required for performance in employment. The NCVQ operates with a narrower definition of competence than that favoured by other bodies such as the Further Education Unit (FEU) and limits it to 'the ability to perform in work roles or jobs to the standards required in employment'.

Clearly, there is therefore an active, performance-related, dimension to competence. It is more than the demonstration of the possession of knowledge and understanding, but must always involve application. So much is common ground, but there remains a fear that what might result, especially at the lower levels of the NVQ framework, is a range of awards certifying rather narrow job-specific skills. Certainly in the early days of NCVQ there were voices claiming to represent industry arguing for just such an approach. But there were also other voices from industry arguing that industry and commerce required awards which recognized and encouraged flexibility of response, problem-solving skills, the ability to transfer to other contexts, interpersonal skills, and so on. To its credit, the NCVQ has accepted this latter approach in its published document. *National Vocational Qualifications: Criteria and procedures*, although some would argue that its accreditation practice has fallen well short of its published policy.

Who, though, determines the needs of employment and the standards required therein? Much passion has been spent, and much ink spilt, on the issue as to whether these standards should be employer-led. The NCVQ's published policy is clear: responsiblity for the specification of standards of competence rests with representatives of employers, employees (including trades unions) and professions, and their advisers, acting together as appropriate in 'lead' or standard setting bodies recognized for this purpose.

The RVQ Group felt that it was essential for the success of the new NVQ system that such representative groups be created, that they accept responsibility for specifying standards within their occupational sector, and that they would carry sufficient clout within their sector for those standards to be acceptable to all. In this way, industry – including employers within those industries – would no longer be able to claim that the education and training schemes were not equipping students and trainees with the required skills and competences; for it would be industry itself in future which would have specified the standards. For this to work, the credibility of the members of the lead body whithin their own sector is crucial.

The RVQ Group went further however. It wanted the NCVQ to establish a clear focus for national action to secure the specification of standards of competence, probably by appointing a high-level group to oversee arrangements. This has not been done. Moreover, it wanted arrangements to secure this action in a way which provided *comprehensive* coverage of industry and occupational groups. It proposed that the NCVQ and the Manpower Services Commission (MSC) should act together to propose a more limited number of standard setting bodies which between them would provide comprehensive coverage, make appropriate proposals for the important cross-sector occupational groupings, and establish formal working relationships between each standard setting body and one or more of the examining and validating bodies accredited by the NCVQ. No one seems to have produced a clear map of the total territory to be covered, nor to have identified appropriate bodies in each sector. Indeed, there has been a tendency to encourage the creation of rather more than the limited number of bodies envisaged by the RVQ Group. Furthermore, especially in the cross-sectoral areas, many observers have doubts as to whether the composition of some of the bodies created is appropriate. The lead bodies must have credibility, must have clout, must be able to deliver those whom they claim to represent. In some areas, the membership of the lead bodies seems insufficiently weighty to achieve these purposes, and seems to rely heavily on 'advisers' rather than on genuine representatives of employers and employees.

Rationalization

Implicit in the RVQ proposal that there should be a more limited number of standard setting bodies, providing between them comprehensive coverage, was the concept of rationalization. The Working Group had emphasized that 'action must be taken to reduce the confusion of present provision'. However the word 'rationalization' was not one which appeared in the RVQ recommendations, in the tasks given to the NCVQ by the 1986 White Paper, or in the NCVQ's own stated aims. Presumably, the creation and implementation of the NVQ framework was seen as sufficient to reduce confusion. It is clear, however, that many had expected much stronger action on rationalization than now appears to be forthcoming. Such stronger action seems to have been foreshadowed by the RVQ Group's Interim Report – accepted by the MSC – which, in relation to certification for the Youth Training Scheme (YTS), had recommended the designation of a *limited* number of bodies as appropriate agencies to be engaged in YTS certification, and the establishment of a consortium of designated bodies. The YTS Certificate Board was duly set up with two representatives from each of four examining and validating bodies (the British Technician and Education Council (BTEC), the City and Guilds of London Institute (CGLI), the Royal Society of Arts (RSA), and the Scottish Vocational and Education Council (SCOTVEC), with an independent chairperson. The creation of this body, together with the emphasis in the RVQ on approval of awarding bodies and quality control relating to the accreditation of qualifications, was seen by most commentators as indicating that only a comparatively small number of certificating bodies would receive the NCVQ endorsement. The commentators were to be proved wrong.

From various possibilities, the NCVQ had chosen for itself an 'all-embracing' role whereby as many awarding bodies as possible are persuaded to come into a unified framework of NVQs. In the short term, at least, there is no doubt that this is adding to the complexity and confusion of the vocational qualifications scene rather than reducing them. What has happened is that certain awards and certificates which appeared to be declining in terms of candidate numbers, and which lacked any reputation for quality in the eyes of education and training providers, have been given a new lease of life by the NCVQ! Suddenly they are respectable and some providers are turning to these cheaper and less demanding certificates 'because, after all, they are NVQs too'.

In following this model, the NCVQ has introduced the concept of conditional accreditation which allows it to recognize existing awards where these fall short of the full criteria for accreditation. A further consequence is that in the face of these accreditations, some of the more reputable bodies have had to divert resources from research, development and customer service to advertizing and marketing: hardly a desirable outcome.

In the long run, of course, the NCVQ may be proved right. By effectively waiving quality control in the first instance, by not rejecting any certificating body, it ties all awarding bodies into the NVQ system and obtains their agreement to conditions which require change towards the full criteria for accreditation. Such a strategy certainly holds out hope for rationalization in that all awards will eventually be in the NVQ format. It holds out the hope of coherence too in that the certificates traditionally awarded within the further education system and those traditionally awarded as a result of in-company training will be encompassed within the same framework. It is a high-risk strategy, however, for the danger is that the NCVQ accreditation could be seen as meaningless. If any and every qualification is NCVQ approved, then where is the added value, what does NVQ status imply, and why should it be sought and paid for? The NCVQ was meant to be more than a bureaucratic hurdle and an additional levy on certificates.

The academic and the vocational

So far, then, the NCVQ seems to have made little impact on reducing the confusion of present provision. What about that other role – maintaining effective liaison with bodies responsible for other sorts of qualifications – which was seen as addressing the widespread concern about the unhelpful divide between so-called academic and so-called vocational qualifications? In practice, it is impossible to discern any positive action at all by the NCVQ in this role. It would perhaps be fair to add that from the other side of the divide, no action has emerged either from SEC or its successor, the School Examinations and Assessment Council (SEAC). Opportunities are simply not being grasped. GCSE criteria are under review and, even more relevantly, arrangements for assessing achievement in relation to the national curriculum are being formulated. The bases for these – attainment targets and profile components – offer the possibility of convergence with the NCVQ approach, yet there is a deafening silence from the NCVQ. The advantages to young people and to society of being able to carry forward and accumulate credit towards NVQs on the basis of attainment demonstrated in school, would be immense. Clearly, full occupational compe-tence cannot be demonstrated therein but some relevant achievement can be – and we should not be asking students to undergo assessment again in later years if they have already demonstrated competence in communication, mathematics, computer literacy, or whatever.

The same points should be made even more sharply with regard to the relationship between NVQs and A-levels. Yet the SEAC, in early 1989, produced a consultative questionnaire about A- and AS-levels which fails to raise the issue at all. Can it really make sense to have A-levels in, say, law or business studies, which in no way relate to vocational qualifications? Are there no common skills, knowledge and understanding? The former Secretary of State for Education and Science, Kenneth Baker, as shown by his speech to the Association of Colleges of Further and Higher Education in February 1989 (Baker, 1989), clearly thinks that there could be – but the NCVQ says nothing. Why are the NCVQ and the SEAC not sitting down together to work out principles and criteria that are consistent at least to the extent that they permit or encourage overlap?

Given the current concern about the implications of demography – in particular the decline in the number of 18-year-olds in the population – for higher education, and the level of interest in opening up access to higher education for more mature candidates, it seems remarkable that the NCVQ should not have taken advantage of the favourable circumstances currently existing. There can be no doubt that the credibility, currency and respectability of vocational qualifications would be significantly enhanced if an appropriate level were to be accepted as the standard matriculation requirement for entry to degree courses. In the absence of such acceptance, vocational qualifications will continue to be regarded as second class qualifications. It should perhaps be added that what is being argued here is *not* a suggestion that the design criteria for NVQs should be altered at the behest of higher education, but rather that higher education should accept that the attainments – the competence, knowledge, skills, understanding and abilities – denoted by a vocational qualification at an appropriate level, signify that the individual with that qualification is likely to be able to cope with a degree course.

Of equal importance for the credibility of NVQs will be the relationship with and involvement of the major professional bodies. While the NCVQ has had a fair amount to say on this issue – and the Government too has been involved in the dialogue – not a great deal of positive achievement has resulted. At the existing levels of the NVQ framework (Levels I–IV), the provision of cerification by the important professional bodies has been extremely limited. Where it has existed, it has been based on assessment systems which confine themselves to testing knowledge and understanding. Perhaps surprisingly, there appears to be no centre of expertise on work-based assessment within the professional bodies. As the years go by, if the awards of the professional bodies are to come within the NVQ framework this will have to change. In the shorter term, however, the NCVQ seems to have made little headway on the issue of progression. This has two dimensions perhaps. First, professional bodies tend to specify for entry or exemption purposes certificates such as GCSE and A-levels. NVQ levels need to feature in the same context if they are to be regarded as a worthwhile option. Action could be and should have been taken on this issue. Secondly, and more problematically, NCVQ policy states clearly that there shall be no barriers to access to NVQs. Professional bodies, on the other hand, almost invariably deny entry to their examinations to those who lack certain pre-requisite qualifications. (Note here that it is not being suggested that professional bodies cannot have entry requirements for *membership*; merely that they should not restrict access to the *examinations*.

To sum up, the NCVQ's role in this area was seen by the RVQ Group as bridging the academic/vocational divide, guaranteeing equal status for vocational qualifications with academic ones, and opening up access for holders of vocational qualifications to higher education and the professions. To date there is no evidence that the NCVQ is carrying out this role. Indeed it seems, whether deliberately or not, to be encouraging a form of qualifications apartheid. In this writer's view this can only damage the public usage of vocational qualifications. In turn this will deter many from following the vocational qualification route and, in turn, the potential economic benefits anticipated will not be capable of achievement.

More and better

The RVQ Group, the White Paper and the NCVQ itself all saw or see the aims of the NCVQ as including the creation of a greater number of better qualified people by encouraging the provision of more and better vocational education and training. Ultimately, perhaps, one decries the objective of a 'credentials' society, where the possession of a licence to practice will be a legal requirement. In such a situation, only those possessing the necessary vocational qualification could undertake particular work (ie what is true now of a doctor should become true of a plumber, double glazing installer, and word processing operator), and that vocational qualification would denote genuine competence in the occupation. If the qualifications are based on valid and reliable methods of assessment, this should certainly result in better qualified people; if the qualifications are open of access and attainable, it should also result in greater numbers of such people. There are challenges ahead for the NCVQ however: how will it ensure open access and prevent restriction of entry? Will a credentials society become a restrictive practices society, with endless scope for demarcation disputes?

Related practical and ethical issues arise if industry training organizations also become NVQ-awarding bodies. If a Training Board is the designated lead-industry body, then it is difficult to see how it can take an objective view of the certification offered by itself. Yet Training Boards are being allowed to nod their own qualifications through. Furthermore there is some evidence that in these circumstances, such Training Boards, acting as lead-industry bodies, are proving reluctant – to say the least – to approve qualifications offered by other bodies. Reasons for this reluctance do not seem to be connected with issues of standards and quality control. Such a market stranglehold, with the possibility of self-created monopolies, sits oddly with current government policy on the market and competition, is at variance with the NVCQ's policy that it will not normally give exclusive rights to an awarding body for an NVQ in a given area of competence, and raises ethical and moral issues too. Yet in some occupational areas – hairdressing is an obvious example – such a situation has been allowed to occur.

Self-judgement also seems to offer few safeguards as far as quality is concerned, although quality control is a wider issue, too. In particular, there is cause for concern about quality control in relation to assessment. NVQ criteria require that 'performance must be demonstrated and assessed under conditions as close as possible to those under which it would normally be practised. This should be done whenever possible by observing demonstrations of performance in its natural setting, the workplace'. In fact, experience and expertise in the assessment of work-based learning is very limited indeed in this country, and can only be found within a very few awarding bodies. There is no doubt at all that many of the bodies approved by the NCVQ, even if conditionally approved, lack this experience and expertise so that we are likely to see a reduction in quality and standards at least in the first instance. The very small numbers of staff employed by the NCVQ also mean that advice and quality control to approved bodies cannot easily be provided.

Another dimension to the quality control debate relates to a prevailing confusion between qualifications and programmes of education and training which may enable individuals to acquire those qualifications. The NCVQ has made it clear that it is concerned with the qualification, with the demonstration of competence. No particular form or forms of education and training are prescribed therefore, nor indeed is participation in education and training a requirement if an individual can demonstrate the necessary competence. As suggested above, the whole burden of quality therefore falls upon the assessment process as far as NVQs are concerned. For education and training providers, this requires a change of focus. Their thinking tends to concentrate on the course or programme, and systems are, should be, set up to ensure quality of delivery, for example, by a validating body such as BTEC, or by the DoE through mechanisms such as 'approved training organization' status. There is a clear need for such systems to be continued and improved, but for NVQs they do not go far enough. In the past, educational providers have often seen 'successful completion of the course' as sufficient for certification. In the NVQ system, where qualifications are broken down into units with their contributory and compulsory elements and performance criteria, this will not do. It is necessary instead to be satisfied that each and every individual has reached the required national standard in each element. Nor can 'compensation' be permitted; that is, the process operated in GCSE and other examinations where poor performance in one aspect can be compensated for by a higher standard of performance in another. Assessment to this level of detail is not something to which most deliverers of education and training are accustomed.

Conclusion

If one refers back to the concerns identified by the RVQ Group, the tasks allocated to the NCVQ by the White Paper, and the NCVQ's own stated aims, it is clear that there is still a long way to go – with no certain prospect of success. Confusion still prevails, the academic–vocational divide still exists and may even be widening, best existing practice is being diluted by an open-door accreditation policy, and serious skill shortages still exist. Vocational qualifications may, however, now relate more directly and clearly to competence required in work: this will of course be true only if those given the task of identifying such competence have been able to do so accurately and efficiently. Even then, whether the competence identified as currently required will prepare individuals for changes in technology, markets and employment patterns is a further question.

The NCVQ was established with widespread support and good will, to carry out a role which all concerned felt was essential both for indivuals and for the national economy. It retains that good will, but some are starting to question whether its tactics can achieve the desired results. If they do, much will be forgiven: if they do not, they will actually have worsened the situation and aggravated the deficiencies identified by the RVQ Group.

Chapter 13

The History and Development of CPVE

Pauline Green

One of the more curious things about the Certificate of Pre-Vocational Education (CPVE), now more than five years old, has been its capacity to stimulate heated argument not only among those with radically opposing ideas about education, but also, and especially, among those on the same 'side'. If some of the heat has now gone out of the argument – certainly in terms of media coverage and probably academic attention – it is not because the problems of CPVE have been resolved: rather it is because the ballyhoo is now about GCSE, the national curriculum, benchmarks and testing, and sundry other centralist tendencies; and curriculum initiatives which are more than five years old have a habit of becoming part of the landscape rather quickly.

The questions surrounding CPVE – its ideological stance, its role in post-16 education and its validity as an educational experience – have not gone away. The major current issue perturbing many of its supporters is that of progression and the problem of ensuring, without formal traditional credentialling, that what students have achieved is properly valued and leads them on to further things. Allied with this is the problem of the client-group and the ever present (ever increasing?) danger of tripartism, even, as Ranson warned (1984), of educational apartheid. Specific as these problems are however – and to teachers in daily contact with CPVE students they are concrete, real and often painful – we are still faced with that equally awkward question: Is CPVE what we should be doing anyway?

CPVE itself is somewhat protean. In 1985, in attempting to work out whether CPVE was a 'good thing' or not, the Communist Party produced a small pamphlet. Here, with disarming simplicity, they wrote:

> The CPVE guidelines allow both good practice and bad practice to take place (CPGB, 1985, p. 13)

In fact, this 'allowance', if that is what it is, strikes at the heart of the ambivalence and anxiety with which many teachers view CPVE. Barker has noted the:

> . . . unsatisfactory admixture of progressive ideas and behavioural objectives . . . (Barker, 1987, p. 9)

which tends, in fact, to characterize all pre-vocational education. Since its inception in 1984–5, and indeed since the coming of the 'new vocationalism' generally, educationalists and teachers have worried about CPVE. Could it be worked up into the positive, liberating experience many 17-year-olds had never before been given? Could it be the 'genuine alternative to the academic organisation of knowledge' and 'reform the whole curriculum' as Michael Young (1987) feels it could? Or is it really just another way of teaching people once more to know their place? The faintly pleading tone of Brockington, Pring and White in 1985, calling to teachers to domesticate CPVE (and other similar initiatives), set what has become I believe, the prevailing attitude. Because very few things are wholly, bad, because teachers know how to domesticate the most ill-conceived ideas, and because most teachers do tend to put the students' needs first anyway, these ideas *have* been domesticated and many a CPVE or Technical and Vocational Education Initiative (TVEI) scheme is admirable in its conception and its practice and many a student has no doubt gained a great deal.

If CPVE were demonstratively 'comprehensive' in its philosophy and its practice, if it did not 'allow bad practice' quite so easily through its ideological ambivalence, and if it were not growing into a socio-political context so apparently committed to social specification, then issues of progression, say, might the more easily be resolved. The curriculum innovation which did *not*, in real life, produce both good and bad practice would be a rare thing indeed. What will be attempted in this evaluation is a discussion of some of the problems which have become apparent in the development of CPVE and an analytic return to the CPVE literature itself to establish how far these very problems are inherent in its theoretical framework and design.

The origins of CPVE

The establishment of CPVE on the post-16 agenda (how successfully and permanently only time will tell) was due to a particular configuration of circumstances which may be summarized as follows:

1 The growth in the sixth forms of comprehensive schools of the number of non-A-level students wishing to extend their education for one more year at least.
2 The arrival in further education (FE) colleges of numbers of students unqualified for, or uncommitted to, the vocational (or academic) courses on offer.
3 The problem of what curriculum such students should have.
4 The rise in youth unemployment.
5 The desire of governments, especially since 1979, to establish more utilitarian values in education; to link it more closely to the 'world of work'.

The situation which has pertained to the education of 16–19 year olds in Britain has never, by general agreement, been satisfactory. The Further Education Unit (FEU) booklet *Signposts '85: A Review of 16–19 Education* gives a detailed and interesting survey of the scene. Things were bad in 1980; by 1985 they had got worse:

> In 1980, when the first edition of this book was produced, it was common to hear the arrangements for the education of 16–19 year olds referred to as a 'jungle'. Looking back from the position in which we now find ourselves [May 1985], the map of 1980 seems like highways through a desert – clear for miles and a model of simplicity – compared with the tangle of paths now produced by competing planning authorities. (FEU, 1985a, p. 1)

The planning authorities have continued to compete and the scene in 1991 is arguably even worse, with the added difficulty of ever higher hedges now separating the paths.

A myriad of courses had arisen in sixth forms and colleges for the 17-year-old student: new O-levels, re-take O-levels, re-take CSEs, Certificates of Extended Education (CEEs), The City and Guilds of London Institute (CGLI) 365 or foundation courses, vocational preparation courses by the Royal Society of Arts (RSA) and CGLI, CFE, the British Technician and Educational Council (BTEC) and so on. In terms of curriculum trends, two main paths were developing: first, the 'academic' path exemplified by the CEE – single-subject courses mainly in sixth forms and sixth-form colleges; and second, the 'voc prep' path exemplified by CGLI foundation and 'vocational preparation (general)' courses, mainly in FE colleges. The split between institutions and types of course is not without significance here. Each path was duly explored by a committee and reported on in 1979. The Keohane Report (DES, 1979), advocated that CEE receive the official approval it had never in fact had and suggested that the single-subject exams could be combined with vocational preparation, social skills and careers education. (Ironically, this is a position many schools may well return to with the coming of GCSE Mature courses).

The FEU Report *A Basis for Choice (ABC)* (FEU, 1979), proposed a unified full-time course consisting of a 'common core' designed to fulfil 12 stated aims, vocational studies, some integration of the two, profiling and work experience. Although CEE, with its strong support among teachers and sixth-formers, continued in spite of its lack of accreditation, the die was really cast by the Macfarlane Report in October 1980 *Examinations 16–18: A Consultative Paper* (DES, 1980a), which came down in favour of a course along the lines of ABC and against the further development of CEE. The various examination boards were quick to develop courses along ABC lines and for the first time in earnest, the boards which had hitherto serviced the more vocationally-orientated FE system, came into schools via course like CGLI 365. But the 'tangle of paths' was worsening such that in its May 1982 policy statement *17+: A New Qualification* (DES, 1982b), the Government proposed the setting up of the Joint Board for

Pre-Vocational Education. This was to be composed originally of representatives from BTEC, CGLI, RSA and the GCE boards; in the event only BTEC and CGLI became the joint secretaries. The absence of any representatives of those boards traditionally involved in school examining has proved highly significant. As Pratley says:

> The development of CPVE marks the culmination of a powerful movement in curriculum development which has had far-reaching effects. (FEU, 1985a, p. 35)

The CPVE is the most important manifestation and institutionalization of what has become known as 'pre-vocationalism'. Its essential features are:

- The curriculum as 'framework' rather than a syllabus.
- A set of ten core areas (with 200-plus core competences to be satisfied):
  personal and career development;
  industrial, social and environmental studies;
  communication;
  social skills;
  numeracy;
  science and technology;
  information and technology;
  creative development;
  practical skills;
  problem-solving.
- Vocational studies (from five broad areas) – to be taken in modules in ascending levels – introductory, exploratory, preparatory. Vocational studies and the core areas are to occupy 75 per cent of the time and are to be integrated for 20 per cent of that time.
- Additional studies – to occupy no more than 25 per cent of the time. Students may supplement their CPVE course here in any way they wish. Many students use this time for traditional exams such as GCSE.
- Work experience – real or simulated for 15 days.
- Formative and summative profiling (of the core competences).
- Experiential learning.
- Negotiation.
- Counselling.

The 'admixture' which Barker refers to is thus apparent even from this simplified list. Providing only a 'framework' rather than a syllabus has strong implications for teacher control of what is actually taught; the use of progressive-sounding terms like 'negotiation', 'experiential learning' and so forth, suggests a desire for an open kind of pedagogy, a 'process'-oriented curriculum. On the other hand, the stress on skills, core-competences, vocational studies and their 228 learning objectives as outlined in the 'Blue Books' is more indicative of a behavioural-objectives curriculum model.

At the very least then, CPVE came across as a kind of hybrid, meeting with a mixed reception in both the main contexts – sixth forms and FE colleges – where it was to be delivered. As will be shown later, the far from unequivocal acceptance of CPVE has been very much affected by these two contexts with their very differing traditions, philosophies, experience of students and teacher attitudes. This has affected not only progression but also delivery. Where CPVE has not been embraced with good grace, each context could be accused of inertia, vested interest or resistance to change. CPVE does at least raise the need for a redefinition of 'education'. But the unhelpful dichotomy between 'academic' and 'vocational' persists; all seem to deplore it, few do anything about it. Whether the notion of 'prevocationalism' as embodied in CPVE is likely or able to mend this dichotomy, or whether it exacerbates it, remains to be seen. The worse scenario which most fear is an unchallenging marginalized curriculum for anyone outside of a mainstream.

If CPVE was approached cautiously from the outset, it is no wonder. What, in CPVE, was a student expected to learn? What kind of student was envisaged? What kind (and level) of skills were to be acquired? What kind of values were to be transmitted? And most important, what kind of ideological stance was underpinning it all? The aims of CPVE were clearly stated:

- to assist the transition from school to adulthood by further equipping young people with the basic skills, experiences, attitudes, knowledge and personal and social competence required for success in adult life including work;
- to provide individually-relevant educational experience which encourages learning and achievement;
- to provide young people with recognition of their attainments through a qualification which embodies national standards;
- to provide opportunities for progression to continuing education, training and/or work. (Blue Book, part A, p. 3)

It is of course a very wise (or foolish) person who can claim to *know* what are the skills, experiences, attitudes, knowledge, competences and so on which make for success in adult life. The first two aims cited above are doubtless as worthy and as philosophically problematic as the pursuit of happiness itself. The second two aims above quickly became extremely troublesome leading to the crisis of progression which Spours discusses elsewhere in this book.

Responses to CPVE

To begin with, there were no clear alignments in terms of who supported or opposed CPVE or what ideological position they were coming from. As I have written elsewhere:

In both camps . . . there are strange bedfellows. Each 'side' attracts people from radically different ideological and political positions. Opponents may include those who fear educational tripartism or apartheid, or the provision of an impoverished experience or who see the vocational elements as antipathetical to 'education' itself, or the 'integration' implications as a threat to their subject 'purity'. Advocates too come from similarly erstwhile polarised positions; progressivists who welcome the student-centred approach join with more reactionary forces who see here a golden opportunity for a differentiated curriculum, usefully vocational, tailor-made to suit the economic aims of a brave new world. (Green, 1987, p. 5)

Manifestly, a hybrid, people tended to take from CPVE and emphasize what they wished to. Wary of the overt vocational orientation, the emphasis on social skills, and attitudes which seemed to favour employers and aims like – Know and appreciate the expectations of employers and the public, in relation to entry level workers in this field' – teachers with different views on education remained concerned:

I'm not saying there doesn't need to be an alternative to the old 'A' level, 'O' level, university board monopolies . . . there certainly does. But the question is whether this is it. I think it's very dangerous when they start talking about relevance. The old Chartists used to demand a relevant education and that was teaching working class kids really useful knowledge. That was 'Why are we poor? Why is the system like it is?' It was that sort of relevance . . . whereas this seems to be simply relevance to the economy . . . learning skills which employers would find useful. People might actually receive training in how to behave . . . learning to be polite, how to behave in the work place, things like that which are not necessarily in their interests in the long term. (Teacher)

Worse still, as Raffe has shown, this kind of education:

. . . helps to legitimate the individualistic ideology which blames unemployment on individual failure. (Raffe, 1984, p. 20)

As well as the highly problematic areas of 'skills' and attitudes, detailed analysis of the framework shows 'knowledge' to have a somewhat limited role in CPVE: nothing is specified for study in depth; little (apart from information technology (IT)) is to be approached historically; apart from whatever 'knowledge' is gleaned from vocational study into three areas only – industrial, social and environmental studies (ISE), science and technology (ST) and IT – are condensed all forms of human intellectual endeavour. The vast fields of mathematics and English become the super-serviceable 'numeracy and communication', with frequent use of the word 'simple'. As Green puts it:

The distinctive shift [is] away from 'knowledge and understanding' – as in traditional education – to 'competence' and 'effectiveness'. This is paralleled by a preference for doing and for 'execution' over conception and analysis. General (or liberal) education has been largely replaced by basic skills and personal effectiveness. (Green, 1986, p. 108)

As will be shown later, reactions to this 'shift' and disappointment with it came not only from teachers but also from students who though not always so able to articulate what was happening to their education, certainly noticed that something was lacking.

The notable absence of, or the lack of encouragement towards, the humanities, literature, the arts, or any of those fields which enrich and illuminate life rather than serve it, is one concern. As Benn has pointed out:

There are no suggestions that CPVE students might ever:

1 Write an essay
2 Read a book all the way through
3 Benefit by or enjoy ideological discussion or study
4 Consider the past or events in history in any way at all, let alone systematically. (Benn, 1984)

But the point about the devaluation of knowledge in CPVE may also be made with reference to science and technology. As I stated elsewhere:

By no means a syllabus, what is here to be learnt is on the one hand 'everything' which might be said to constitute the 'scientific method' and on the other a science/technology which is only to be that manifest in everyday life . . . There is something unrealistic about this area. The 27 aims which would be met with difficulty by science and technology students at any level working concentratedly for long periods of time are to be met by CPVE students in passing as it were, in pursuance mainly of other activities. This is not to enter into the integration/separation of the sciences debate. Rather, it is to query exactly what level of cognitive development is likely to be possible – even for more able students. The frequent use of the word 'simple' suggests that scientists are certainly not here to be produced. (Green, 1987, p. 27)

It might be noted here that of all the core areas, it has been science and technology which has experienced the greatest difficulty in establishing a place for itself, in practice, in CPVE:

The FEU evaluation of CPVE involving nearly 900 students in 52 establishments disclosed more problems with Science and Technology than with any other core area. (*CPVE* 7 September 1987)

Those supporting CPVE tended to look less at the inadequacies of the framework in terms of skills, attitudes and knowledge, and more at the possibilities within the pedagogy and the assessment procedures. Glazier, a moderately strong critic of CPVE, wrote in 1985:

And whatever happens now, the new teaching strategies, experiential learning, student-centred approaches, the stimulus to non-academic capability and summative methods of assessment will prove beneficial to education generally. This most people accept. (Glazier, 1985, p. 332)

Titcombe feels the same way:

It is however difficult to deny that the CPVE framework *could* provide a radical synthesis of many progressive developments in assessment and in process-centred curriculum construction. (Titcombe, 1986, p. 49)

The big question of course, which will intrigue the curious, might be why, in 1985, when behavioural psychology and 'objectives' models were taking an ever-stronger hold on management training, social work and most other curriculum developments (certainly in FE), should something that even sounded as 'process-centred' and 'progressive' as the CPVE be given official backing as it were, particularly since progressive teaching in primary and secondary schools was being blamed for many of the country's ills?

The concerns surrounding this radical new piece of curriculum development might be summarized in this way: whether it was likely to be a device for producing 'tractable workers', gentling the masses and for delimiting opportunity by further stratification of the system, or whether its undoubted flexibility would allow teachers indeed to 'domesticate' it and turn it into a new, more vital learning experience for many students. Fears of the former happening might perhaps be quietened by statements like the following from the CPVE Handbook:

Most educational provision has sought to stratify young people into a form of educational class system. It would be close to disastrous if this were encouraged to continue. (Resource sheet *Ammunition for rebuffing the Cynics*, p. 98)

The Joint Board seemed then to be leading the crusade against the divisiveness of provision: CPVE was not intended for the low-achiever.

Problems facing CPVE

In 1986 however, just as the first cohort of CPVE students proper was about to graduate, the first blow to this quasi-comprehensive ideal was dealt, and not by some outside competitor either but from half of the Joint Board itself, BTEC. BTEC, in an apparently blatant reneging on the CPVE philosophy, introduced a BTEC First Award 'for those who had better than average qualifications at CSE but below the four 'O' level requirement for direct entry on to BTEC National'. BTEC First, it was true, was intended for those in FE colleges and not schools, and in some LEAs – Leicestershire for example – it was not allowed before 17 (or the second post-16 year). Nevertheless, messages were being sent to the students, especially those turned down for BTEC First and sent (back to school?) to do CPVE; even greater stratification was back with a vengeance. Kenyon, writing in *The Times Educational Supplement* (9 January 1987), spoke of CPVE withering on the vine; the status of CPVE, never certain, looked set for immediate down-grading. And the problems of progression, ever present, could begin in earnest.

Notwithstanding all this however, CPVE found some favour (or a choiceless niche) with students and teachers alike. From 18,000 in 1985–6, the student numbers rose to 36,000 in 1987–88. It is perhaps highly significant that of these 36,000, 70 per cent were taking CPVE in schools (presumably comprehensive) and only 30 per cent in colleges, significant not only for the academic/vocational debate but also from the comprehensive perspective.

Who were these students? A key issue which leads to the heart of almost all the questions and problems surrounding CPVE is that of the client-group. Much official 'double-think' has actually surrounded this area. In March 1984, in *CPVE 1* (The Joint Board's Newsletter), the target group was described as:

- ... young people who: after completing compulsory schooling, will benefit from further education as a preparation for adult life, including the world of work;
- do not wish at this stage to proceed to 'A' level study;
- are interested in vocational training or work but are not yet committed to, or qualified for, a particular occupation.

A huge target group was thus envisaged, carefully disguising any hint at selection downwards by the suggestion that many students *could* but did not wish to proceed to A-level. By June 1985, in *CPVE 5*, the suggestion was that students were choosing CPVE because it enabled them to take O-levels:

Most students arrived at CPVE because they had chosen the vocational courses that were subsumed within Pilot CPVE schemes [there was no BTEC First Award at this time] or because they had made arrangements to re-take 'O' levels.

The evaluation of the pilot *CPVE in Action* (FEU, 1985c), also noted that students were valuing CPVE because of the chance it gave them (perhaps the only chance) to do O-level within additional studies O-levels.

By May 1987, an FEU report on CPVE progression noted:

- CPVE students seem in general to be those with school qualifications which are often too low to allow them access to other courses.

- Students joined CPVE programmes because:
  - they failed to get on to the progression route they wanted
  - it was the only full-time education option available
  - they could resit CSEs or GCEs

– they saw it as a route to a particular vocation. (FEU, 1987a)

Thus although CPVE began life purporting to be a qualification at 17 for all but A-level students, it certainly has not, as many critics predicted, been working out like this. If it is what you do when you cannot do anything else, is it any wonder that its status remains low and its progression problems intractable? By *CPVE 14* (May 1987), the Joint Board themselves were seen to be worried:

> Much remains to be done about informing practitioners and participants about the status, nature and purpose of CPVE programmes; in particular, it is important that CPVE should not be regarded as the last option for students of lesser ability. The perceived problem of the lack of status of CPVE is made worse by the inappropriate comparisons made with GCSE by some employers and college admissions tutors.

They admit further, that many employers and YTS managing agents had still not heard of CPVE.

It is perhaps ironic that it is in schools, with their supposed academic/anti-vocational bias, that CPVE has put down the firmest roots. It is even more ironic that it is in colleges, with their ostensibly more responsive/pro-vocational bias, that the barriers to progression have been experienced:

> College admissions tutors were willing to consider CPVE but still placed an emphasis on GCE/CSE/CEE. (*CPVE 14*, May 1987)

This must, of course, exclude those local education authorities (LEAs) like Haringey for example, where strong school–college links have been established and local progression routes from CPVE *per se*, well arranged.

Nevertheless, behind these ironies there is a story and this story concerns an attitude of mind and a tradition. The perception of the client–group is very different in an open-access sixth-form say, than in an FE college. The actual design and construction of CPVE may be viewed critically in schools and colleges but for very different reasons.

Apart from tertiary colleges with more flexible arrangements for 'mixing and matching', the traditional FE college has long been a highly stratified institution. Numerous vocational and academic (O- and A-level) courses have traditionally catered for many levels of attainment and the task has been to suit the student to the course. Apart from the breadth of access (varying from college to college) little comprehensive spirit has informed most FE colleges. The clientele for pre-vocational education when it arrived tended to be those at the 'lowest end' – particularly those who did not wish to return to school. (The tension between schools and colleges was not helped here by the feeling in colleges that they were picking up those whom the schools had failed.) Scooping up these students on to one course, the CPVE, especially after BTEC First had creamed off the better qualified, made their ghettoizing even more inevitable, ensuring the further devaluation of the certificate.

Schools have been confronted with a different problem; it is perhaps no coincidence that they are catering for 70 per cent of the CPVE students. First of all, schools needed CPVE or at least something like it. As the historical development of CPVE shows, the need for a curriculum for the one-year sixth-former has long been urgent. Although many schools have, over the last 20 years or so, experimented with vocational and pre-vocational courses (CGLI, RSA, CGLI 365), the provision for these students has never been satisfactory. The one-year sixth form has really tended to contain the clientele of all but A-level students; and to perceive this in a school is to perceive a huge range of ability and need in what may be a relatively small population (50–60 perhaps in a typical school), ranging from those who with one more year might well be in a position to move on to A-level, to those unlikely to succeed in any traditional form of examination.

LEAs and schools have varied in their approach to CPVE, particularly in terms of the relationship with other examinations – initially O-level/CEE, more recently GCSE (Mature). Pushing these into additional studies time (25 per cent) might have seemed logical to the Joint Board and perhaps to the colleges with a narrower range of students, but in schools it presented real problems. CPVE immediately attracted criticism as being anti-education; and indeed in its 'cutting-off' effect, anti-comprehensive. A course which seemed to cut students off from detailed, rigorous study and the routes to higher education, leading them only to the world of work (or YTS), seemed highly divisive:

> I feel personal and career development is a good subject but we seemed to concentrate mainly on how to survive interviews and jobs too much. Don't take me wrong, this is good but not all of us will be going straight into jobs but hopefully into colleges. But we did not do much on colleges etc. (CPVE Student, 1987)

The profiling system too, based on the core competence with their unspecific and often vacuous meanings, seemed questionable. While teachers and students might have welcomed the getting away from the stranglehold of traditional examinations in some respects, having to demonstrate

24.1 Can hold social conversations with friends and colleagues
25.1 Can read words and short phrases
41.1 Can recognise numbers in both figures and words,

was felt by many students to be somewhat demeaning; and there was no formal way in which previous achievement could be accredited. Furthermore, core competence statements like 'C26.4: Can create/organise written material in style suited to purpose' could mean anything from the production of a simple report to the writing of a postgraduate thesis. CPVE seemed to be predicated on the so-called 'least able' student, just as O-level, for example, was predicated on the 'most able' – just as damaging, just as 'uncomprehensive'.

In schools with perhaps 50 or so students to cater for, this led to agonizing decisions. Should everyone do CPVE, thus cutting off from serious study and several examinations those capable of passing them, or at least delaying them a year? Should there be two courses – the 'exam' (O-level/CEE/GCSE) and the CPVE – thus creating stratification (or recreating it in many cases where there had before been City and Guilds 365)? Most schools attempted some partial integration where CPVE could 'borrow' from other courses and indeed do examination subjects as additional studies; others attempted to make parts of the CPVE 'examinable' as it were – calling 'communication' CEE English for example.

At the pilot stage, some schools tried to integrate CEE and CPVE fully. Hilary Radnor in her *Case Studies of Six Schools Related to Participation in a Pilot Scheme CPVE/CEE 1984/85* (University of Sussex/SREB Research Study, 1985) reported:

> Within the teaching group a strong commitment to a general rather than a narrowly vocational education remains and some continue to argue strongly in favour of CEE for this reason. (p. 19)

But the problems were legion; conflicting organizational and time demands; fragmentation of learning; student and teacher confusion.

> CPVE as an integrated and vocationally-orientated course ran directly counter to increased emphasis on teacher specialisation being expressed by the DES in 'Teaching Quality' and the development of GCSE. (Ibid, p. 30)

With the coming of GCSE (Mature) and especially with syllabuses designed with courses like CPVE in mind, the situation might well be ameliorated, given of course the difficulty which newly-named subjects have in establishing credibility with their customers. While some LEAs like Suffolk are solving the problem by excluding GCSE altogether within full-time post-16 provision except as additional studies, (though it should be remembered this is a county which has retained grammar schools), others, like Brent, are attempting a full integration of CPVE with (four) GCSEs, using imaginative team-teaching strategies and so on. The Joint Board's position has manifestly shifted in this respect.

CPVE purists might bewail this move towards dual-certification. If the GCSE (Mature) certificate becomes part of the CPVE portfolio, is the profile then not devalued as the instrument by which the student is supposed to be judged? The answer, realistically, is yes, but there is evidence that the profile, with its elaborate and confusing system of core competence, has not established much (if any) credibility with employers or admissions tutors anyway. Indeed, in the May 1988 press release, The Joint Board partially acknowledged this problem and stated that 'the core competence statements will be revised in simpler language and format'. Where CPVE 'pure' *has* scored has been in the concept of students' portfolios, where (as for the prospective art student) there is real evidence of what they can do, and where their poise and confidence at interview has increased. The problem of credentials is a problem for the credential society: students cannot be denied the opportunity of taking examinations while they are there to be taken. This lesson was learnt long ago by the old secondary modern schools (see Chitty, 1989).

From the FE perspective, it is the pre-vocational rather than the educational aspects of CPVE which have run into difficulty. More even than teachers, but for different reasons, those gate-keepers of vocational and craft standards the FE departments (often strongly vertically as well as horizontally stratified), have viewed CPVE with suspicion. This could mean reluctance either to participate in the delivery of the in-college CPVE course (which by its very nature must be cross-curricular and interdepartmental), or to welcome the CPVE as an entry qualification for other courses, or both. Some departments have eschewed CPVE altogether; in some colleges CPVE has been established and immediately marginalized, recruiting only the 'left-overs', and housed in odd corners not required by other courses. In many cases it was general education lecturers, not those teaching the vocational courses, who picked up on the CPVE.

One of the main problems for FE was the vagueness and lack of specificity in the CPVE vocational studies themselves. Although the objectives in the Blue Books might sound grand enough, there was no clear way of indicating the extent to which they had been met. Secure in the tried and tested BTEC system, the First Award came in to placate the vocational departments. The greatest problem was the preparatory modules which purported to be the most specialized and advanced level of study, but again the accreditation was not clear. Just as schools have sought to establish some academic credence through dual-certification (as well as giving students something to aim for), so colleges especially have been willing to include some dual-certification with City and Guilds/BTEC modules etc.

The de-ghettoizing effect these moves are likely to have is certainly to be welcomed: the mention of A-level students represents something quite radical. The failure of all attempts to date, most recently the Higginson Report (DES, 1988b), to reform A-level has meant that notions of 'comprehensiveness' have never informed the post-16 debate in any real way. It would be ironical if it were through the vocationally-orientated CPVE that this debate were stimulated. The voice of comprehensive education is somewhat muted these days; attempts to vocationalize the higher reaches of post-16 provision could certainly serve to revitalize the arguments.

The notion of the 'vocationalized curriculum' and the more economic and utilitarian purposes of education is a philosophical, ideological and political issue. But if the search for comprehensive education does go on, two further points might be made here. First, it has been in the classrooms of comprehensive schools pre-16 that teachers have developed the mixed ability pedagogy which is a *sine qua non* of a more egalitarian system. They have realized that it is only in a context where all young people are valued, and seen to be valued, that the barriers of class, subject status and all the impedimenta of educational prejudice can be broken down. Second, the barriers between the academic and the practical have begun to be broken down, notably through subjects like craft, design and technology whose problem-solving and evaluative approaches demand rigorous intellectual thought as well as the practical skills necessary for the execution of the outcomes of that thought. Demarginalized and embracing all students, CPVE could no doubt change into something rather different.

Conclusion

The actual educational experience of CPVE for students is hard to measure particularly where few had any choice. In one school, where for the last two years students have been encouraged to talk and write their own evaluations, reactions have varied. Students have complained about disorganization, the slowness of the course, the excessive 'bureaucracy' (usually associated with log books, task sheets and the core competence profiling), the repetition of learning (particularly in areas like numeracy) and the fact that the work was sometimes 'too easy':

> At the beginning of the course I was confused, I didn't really understand it. At first I thought it was because I had arrived late, but when I asked the other students they said they felt the same way. I think it would have been better if they had explained the whole thing better. (Student, 1988)
>
> Information Technology was the fifth biggest let-down. All the work we had done in the fifth year was repeated so I found it boring . . . I didn't work at all in this lesson. (Student, 1987)
>
> The main disappointment was the competence sheet we had to do for every piece of work. It was much harder doing them than doing the actual piece of work. And also, everything wasn't set out properly and we'd get confused. (Student, 1987)

Almost unanimously, however, work experience was hailed as the most useful and confidence-enhancing aspect of the course.

> The best part of CPVE was the work experience. No words can describe the experience it gave. I was in an infants class for three weeks. There I felt so 'grown-up' and mature, it was as if I belonged there all the time. I was treated as an adult, as part of the staff and that made me feel really great about what I was doing. (Student, 1988)
>
> There is one thing that I enjoyed, that was my work experience. I wanted to go to a shop because I wanted to learn what I could on display. This is

probably the only worthwhile thing I did in CPVE. I learned techniques which I never thought existed. I enjoyed it very much. It made me see how a business is run and how important little things are to help build up a business. The most important thing I feel work experience gives you is independence. I'd never worked before and for the first time I was treated not like a student but as an adult going to work. (Student, 1988)

Responses to particular vocational studies and core areas varied. Generally popular were school–college links, particularly as an experience of a different learning environment. Some students complained however of 'too easy work', of being patronized and of being treated as less able than they actually were. This no doubt has something to do with some teachers' and lecturers' perceptions of CPVE students.

In a programme where immense care was taken over progression, many of the students ended by expressing satisfaction with the course; they did, by and large, get to where they wanted, including a reasonable number who secured places on BTEC national courses without the usual 'four O-level equivalents' normally required. A few students went on to persist with the academic route, spending another year on GCSE (Mature).

If the 'new look' CPVE does manage to embrace the widest possible cohort and allow for both academic and vocational dual-certification, then it could well evolve into an instrument for 'comprehensivizing' the post-16 area, at least for the first year. Systems of credit accumulation and modularizing furthermore, could well be the way forward. Much will depend on the NCVQ. Even more, however, will depend on the educational climate.

The pressures on schools to link with industry are increasing. The compulsory cooption of governors specifically representative of local industry is one manifestation; the encouragement of local industrialists – through compact schemes and curriculum projects – to form relationships with schools is another. (In areas where industry/employers are at a premium, this will, of course, encourage competitiveness between schools already exacerbated by prospects of open enrolment and opting out). Whether teachers are able to stand their ground on asserting the non-utilitarian purposes of education in this climate – as opposed to becoming grandiose employment agencies – remains to be seen.

In 1983 Watts wrote:

The basic dilemma – that education can improve the employability of a given individual in the labour market, but can do little or nothing to reduce unemployment on a collective level – will haunt and confuse teachers and students alilke. (Watts, 1983, p. 177)

Of course teachers, as much as parents, wish to secure as far as possible their students' futures. But many teachers continue to strive – stirred by the voices of their own education perhaps – for a curriculum post-16 which puts the student first, not in the impoverished 'personal effectiveness' sense but in a broader sense which embraces concepts like critical awareness, intellectual development, and understanding through knowledge and creativity. The quest really should be for a post-16 comprehensive curriculum which is available to all, which neither stratifies nor selects, which advances knowledge and society, and exists within a common system of assessment.

Chapter 14

A Common Curriculum for the Sixth Form: Two Case Studies

Alan Payne

One of the philosophical problems that comprehensive schools have had to face is the need to acquire an educational rationale of their own. In the early days of the comprehensive system in the 1950s and 1960s, there was a tendency to absorb the structure of the various sections of the tripartite system rather than conceive a new curricular identity. Holt has emphasized the lack of clarity about the educational purpose of the comprehensive school and states that it 'took shape not from a clear education vision, but from a political solution to the problem of pupil selection (Holt, 1978, p. 19). Since then, the idea of a common curriculum and a common culture for the comprehensive school has emerged, though it is arguable whether the patterns and procedures of grammar and secondary-modern schools have entirely disappeared.

Schools have not moved towards a common curriculum in any uniform way because the very nature of change has depended upon the ability and enthusiasm of all the partners in state education. Yet, while the debate about what type of curricular experience a child should be exposed to has continued, the nature of the partnership has changed. In the 1980s, a preoccupation with falling standards, lack of relevance, the need for accountability and the state of Britain's economy all served to highlight the purpose of education to a wider public. With such a wide spectrum of interest within society, there are bound to be conflicting opinions about what constitutes a basic minimum to aim at for every educable child, and about what knowledge, skills, dispositions and concepts a common curriculum might include. On the other hand, it is difficult to deny our young people the concept of education as a human right whatever the calls for greater efficiency in education might be, Golby has provided one example of extreme opinions in 'the tension between those who see the curriculum as an instrument for social ends such as equality of opportunity within a meritocracy and those who advocate a common experience . . . as a building block of common culture, (Golby, 1980, p. 4). He points out that this polarization of views is exemplified in the philosophical differences between the Department of Education and Science's (DES's) *A Framework for the School Curriculum* (1980c) and HMI's *A View of the Curriculum* (1980). The meritocratic tradition of education which sees ability as a resource to be developed in society's best interests is the essence of the DES philosophy and is the tradition which many comprehensives took on from the grammar schools. Nowhere can this be better observed than in sixth forms. Traditionally coping for more able students taking A-levels, they have tended to be exempt from the discussion on comprehensive schools and the common curriculum.

Although those pupils staying on full-time education after the age of 16 do so from personal choice, it can be argued that a common curriculum is just as valid post-16, especially since many institutions operate an open access policy. The main problem stems from the status of those young people attending post-16 institutions. In some centres where they form part of a comprehensive school, they are a distinct group, in others, they are required to integrate and form part of a whole community. Unfortunately, the maintained 16–19 sector is rife with structural variations that simply underline the lack of agreement about the aims of education for that age range. Whatever structure a local education authority (LEA) chooses to effect, a common curriculum is bound to come low down on the list of priorities after budgetting and course provision. A tertiary college might seem to be in the best situation in that it can claim a greater wealth of courses, but it is the variety of provision, not necessarily any common element, which often takes priority. Certainly in sixth forms, the common curriculum is neglected. Principles which uphold a democratic tradition, an assertion that pupils have a right to experience a common curriculum as members of a whole community, the promotion of humane dispositions, and an understanding of both science and the arts, tend to be taken for granted as part of post-16 courses.

For years 16–19 centres have played around with the idea of a common curriculum by virtue of a general studies programme, but they have not been encouraged to think in terms of a common curriculum whether by LEAs or by central government. The legacy of the grammar school still lingers on in a functional curriculum geared towards the professions and higher education. Numerous attempts to challenge the status quo have proved ineffective. For example, Reid and Filby believe that the reluctance to change the sixth-form curriculum after the last war 'was linked with the acceptance of an ethos of competition rather than cooperation, of loyalty rather than questioning, of authority rather than democracy' (Reid and Filby, 1982, p. 141).

The Crowther Report into 15–18 education (Ministry of Education, 1959) did nothing to alter the curriculum despite recognizing an increase in the number of sixth-formers. Specialization was still considered desirable. In fact, the main argument was when it should begin. Neither were comprehensive school sixth forms expected to make an impact: 'What is true of sixth forms in grammar schools will be true of comprehensive schools, and the views we hold about the one, we should expect to hold also of the other' (paragraph 304). Nearly 30 years later, the present Government has at last realized the need to add breadth with the introduction of AS-levels, but these are clearly aimed at the students of highest ability. With the possible exception of the Technical and Vocational Education Initiative (TVEI), the ability range of the whole 16–19 clientele has not been addressed. A-levels still reign supreme as the rejection of the findings of the Higginson Committee (DES, 1988b) indicate. Yet it is unlikely that the Higginson proposals would have done anything about providing a common curriculum. Its recommendation that students follow a five-subject curriculum would add breadth, but at the same time attack the time given to non-examined courses. What is worrying is the failure to scrap the present system and start again from a much broader base. Widening the experience by adding on a few extra subjects here and there is not the answer. The need to attach commonality as well as breadth to the curriculum is left to individual institutions to recognize and to respond to. Unfortunately, because many sixth forms are not in a position to fulfil that desire owing to their small rolls and stringent timetabling demands, they may continue to justify their existence purely in terms of A-levels. The Certificate of Pre-Vocational Education (CPVE) and GCSE come second if at all, followed by supplementary, complementary or general courses. They can scarcely be blamed for operating within market forces.

Meanwhile, the expansion of post-16 education in the last 20 years, and the increase in the ability range of the clientele, continue to throw doubt upon both the structure and the curriculum of 16–19 provision. It is strange that post-16 courses have introduced a divisiveness which comprehensive schools have sought to eradicate pre-16. The distinction between the academic and vocational curriculum simply underlines this. It could be argued that the common curriculum is totally inapplicable to the 16–19 age group. This paper questions that view and argues that the completion of compulsory education does not mean an end to a democratic right to certain minimum learning opportunities. There is certainly evidence that many practitioners are aware of common needs. Take for example *A Basis For Choice* (Further Education Unit (FEU), 1979), which sets out a common core of studies for post-16 students no longer motivated by academic subjects. It suggested that various areas of learning ought to be grouped around a common interest. There are implications, however, for all young people and the document admitted the need to give the most academically gifted a process of vocational preparation. Pre-employment courses can be applied to all students, including those taking A-level, which is just as vocational as any other course. In Australia, the Victorian Ministry of Education (1985) has recommended in its review of post-compulsory schooling that all students have access to a comprehensive curricular range, in which the arts and humanities figure alongside science, technology and mathematics. The theme which runs through the report is commonality of experience and a far-sighted view of the young person embarking upon what is just the beginning of post-compulsory education. There are ideas here for formulating a statement which indicates how education, training, work and the community can be united into producing a common curriculum.

There is no doubt that there exists a willingness to explore the issue. Holt has stated that the staff at Sheredes School, where he was headteacher in the 1970s, agreed to pursue the same objective of a broad general education for all pupils into the sixth form:

> Education (for the first five years) is a statutory provision, and to see it as offering all pupils access to our culture is both to discharge a duty and to allow them to discover their own strengths. Thereafter, whether at school, at college or at work, we accept that they will more closely bring into focus those studies and activities which appeal to them. But we are anxious that the idea of continuing education should not be lost and in the sixth form we want to prepare them for adult decisions and ensure that their understanding is not exclusively confined to too narrow a field. (Holt, 1978, pp. 151–152)

This approach seems particularly relevant to those students whose choice of career or higher education is still undecided and for whom it is desirable to keep options open by way of a common curriculum. The age of 16 may constitute a legal conclusion to comprehensive education, but it is no longer as significant as it used to be. For one thing, more pupils are staying on at school or college, and central government is well aware of the extent to which the country is falling behind our competitors in terms of the post-16 student population. However, while institutions may recognize the need for some common curriculum, any formulation of an agreed conceptual framework rests on practicalities within each institution. The move towards an open-access education system for 16–19 has created varied provision throughout England and Wales both across authorities and within them. The aim of the discussion here is not to argue for one post-16 scheme or another, but rather to focus attention on the provision of a common curriculum in the 16–19 age range, especially as it affects two sixth forms with which I am familiar.

Both illustrate attempts to incorporate a common curriculum. One is a sixth form within a comprehensive school and the other is a sixth-form college. Though neither institution caters for the complete ability range and could ignore the issue of a common curriculum if it wished, they have both recognized the narrowness of the traditional post-16 curriculum. The lack of balance in the accounts is unfortunate, but then the experience of each institution is very different. What matters is that they show how the final curriculum depends upon the values and ethos of the institution, the teachers themselves and the practicalities. The structure of 16–19 education has tended to dominate curriculum practices so that the implementation of a common curriculum has reflected mainly local circumstances. The way that two sixth forms have faced up to the issue will be the principal focus. Since no definition exists of an ideal curriculum, it would be meaningless to describe either as examples of 'good' or 'bad' practice.

Case study one: the 11–18 school

This is a coeducational, purpose-built comprehensive school of over 1300 pupils, including about 145 in the sixth form. It is located in an urban residential area and has a mixed social and ethnic intake. For its post-16 provision the school has to fit in with arrangements for the town as a whole, so that young people are able to choose from a coordinated range of opportunities offered by many establishments. As a TVEI pilot school, it can offer a one-year CPVE course as well as technology, business studies and art at A-level which also come under the TVEI umbrella. Thirteen other A-levels are on offer, while the range of GCSE courses varies according to demand. The school does not offer a full-time course solely for the retaking of fifth-year public examinations.

Although recognizing the need to create varied opportunities for its sixth-formers, the school has to face up to the problem that any particular sixth-former's programme lacks breadth and balance. Until 1988, an accredited system of complementary studies was made available to all students in the lower-sixth and occupied a fifth of the timetable. Designed to complement academic studies, the course consisted of a mandatory core element comprising modules such as communications, government and industry, power and politics, art and society, science and society, opinions and beliefs, and computer literacy. The remainder of the course allowed a choice from games or community service, and keyboard skills or survival skills. Each module had individual assessment patterns and from this, credit was given to students in the form of a profile. Although it worked in mixed-ability groups and incorporated a modular structure, the course in complementary studies has now been discontinued. The reasons for this decision centre upon the lack of staff and student conviction. The course was not taken seriously by staff and the merit system was abused by students. Although in its last year attendance was more effectively controlled by having complementary studies at a set time of the week, there were still feelings of coercion and apathy.

Complementary studies were never described as a common course but, in practice, that was the reality. The decision has now been made to make more use of the programme of personal and social education (PSE) and to add more choice to the non-examination provision. Sixth-formers will have to opt for courses taking up a minimum of 32 (out of 40) periods a week. Within that, two periods of PSE are compulsory. It would appear that the common element has declined and is centred upon PSE in a restricted way. The school argues in defending the change that it is responding to market forces and giving the sixth-formers what they want. Competition from other sixth forms cannot be ignored. Additionally, the end of complementary studies identifies a pragmatic approach to the problem. Teachers are still subject-oriented and do not see the common course as an immediate priority. Furthermore, it is assumed that anyone can teach it, which is far from the truth. Unless the enthusiasm exists and the in-service training is provided, then the common curriculum is dead. The obvious question remains. Will PSE be any better? It too needs careful INSET and the objectives can be difficult to determine. As in complementary studies, presentation can be individualistic.

There are, however, two important aspects of the curriculum which need to be taken into account. First, there is the ethos of the sixth form. Students are expected to play a full part in sixth-form activities and to accept responsibility in a variety of situations. There is an agreed uniform and sixth-formers are required to provide acceptable models of conduct for younger pupils. Life is characterized by a great deal of autonomy with regard to learning. The role of the group tutor, both within and outside the PSE programme, to give guidance is paramount. Second, there are the knock-on effects of TVEI to be assessed, not least the change in teaching styles. Within the PSE programme will come records of achievement, a counselling service and two weeks' work experience for all sixth-formers. Here may lie the common curriculum of the future, one which can be more satisfactorily managed by staff.

The problem remains as to the extent to which PSE as a common element provides that unity and coherence in the curriculum. PSE is peripheral to the sixth-form curriculum and scarcely provides a focal point. Unity has to come from the sixth-formers themselves, by acting as a tight community and by establishing their own base – a library and a common room, and by engaging in social events. Scope exists to build upon this ethos but there is an implicit acceptance by staff of the fact that students of high ability need concentrate only upon their A-levels.

Case study two: a sixth-form college

This case study refers to a sixth-form college of 600 students and 60 staff. It also has an urban location. The college's principal aim is 'to give every student the chance to develop as fully as possible his or her own potential in a friendly, enthusiastic, academically stimulating and socially responsible environment'. There is an undeniable attempt to support an egalitarian ethos and promote the enjoyment of non-examination courses. Most staff support a liberal/progressive ideology. Without seeking to acquire a high-flying academic profile, the college has little problem in attracting A-level students.

The college accepts students for A-level and GCSE courses. Until 1988, CPVE was also offered but because of low numbers, the course is no longer viable. By arrangement with the other local 16–19 institutions, the college does not put on a complete range of post-16 courses. There are approximately 25 A-level courses on offer and about the same number of GCSEs. To counter the academic content of student experience, general studies (GS) is very strong and it is in this context that a common curriculum has taken shape. GS consists of a core programme and 41 optional activities for the lower-sixth. Students do not initially like the core and have to be convinced of its potential by an enthusiastic staff. A policy for the course was laid down in 1981 and wished to:

- devise, monitor, refine and evaluate a compulsory core course of really useful knowledge;
- enable individual students to devise, evaluate and refine their own learning programmes.

In the college there is concern with the low esteem in which non-examination courses are held and the priority that is inevitably given to examination-status courses. This low esteem is not inevitable; nor is it sufficient ground for conceding the case for public examinations. The course material chosen by the staff is considered to be of sufficient importance to obviate the likely response to non-examined courses. Discussion originally centred upon what was 'useful knowledge', and it was decided that in the case of a sixth-form college the answer had to rest with the students themselves. One obvious difficulty was to discover how students would perceive 'useful knowledge' and whether their choice reflected the fact that they were weighed down with the pressures of examination work. A questionnaire was circulated which consisted of a list of 47 topics, about half of which might have fallen within the nineteenth-century radical definition of 'really useful knowledge', for example the police, careers, planning, politics; the other half focused more on activities and forms of learning, for example car maintenance, drama, sport and cookery. Students were asked if they had ever taken part in a course dealing with a particular topic. The results were very inconclusive since they revealed not only a variety of experience across the 16 feeders schools but also variation within each establishment. It was obvious after further research by the college staff that students were unable to tie together the experiences they had encountered over five years or more. Rather than discount the results of the questionnaire, the college realized that the complexity of experience could itself be incorporated into the course. Meanwhile a group of 15 staff had expressed interest in GS, and it then became possible to marry up the topics at the top of the students' rank order with topics in which the staff themselves had expressed an interest. Course materials and objectives were then devised by staff working in teams. The objectives were more or less common to all teams and subject areas and derived from the nature of the situation and the students rather than from specific topics. These can be summed up as follows:

- to enable students to discuss, share, value and make use of their own experience;
- to give students access to aspects of the world from which their status as students is liable to cut them off, vis-a-vis their contemporaries;
- to enable students to consider where their future might lie, and where it fitted in with the future of society;

- to encourage students to believe that learning can be useful, satisfying, life-long and not necessarily limited to the value that others (for example employers, parents, higher education) place upon it;
- to encourage students to participate, by encouraging, circulating and making use of their comments and criticisms.

Emphasis is laid upon the student reaction to the various topics rather than a consideration of whether there is sufficient time to cover an exhaustive informational input in a single lesson. 'Discussion' and 'critical rationality' are the watch-words.

The GS core course has continued to maintain its central role within the curriculum. All lower sixth-formers take part, though out of about 350 students there may be 30 who have timetable clashes because of GCSE or a fourth A-level. Provision is made for the latter in the upper-sixth. Five units are covered – rights, economics, health, education and handling information – which are, in turn, divided into separate issues. Staff are not trained in GS but this is not regarded as a handicap. In fact, subject specialists are viewed with suspicion, so that for example, the unit on health is not taken by biologists. This standpoint has the advantage of allowing staff to adopt a neutral position without any subject influence, but having said this, it does undervalue a teacher's capacity to use common sense in utilizing his/her own subject expertise. The course is cyclical in that students attend a six-week unit and then move on. Teachers repeat the unit with a new group of students. The aims continue to be integrated with the anti-elitist, egalitarian attitude of many staff. It therefore avoids the description of being supplementary or compensatory. Rather, it is a corrective to the individualistic emphasis of most academic work.

Outside the core, there are a number of options which have been built up partly from the suggestions of students. They include art, architecture and cookery at one extreme, and yoga, beginners' piano and a jazz group at the other. The options chosen by students partly depend upon the academic pressures on them. Those taking three A-levels have to achieve 85 credits in the lower-sixth, while that figure increases for a two A-level student. Each credit equals one hour's attendance, though this can be forfeited by lack of attendance and participation. Credit can also be gained from activities outside the college by negotiation with group tutors. The upper-sixth no longer experience the core but they continue to accumulate credits within the options.

The present feeling is that the core needs to be revised in two fundamental ways. Firstly, the inclusion of an aesthetic and spiritual component would repair an important omission; and secondly, more responsibility could be devolved to group tutors within a newly- devised tutorial programme. This raises vital issues of INSET and control for the future. Evaluation, too, is difficult considering that the core is regarded as part of an on-going educational experience. Nevertheless, in this establishment there is a fully articulated common experience in which all lower sixth-formers are expected to participate. A great deal of time has been spent on achieving agreement on the aims of the course; namely that there are types of knowledge and experience which ought to be a part of every student's, if not every person's, own resources for dealing with the world. The emphasis is very much upon problems and issues which may confront people over the ensuing years. There is an implicit assumption that at 16-plus most students are ignorant of some vital information which may be necessary for their personal well-being. The college cannot assume that student awareness of social issues is uniform. Yet to handle information in the same way as is done in examination classes is to risk alienation. There are no examination goals and pressures. Where the college has been successful is in being able to accommodate its aims within the timetable, and to use the staff that the head of general studies wants. At the end of the course, students are asked to evaluate the course in written form. The data is fed back to staff for deliberation about the following year's commitment.

Conclusion

Neither institution can call itself comprehensive in terms of ability. Regulations relating to student intake are made by the respective LEA. While the college has been able to evolve a programme common to all students with the resources and philosophy to accompany it, the school has moved towards a limited course which is practically more efficient than before. There is a clear message here for the respective local authority which has never really been debated. Is 16–19 provision meant to maintain the comprehensive ideal of the 11–16 phase or not? If it is, then what are the implications for a common curriculum? At present no policy exists and the subsequent choices open to institutions rest firmly on the resources available and on the interests of individual teachers. Both establishments recognize the need to provide a common experience but the size of the sixth-form college and the more favourable pupil–teacher ratio enable it to fulfil its demands more successfully. One ought not to conclude from this that a sixth-form college, or for that matter a tertiary college, is automatically preferable. Certainly, a new start at 16 has the advantage in that assumptions about students need not be carried forward. Rather, the exercise highlights the disparities that exist within 16–19 education and the inevitable downgrading of the common curriculum vis-a-vis public examinations. The entitlement curriculum which characterizes compulsory education is ignored at 16. Given the resources and LEA support, there is scope for institutions not simply to explore issues such as breadth and balance in the sixth form, but to start from the basis of the common curriculum.

Chapter 15

Ethnicity, Achievement and Progression at 16: The Tower Hamlets Bangladeshi Community

Sorrel Pindar

Tower Hamlets in the East End of London is distinguished on two counts. It is one of the most deprived boroughs in the country and it is home to a large Bangladeshi community which is said to be the most disadvantaged ethnic minority group in Britain (Home Affairs Sub-Committee on Race Relations and Immigration, 1987). Unsurprisingly, Tower Hamlets has almost the lowest rate of participation in post-16 further and higher education. However, staying-on rates are higher among Bangladeshi than they are among white pupils. The Bangladeshi community provides us with an interesting perspective on the link between ethnicity, social disadvantage and access and attainment within education.

In this paper, some research findings are presented from the Tower Hamlets Career Decision Study, a study of the process through which 16-year-olds in Tower Hamlets make decisions about their post-16 plans.[1] The findings are placed in the context of what is known about Tower Hamlets and its schools as a setting for young people's experience of education and vocational/educational choices. Thus the approach is to consider young people as occupying a position within a nexus of structures which affect both the quality of education and youngsters' expectations for the future.

The communities of Tower Hamlets

Tower Hamlets is one of the most deprived boroughs in the country, as measured by a number of social indicators (DoE, 1983). It is very much a working-class borough. In the 1981 Census of Population, manual workers totalled 53.3 per cent of the economically active population, while there were only 0.7 per cent of professional people. The corresponding figures for inner London as a whole were 40 per cent and 3.8 per cent. Similarly, the percentage of men with higher education qualifications is the lowest of any local authority (5.2 per cent), and the figure for women is only a little higher (8.7 per cent) – the figures for inner London are 15.1 per cent and 16.2 per cent respectively (London Regional Manpower Intelligence Unit, 1985).

Side by side with its white residents, Tower Hamlets has a tradition of immigrant communities: Huguenots, Irish, Jews, Somalis, Africans, Caribbeans and Chinese, in the past; and more recently, Vietnamese as well as the Bangladeshis. The borough currently contains a number of ethnic minority groups, much the biggest group being the Bangladeshis, and the second largest the Afro–Caribbeans. Unfortunately, apart from a recent count of the Bangladeshi community, there are no figures on the ethnic mix of the borough since the 1981 Census.

The early Bangladeshi settlers in East London were mostly seamen, and the settlement of their families did not begin until the 1960s. So the community is relatively new, and it has continued to grow considerably in the 1980s (Carey and Shukur, 1985–6). The 1981 Census counted an estimated 12,600 Bangladeshis living in the borough, constituting 9.2 per cent of the population; a recent estimate put the Bangladeshi population at between 23,400 and 27,100, which is 15.1–15.5 of the borough's population (London Borough of Tower Hamlets Planning Department, 1987). Approximately 50 per cent of Bangladeshis are below the age of 15 and in 1985–6 they constituted 40 per cent of primary-school children who will of course be entering the secondary schools in the next few years (Home Affairs Sub-Committee on Race Relations and Immigration, 1987).

Attainment and post-16 participation in Tower Hamlets

Tower Hamlets has one of the lowest rates of participation in post-compulsory education in the country. It also has some of the lowest levels of school achievement. These trends are documented by figures published by ILEA research and statistics and the careers service. However the figures do show a slight upturn in recent years and suggest that the educational situation may now be starting to improve.

Participation in post-compulsory education
The low take-up of post-compulsory education at 16-plus is documented by the Tower Hamlets careers service, and by some ILEA studies. The latter show a history of low school staying-on rates in Tower Hamlets from 1977 onwards, though with some sharp fluctuations, for instance between 28.1 per cent in 1977 and 23 per cent in 1978 (ILEA, 1980; 1981; 1983a).

The ILEA careers service figures for 1988 show that 27.2 per cent of fifth years remained at school for the sixth form, and that a further 11.5 per cent went to a college of further education. Thus the total percentage of students continuing into post-compulsory education was 38.7 per cent. This is an increase over the percentage of students who remained in education in the preceding years; for instance the figures for 1988 were 34.1 per cent, and for 1987 only 32 per cent (ILEA careers service, 1986; 1987). Unfortunately, the total participation rate (schools and colleges) for ILEA as a whole is not available for 1988, but the figure for 1986 was 43.8 per cent (ILEA, 1986a), so it is clear that Tower Hamlets has had a low staying-on rate even compared with the rest of inner London.

However, while the staying-on rate has been particularly low in Tower

Hamlets, there is variation between the different ethnic groups. The 1988 careers service figures show that 48 per cent of Bangladeshi pupils remained in education after the fifth year. This is a considerable increase over the figures for 1986, when only 36 per cent of Bengali fifth-years continued their education post-16 (Bangladesh Youth League, 1988), but even this figure was higher than that for all students in Division 5 of the ILEA (34.1 per cent).

The careers service report also provides entry rates of sixth-formers into higher education for Division 5: in 1988, out of a total of 171 students leaving school at the end of the upper-sixth, 55 obtained places at universities and polytechnics. This represents 2.7 per cent of the cohort of students who were on roll in the 5th year two years previously,[2] which can be compared with a national age participation rate of 14.2 per cent in 1986 (DES, 1987a). It should be noted that the participation rate in Tower Hamlets has increased over that for previous years; it was approximately 2 per cent in 1986.

Eleven of the students going on to higher education in 1988 were Bangladeshi (slightly less than a quarter of those who were leaving school). Unfortunately, it is not possible to calculate the percentage of the cohort from this figure, as we do not know the number of Bangladeshi students in the cohort. But we do know that 23 of the 66 Europeans who were leaving school went on to higher education; ie over one third. Thus while compared to Europeans, Bangladeshi students are remaining in education in larger proportions at 16, and of those who do stay on and who are still there at the end of the upper-sixth, a smaller percentage remain in education after 18.

Attainment at 16
Tower Hamlets has a history of low achievement, affecting white working-class children and ethnic minority children alike. Figures for 1987 show that Tower Hamlets had the second lowest 5th-year performance score of any ILEA division (ILEA, 1988b). Tower Hamlets' score of 12.8 is worth a little less than three CSEs at grade 3 and one at grade 2 (the ILEA average was 16.5, a little more than four grade 2 CSEs). Another way of looking at the figures is to look at the percentage of students earning a certain number of grades. In Tower Hamlets only 33.7 per cent of fifth years earned one or more O-level equivalents (grade 1 CSEs or O-levels grade A–C). This is the lowest percentage of any division. Six and a half per cent obtained five or more O-level equivalents, while 31.1 per cent either sat no exam or failed to pass any. The ILEA averages were 43.3 and 21.6 per cent of pupils, respectively.

Levels of achievement among Bangladeshi students are not as high as they are for Tower Hamlets as a whole. However the date for Bangladeshi pupils show that while in absolute terms their achievement levels are very low, they are nonetheless doing better than is predicted when their circumstances are taken into account. In 1987, ILEA released a report which analysed the fifth-year results of ILEA pupils from different ethnic groups. Bangladeshi pupils, the vast majority of whom live in Tower Hamlets, were easily the lowest achievers, with a mean performance score in 1986 of 9.3 (which is worth about three grade 3 CSEs or three grade E O-levels).

However, the report compared this performance score with the score that is predicted if controls are made for the pupils' sex, and with the score on the ILEA test of verbal reasoning which children take at the end of primary school (the two variables which the ILEA found to be the best predictors of achievement). Bangladeshi pupils were among those groups whose actual mean performance score was significantly higher than their predicted score. This suggests that although Bangladeshi pupils begin secondary school at a terrific disadvantage, they actually improve their level of attainment considerably more than do some of their peers. But the question arises as to why these children did so poorly on the verbal reasoning test, and whether or not this is a useful measure to apply to children who do not speak English fluently.

Explaining patterns of achievement and post-16 participation among Bangladeshi pupils in Tower Hamlets

As we have seen, there are low rates of participation in post-compulsory education among all students in Tower Hamlets. However while the participation rate is low among Bangladeshi young people, it is not as low as it is among Europeans. Thus it is necessary to examine the reasons for the generally low participation rates in Tower Hamlets, while at the same time looking at why Bangladeshi (and other ethnic minority) pupils are more inclined to remain in education than are their white peers.

The ILEA (1981) examined some possible factors affecting staying-on rates on a school-by-school basis, and found that staying-on rates were related to the school's success rates in 16-plus exams, the percentage of children scoring in the lowest band on the verbal reasoning test, and the percentage of children eligible for free school meals. However, even after all these variables were controlled, there was still significant variation between the different geographical areas with lower than expected staying-on rates in Tower Hamlets, Greenwich, Lewisham and Southwark (all in East and South-East London). This suggests that there may be some locally-specific processes which affect achievement and staying-on rates, which may be linked to characteristics of both the schools and the communities to which students belong.

The socioeconomic situation in Tower Hamlets

As I noted above, Tower Hamlets is one of the most deprived boroughs in the country, on almost any indicator of social and economic disadvantage. In the discussion below, we outline the situation for Tower Hamlets as a whole and for the Bengali community in particular.

Employment in Tower Hamlets In the past, the Tower Hamlets economy revolved around the docks and the garment trade, but it has for some time been undergoing a major transition. While certain industries (notably the garment trade) provide some continuity with the past, the old industrial economy has largely disappeared and is now being replaced by the new commercial developments in the Docklands areas. By 1981, only 33.5 per cent of jobs in Tower Hamlets were in manufacturing, construction or extractive industries, with 65.4 per cent of jobs being in the service sector (London Regional Manpower Intelligence Unit, 1985).

Between the 1971 and 1981 Censuses of Population, there was a decline of 27 per cent in the numbers of residents in employment, which was almost twice the decrease in the population. More recently, between November 1982 and July 1985, there was an increase in unemployment among men of 19.3 per cent and of 37.4 per cent among women (London Regional Manpower Intelligence Unit, 1985).

Bangladeshi people occupy a particularly unprivileged position in the labour market. As a result of their lack of fluency in English, along with the discrimination they face from employers, Bangladeshis are concentrated in the lower ranks of the labour force. Most Bangladeshi men who are employed work in catering, the garment trade or other factories. A 1982 survey revealed that 69 per cent were in unskilled or semi-skilled manual work, while only 16 per cent of whites were in such work (Home Affairs Sub-Committee, 1987). Many of the women are employed as homeworkers in the garment trade, and as such are among the most exploited workers in the economy (Carey and Shukur, 1985–6). Recent ILEA data indicated that between 50 and 60 per cent of Bangladeshi secondary-school pupils have no parent in employment, compared with 17.2 per cent for other groups (ILEA, 1987).

Unemployment, underemployment and low-paid work all put pressures on families which make it difficult for parents to offer support to their children with their school work. Furthermore, children who live in a community with high levels of unemployment and where most residents can get only low-status work, may feel that school has little relevance to their future or that it will make no difference to their prospects. This is likely to be accentuated in ethnic minority pupils who see adults in their community being unable to get employment commensurate with their qualifications – often as a result of discrimination.

Housing Tower Hamlets' history as a mainly working-class borough and the consequently heavy demand for public housing, combined with an extensive post-war rebuilding programme, has produced a borough landscape dominated by council-owned housing blocks. In 1987, the tenure mix of the borough's housing was 4.6 per cent owner-occupied, 9 per cent private rental, about 81 per cent council-owned, and 4.7 per cent housing association units (London Borough of Tower Hamlets, 1987). Housing in the borough is currently in a state of crisis and for the Bangladeshi community the situation is even worse. According to the

Docklands Forum (1987) there was an increase of 120 per cent in the number of homeless people in the Docklands boroughs between 1981–2 and 1985–6, compared with an increase of 38 per cent for inner London as a whole. Because only half of applicants are housed by the council and those accepted as homeless have to wait for long periods before being housed, many are forced to squat in overcrowded, derelict housing with another family, or to continue living with their parents. The number of shared and concealed households in Tower Hamlets is estimated at nearly 30 per cent of the total number of households (Docklands Forum, 1987).

The condition of housing in Tower Hamlets is also very poor. The Docklands Forum reports that in April 1986, 50 per cent of all dwellings in Tower Hamlets were in an unsatisfactory condition. The situation is particularly bad among housing association and private sector stock, of which 46 per cent and 50 per cent respectively were found to be either unfit for human habitation or lacking basic amenities. Ten per cent of local authority stock was unfit or lacking amenities, but another 40 per cent was in need of substantial renovation. The situation has worsened dramatically since 1980 when 23 per cent of the total housing stock was considered unsatisfactory.

The poverty of the Bangladeshi community has combined with discrimination on the part of Tower Hamlets Housing Department allocations to confine them to some of the borough's poorest housing (Commission for Racial Equality, 1988a), and while Tower Hamlets has a serious housing crisis which affects the non-Asian communities, the Bangladeshi community is the hardest hit. Bangladeshis are disproportionately represented among the homeless and those living in overcrowded housing and 'temporary' hotel accommodation. In 1987, the Tower Hamlets Homeless Families Campaign reported that there were 700 Tower Hamlets families living in hotel accommodation, and estimated that 90 per cent of these were Bangladeshis.

In Spitalfields, which has a 50 per cent Asian population, Asian households make up 95 per cent of those which are statutorily overcrowded, 85 per cent of those lacking basic amenities, 81 per cent of those which have no security of tenure, and 78 per cent of those on the housing waiting list. The Docklands Forum suggests that the 'political will to resolve [this] problem has not appeared to be present', and this is borne out by the recent Council evictions of Bangladeshi families for the reason that they had made themselves 'intentionally homeless' by leaving Bangladesh.

Research on ethnicity, achievement and participation

The implications of urban deprivation for the educational attainment of Bangladeshi young people can be better understood in the light of related educational research. This review includes not only research on Bangladeshi young people but also that concerned with other South Asian groups. This is because there is actually very little research which looks specifically at

Bangladeshis and therefore it seems sensible to examine the other research for clues to the situation of Bangladeshi youth, while being careful not to generalize unduly.

Patterns of achievement First we should note that studies have shown that Bangladeshi children are unlike other South Asian children in terms of achievement. The Swann Report concluded that, on average, South Asian children perform on a par with white pupils except Bangladeshis, who perform well below the level of whites and other Asians (DES, 1985). The finding that the achievements of Bangladeshi pupils are below those of other Asian groups was replicated by a study of young people in Leeds and Bradford (Verma and Ashworth, 1986). Thus we see that the low achievement of Bangladeshi children is not confined to those living in Tower Hamlets.

The relationships between achievement and ethnicity are complicated by variables such as social class and neighbourhood: some studies have been criticized for not controlling for social class; that is to say, comparing middle-class Asian children with working-class white children. When social class is taken into account, the findings generally show less clear-cut ethnic differences. For instance Brewer and Baslum (1986) in an analysis of the Child Health and Education Study[3] found that the attainment of Asian pupils was related to certain indicators of social disadvantage, notably parents' qualifications and skills, as well as overcrowding and dependence on Family Income Supplement.

On the other hand, Verma and Ashworth (1986) suggest that social class effects may differ among ethnic groups – they found social class a good predictor of achievement (in fifth-year exams) only for white and Pakistani children. Thus although the achievement of all pupils was related to their attendance at school, there was no other predictor of achievement common to all ethnic groups. Among Bangladeshi pupils, the single other variable which predicted achievement was the level of paternal interest in their child's education.

First- and second-generation youngsters may also suffer particular educational disadvantage. Several studies have found that UK-born South Asian children do better at school than those born abroad, and that among Asian children born outside Britain, those who have been longer in Britain are the higher achievers (Essen and Ghodsian, 1979; McEwan, Gipps and Sumner, 1975). Furthermore, those Asian children who have lived longest in this country have been found to do better than their white peers (Ashby, Morrison and Butcher, 1970).

There is also a relationship with use of English: two studies indicated that those children who spoke English at home did better in school than those who used only their mother-tongue (McEwan, Gipps and Sumner, 1975; Robinson, 1980). However, Verma and Ashworth (1986) found this variable was a significant predictor of achievement only among Pakistani pupils.

However, as Tomlinson (1980a) points out, it is also important not to fall into the trap of attributing the depressed achievement of ethnic minority children to their social background, while reserving any explanation in terms of school shortcomings for white children alone.

Motivation, aspirations, and participation in post-compulsory education
The other important questions for discussion are how Bangladeshi young people respond to their social and educational disadvantage, and whether they regard education as being of value to them when they enter the labour market. Driver and Ballard (1979) found that Asian pupils, particularly the girls, were more persistent at staying the course than were white pupils and were more likely to enter further education. Fuller (1983) found that Asian girls were highly motivated at school because they regarded education as a route to some independence and a way of avoiding early marriage, and of getting a better choice of marriage partner.

Official agencies as well as schools hold contradictory beliefs as to whether Asian young people have unrealistically high ambitions. Gupta (1977) found that Asian pupils did have higher aspirations than their white peers in terms of continuing their education and the kind of job they hoped to get. Asians whose fathers were in lower status jobs than the fathers of their white peers, also aspired to greater social mobility than did the white pupils. However, he does not tell us whether the Asian fathers were in jobs appropriate to their level of education.

Continuing the trend of motivation and persistence, Asian students actually enter post-16 education in greater proportions than do white students, although in some cases this is because Asian school leavers cannot get jobs and so return to education (Craft and Craft, 1983; Eggleston, Dunn and Anjali, 1986; Fowler, Littlewood and Madigan, 1977). However, commensurate with the findings of lower achievement among Bangladeshi pupils are the results of a study by Ballard and Vellins (1985) based on data from the Universities Statistical Record and the 1981 Census. An analysis by country of birth showed that the percentage of Bangladeshi 18-year-olds going to university was much smaller than the percentage of other South Asian sub-groups, or of UK students. But, interestingly, while among other Asian groups two to four times as many boys as girls went to university, among Bangladeshis the percentages were 1.8 per cent of boys and 1.6 per cent of girls. This is an interesting finding in light of the widespread perception that Bangladeshi (and other Muslim) parents to not like their daughters to attend mixed-sex colleges. However, it may be that this consideration carries less weight in the case of universities, because of the higher status of these institutions. On the other hand, the tiny proportion of Bangladeshi university students may be drawn from middle-class or better-educated families who may take a different view of mixed-sex colleges.

Implications of the research for Bangladeshi students in Tower Hamlets
This research suggests that Bangladeshi pupils may be disadvantaged by more

than just urban deprivation: first, if they were born outside Britain and entered the British educational system later in life than did their indigenous peers; second, if they do not speak English in the home; and third, that they or their parents have emigrated from a country where the educational system is still young and poorly developed.

Although Verma and Ashworth found that social disadvantage was not related to achievement among Bangladeshi pupils, this may have been because there is such little variation in the extent of that disadvantage. In a community in which social disadvantage is so widespread, we may expect it to have a fairly uniform effect in depressing achievement. But the other consideration is that if we regard a community as responding collectively to socio-economic pressures, rather than as a group of individuals each responding separately to those pressures, then we may indeed find a strong connection between social disadvantage and low achievement, but at a group level. After all education is a group process and children benefit from each other's learning and are therefore affected adversely if the learning of their peers is depressed by the pressures of social and economic disadvantage.

Research shows that Asian children who have lived longer in this country do better at school than do more recent immigrants. This may be either because the more recent immigrants speak very little English, or because they have been educated in a different system before entering Britain. As a result of the continuing reunification of families, there is always a large number of Bangladeshi pupils starting primary and secondary school who speak little or no English. ILEA (1983b; 1984; 19877) figures show a continued increase in the number of Bangladeshi pupils in Tower Hamlets' schools, with a substantial proportion of recent immigrants joining each year. A recent survey of Bangladeshi mothers of primary-school children found that 79 per cent of the children had been born in Bangladesh, and that of these, 57 per cent had arrived in Britain after the age of five (ILEA, 1986b). Of course, these newly-arrived children speak little or no English when they enter the schools and therefore need substantial language support.

There are large numbers of bilingual students in some schools, most of whom are Bangladeshi. The ILEA Language Census of 1985 showed that 31.9 per cent of Division 5 secondary-school pupils spoke English as a second language (ILEA, 1986c). Again, this is the highest figure of any division and compares with an ILEA average of 16.8 per cent. In line with this high proportion of non-English speakers is the 22.9 of pupils who did not speak English fluently, compared with 7.4 per cent for ILEA as a whole. Among Bangladeshi pupils only 10 per cent were fluent in English in 1987 (Bangladesh Youth League, 1988). Bangladeshi students who face this additional obstacle of having to learn a second language need more time to realize their potential. However the financial costs of extended education militate against continuing it beyond the minimum school-leaving age.

Additional problems facing Bangladeshi pupils arise mostly from the racism they encounter inside and outside the school. Racial hostility impairs children's confidence and ability to take advantage of the schooling on offer (Commission for Racial Equality, 1988b; Home Affairs Sub-Committee, 1987). Racial harassment in the street or at school may lead to anxiety which prevents a child from concentrating on her studies or may even keep the child away from school – certainly many after-school events are closed to Asians in the dark winter months because of the fear of attack. On the subject of racism, it should also be noted that discrimination in the labour market may be a powerful disincentive to some Bangladeshi youngsters when they see older people with qualifications who are unable to get jobs commensurate with their education. Furthermore the Home Affairs Sub-Committee notes that 'there is evidence that many Bangladeshis regard further and higher education as closed to them'.

It is important not to fall into the trap of attributing the underachievement of Bangladeshi children to their families. But although most Bangladeshi parents are concerned about their children's education and want them to achieve, for many of them insufficient English, lack of education and limited knowledge of the British educational system make it very difficult to assist their children.

Education is often regarded as a route out of poverty and social disadvantage, and this seems to be as true of the Bangladeshi community as of any other. The critical role played by education in the aspirations of the community is demonstrated by the level of activity that has been generated by the recent transfer of power from the ILEA to the local authority. But can we assume that this is a view held by parents as well as by community activists? If Bangladeshi parents do regard education in the same way as do previous immigrant communities, we may find that their children are more persistent at school and have higher aspirations for social mobility than do white East Enders.

The secondary schools
In providing a service to both white and Bangladeshi youngsters, and to the borough's other ethnic minority children, the education system of Tower Hamlets faces a complex challenge. Among white young people, low levels of achievement are combined with low levels of aspiration, while among Bangladeshis there is the further dimension of language difficulties combined with social disadvantage even more severe than that suffered by the white population. Unfortunately, the schools are experiencing problems of their own, particularly in staffing, as detailed below.

There are 14 secondary schools in Division 5: three girls', four boys', seven coed; seven voluntary and seven county (plus special schools). With very small sixth forms, no school is able to support a full offer of sixth-form courses, and so the schools operate a consortium focused on the sixth form centre which now provides the vast majority of the A-level courses on offer in the borough. The City and East London College of Further Education coordinates with the Sixth-

Form Centre and some sixth-formers also take courses there. And of course a proportion of 16-year-olds enter further education instead of staying on at school.

Commensurate with the predominance of working-class and bilingual children, the pupil intake into Division 5 secondary schools is skewed towards the lower end of the attainment range. For instance in 1984, of all divisions, Tower Hamlets had the lowest proportion, (20.1 per cent) of fifth years who had been in the highest academic band (as measured by the ILEA's test of verbal reasoning at 11), and the third highest proportion (27.2 per cent) in band 3 (ILEA, 1985). In 1987 the balance had shifted even further towards the lowest band, with Tower Hamlets having the second highest proportion in band 3 (32.7 per cent) and the lowest proportion (14.2 per cent) in band 1 (ILEA, 1988).

While there is no doubt that many of the schools have developed good practice for working with ethnic minority pupils and that there are some very committed and effective teachers, resource constraints and staff shortages seriously limit what is possible nonetheless. Moreover, some pupils' achievement is depressed by the low expectations of some teachers and by the lack of continuity in the child's education brought about by the very high rate of staff turnover. And equally important is the fact that so few Bengali staff are employed even in schools with a majority of Bangladeshi pupils.

Staff shortages The Division 5 schools have experienced great difficulty in attracting new staff to the area, and there is always a large number of unfilled posts; recently the vacancy rate has stood at 10–15 per cent (Twomey, 1988). Some schools, though by no means all, also have trouble keeping staff. Consequently there is a high level of staff turnover (about 30 per cent). This has been mostly among younger staff, but more recently has also affected the 28–38 age range and thus is reducing the numbers of experienced staff and necessitates a heavy reliance on supply staff. Furthermore, there are 150–200 probationers entering the Division every year, and with such a high level of staff turnover and vacancies, they are not able to get the support and guidance they need (Twomey, 1988).

In interviews for this study, teachers at 7 out of 11 schools said that their school has a high or medium-to-high level of staff turnover, and they pointed out that the discontinuity in teachers affects course work, with some subjects being taught by supply teachers for the best part of a year or even longer; and that there is an adverse effect on course planning, pastoral care, discipline, pupils' motivation and attendance.

In the late 1980s, 10 out of 14 schools have had a new head teacher appointed, with 5 of these appointments being made in the academic year 1987–8. As many of these appointments were preceded by a period in which a deputy was serving as acting head, and therefore another senior member of staff was acting deputy head and so on down the line, it can be appreciated that there has been a good deal of instability in some schools. As the Twomey Report points out, this level of turnover among staff and headteachers creates insecurity in pupils and undermines both achievement and standards of behaviour. Discipline over racist attacks for instance may become lax due to lack of continuity among senior staff.

The reasons for the difficulties in recruiting and keeping staff include the cost of accommodation in London, particularly since property prices have shot up in Docklands, and the cost and time involved in travel to work (Twomey, 1988). Enormous difficulties in some schools have led to low morale which has also contributed to the high staff turnover. These include material problems, particularly overcrowding, which inevitably have a depressing effect on staff and students.

Bilingual staffing Although two secondary schools have been closed in Tower Hamlets in recent years, rolls are now rising in several schools due to the increasing Bangladeshi population. There is also a bulge in the number of primary-school age Bangladeshi children, such that hundreds have been unable to obtain places in school (Twomey, 1988), and these children will soon be contributing to an increase in the secondary-school rolls.

Because of the large number of Bangladeshi pupils, the borough has always attracted a large amount of Section 11 funding. Section 11 funding enables schools to hire extra teachers and instructors to provide English as a second language (ESL) and bilingual teaching and other support for Bangladeshi and other eligible children. Furthermore, with such a large proportion of Bangladeshi pupils in the schools, it is important that there are Bengali staff teaching mainstream subjects and providing role models to the young people. However, there is a serious shortage of bilingual teachers with UK qualifications, and while there are numbers of Asian teachers and staff from other ethnic minority groups, there are not yet enough Bangladeshi teachers. Most Bangladeshi staff are employed as instructors, and can provide only support to mainstream teachers.

Educational and occupational decision-making at 16

Having outlined the context within which Bangladeshi and other young people in Tower Hamlets experience their childhood and youth, we now approach the question of how they make decisions about the phase of their life which follows the end of compulsory schooling. This was the central question of the study from which the results below are derived. It should be noted however that by the middle of the fifth year, when many students are making these 'career' decisions, a large number of their peers have already made an effective choice by truanting from school.

Careers education, counselling and advice

In making decisions about what to do at 16-plus, students have the aid of the Tower Hamlets careers service, which offers a vocational and educational guidance and placement service to young people from the fourth year until they are 19. Each fifth year is entitled to at least one interview with a careers officer (CO), and many receive two or more depending on their needs. However, due to recent cuts in funding and the reduction in staff numbers, personnel and resources are stretched to the limit. This means that many COs can offer only what they consider to be a barely adequate service to young people. Furthermore, the school should, through its careers education programme, ensure that students are prepared for their interview with the CO. However there is considerable variation in the staff time and resources allocated to careers education, and therefore both the quantity and quality of the careers work varies among schools.

In interviews with COs for the Career Decision Study, it emerged that in only one-third of schools were the students well-enough prepared for their interviews with the CO. One CO commented on the lack of college prospectuses or leaflets in the school; another commented that the students at one school were not at a point to have a typical careers interview, and went on to point out that few schools are good at keeping up-to-date careers information and that until careers teachers are given what *they* consider to be adequate status, support, time and resources, they will not be able to provide a proper careers programme.

There are further problems in offering a service to Bengali young people; there are no Bengali COS and with only two Bengali-speaking staff, non-Bengali COs do not have the support they need for communicating with pupils or parents who speak little or no English.

For many young people, their parents are an important source of advice and a major influence on their career plans (Cherry and Gear, 1987; Eggleston et al, 1986; Verma and Ashworth, 1986). Verma and Ashworth found a very high degree of congruence between Asian students' occupational aspirations and those their parents held for them; this was particularly so for Bangladeshi young people. Furthermore, Tomlinson (1980b) found that the majority of Caribbean and Asian parents wanted their children to remain in education beyond 16, but that they often did not understand which qualifications would be most useful. Three out of five teachers interviewed for the Career Decision Study said that more Bangladeshi than English/Scottish/Welsh (ESW) parents wanted their children to stay on at school or college; only one teacher said that more ESW parents wanted their children to stay on. It is also interesting to note that five out of six teachers said that more Afro–Caribbean than ESW parents wanted their children to stay on.

Deciding whether to continue education after the fifth year
In a survey carried out in the spring of 1987 for the Career Decision Study, 212 young people enrolled in fifth-year classes in eleven secondary schools in Tower Hamlets responded to a questionnaire about their plans for the following year, their reasons for leaving or staying on in education, their opinions of 'stayers' and

'leavers', and the information available to them for making a decision about what to do after the fifth year. In most of the schools, the students were all members of the same mixed ability class. But in one school they were volunteers from several classes, and in another, they were selected from two classes by the teachers on the grounds that some of the students would be too disruptive and therefore should not be included; in a third school the entire fifth year who were in school on the day of the survey were included.

The questionnaire was based partly on the one used by the ILEA Research and Statistics Branch in their survey of Tower Hamlets' fifth years the previous year (ILEA, 1988a). Thus the present study was designed in part to replicate the ILEA findings on students' reasons for staying or leaving and their opinions of stayers and leavers. In several schools there were Bangladeshi students who were either not literate or not fluent in English and therefore were given help either in reading or in interpreting the questionnaire into Bengali.

The pupils who participated in the study included 112 boys and 100 girls. The majority were ESW students, a large percentage were Bangladeshi, and the rest a cross-section of different ethnic groups, including African, Caribbean, Chinese, Vietnamese and others. The focus of this report is on three groups: Bangladeshi, Afro-Caribbean and ESWI (including Irish) students.

Unfortunately, many students were out of class or out of school on the day the questionnaire was administered. Some students were attending oral examinations or had other commitments which kept them out of class. The number of students who were absent from class for the questionnaire varied considerably from school to school. The lowest attendance was at a school where only 27.6 per cent of the fifth year were in school on the day the questionnaire was administered and all but one of these students filled in the questionnaire. The highest attendance was 84.6 per cent and the mean attendance was 56.7 per cent. The fact that the sample cannot be regarded as representative of fifth-year students as a whole is made clear by the fact that data which was collected subsequently from five of the participating schools revealed that only 3.31 per cent of the students who were present for the questionnaire left school at Easter, while 28.13 per cent of those who were absent left at Easter. Thus this must be considered a study of young people who were still regular attenders in the Spring of their fifth year.

GCSE entries

We start with an analysis of the number of GCSEs students were expecting to enter as this gives an approximate guide to the level of achievement they were hoping to attain. However, it should be borne in mind that we do not know how many exams each student passed or what grades they obtained. We found that the majority of white students were planning to take seven GCSEs, while the distribution for Bangladeshi and Afro–Caribbean students was bimodal, the majority taking seven, but the next largest proportion taking only four GCSEs.

Further analysis of these distributions shows that there is an interaction with sex, since among Bangladeshis and Afro–Caribbeans the distributions for boys are more skewed towards lower numbers of GCSEs, while for girls the skew is towards a larger number of GCSEs (and the distribution for Afro–Caribbean girls is near normal). On the other hand, among white ESWI students, the difference between girls and boys is in the range of the distribution (wider for boys).

We might infer from the bimodal distribution for Bangladeshis and Afro–Caribben boys that these young people had channelled themselves (or been channelled) into two groups: the academic and the non-academic. It may be that many of the non-academic white students had already effectively dropped out of school and thus were not there for the survey. On the other hand, Bangladeshi and Afro–Caribbean students might have opted to take extra GCSEs in the sixth form rather than attempting the full complement in the fifth year. It is possible to explore the intentions of the students further by looking at their post-16 plans.

Students' post-16 plans
The results reveal a significant difference between the three ethnic groups, with four-fifths of Afro–Caribbeans planning to remain in education, while the white students were planning to leave or stay in roughly equal proportions. But among Bangladeshis, the results are complicated by the fact that nearly a quarter had not yet decided whether to stay or leave education. Nonetheless, a greater proportion of Bangladeshi than of white students had already decided that they wanted to remain at school.

There were no straightforward sex differences; however there was some indication that there might be an interaction of sex with ethnicity. While roughly equal proportions of Bangladeshi boys and girls were planning to remain in education, and there is also a balance between white girls and boys, most of the Afro–Caribbean leavers were boys.

A further analysis was carried out to examine the plans of students falling into each of three groups: those taking 0–4 GCSEs (low GCSE group), those taking 5–7 GCSEs (middle group) and those taking 8–10 GCSEs (high group). The majority of Bangladeshi and Afro–Caribbean students in each GCSE group were planning to remain in education after the fifth year (though these majorities were greater in the middle and high GCSE groups). However, among the white students, 90 cent of those in the low group were planning to leave, and equal proportions (44 per cent) of those in the middle group were planning to leave and stay; only in the high GCSE group was there a significant percentage (50 per cent) who were planning to stay in education. This indicates that even when controls for expected achievement are made, the educational aspirations of Bangladeshi and Afro–Caribbean students are higher than those of white ESWI students. There are also some interesting differences in the ordering of the items. Most particularly is the much lower ranking given by Bangladeshis to the last item, 'I've been offered a job I want to do', possibly because fewer of them had been offered jobs.

Finally, while there were no significant sex differences, there was a significant sex-by-ethnic group interaction on one item, 'Many of my friends are leaving'. The ethnic difference on this item is accounted for solely by the fact that it was very much more important for Bangladeshi girls than for any of the others.

Findings and conclusions

This survey of Tower Hamlets' fifth years for the Career Decision Study yielded results indicating that the staying-on rates of Bangladeshi and Afro–Caribbean students were higher than those for white students. But in attempting to explain this pattern of staying-on rates, it revealed considerable common ground between all three groups of young people and only a few differences. Naturally, we should not assume that there are not other differences which the questionnaire did not reveal. However, these results suggest some interesting patterns which could be explored further.

The evidence seems to reveal a difference in the value placed upon education by Bangladeshi and Afro–Caribbean young people, compared with the white students. However this is not a straightforward difference. Although all three groups agreed that personal effort (ie qualifications, confidence and trying hard) was the most important factor in getting a job, Bangladeshi young people nonetheless displayed less confidence in the power of personal effort in that they did not rate it quite as important as Afro–Caribbean and white young people did. On the other hand, both Bangladeshi and Afro–Caribbean students accorded more importance to discrimination than did white students. Thus the ethnic minority students show a certain amount of scepticism about equality of opportunity in the labour market. However, this scepticism does not lead them to the conclusion that education is of no value. Rather it seems to lead to the opposite conclusion that 'it is important to get more of it'. Thus Bangladeshis are inclined to regard young people who stay on even more positively than do white or Afro–Caribbean students and, along with the Afro–Caribbeans, to regard those who leave education at 16 somewhat more negatively than do white students. It should be noted, however, that in general all students regard stayers more positively than leavers.

These findings begin to answer the question of why Bangladeshis and Afro–Caribbeans stay on in greater proportions than do whites, but they do not answer why it is that nonetheless the majority of all three groups actually leave education at 16. To find some answers to this question and to further our understanding of why ethnic minority students are more inclined to stay on, we must look at the reasons why individuals chose to leave or stay.

Both leavers and stayers attach greatest importance to job-related reasons for their decision, for example 'I am staying on to get the qualifications I need for the job I want'; or 'I am leaving because I want to start to earn money as soon as possible'; or 'I've been offered a job I want to do'. Thus it seems that the underlying rationale for both leaving or staying is the ultimate goal of getting a job, and there are no other major incentives to stay on. The critical question, then, is whether the young person sees a pay-off in staying on to obtain some further qualifications.

However, if we compare the stayers among the three ethnic groups we find that there are three items which are more important for the Bengalis than for the Afro–Caribbean and white students: that their parents want them to stay, that their teachers have encouraged them to, and that they enjoy staying. This may suggest that Bangladeshi young people and their parents actually identify more strongly with the school or education *per se*, as well as a means to the end of getting a good job. Furthermore, the sex-by-ethnic group interaction for one of the job-related items suggested that while the utility of qualifications for getting a job seems to be particularly important to Afro–Caribbean and white girls, it is of less importance to Bangladeshi girls than it is to their brothers. This may reflect the lesser importance of work to Bangladeshi girls or it may suggest that white and Afro–Caribbean girls have a clearer idea of what kind of job they want.

The results for leavers mirror this pattern: for Bangladeshi students, being no good at studying was more important than for either of the other two groups, while teachers' advice to leave was less important. A third factor was much more important for Bangladeshi girls: whether or not their friends were leaving.

Perhaps, then, the greater propensity of Bangladeshi students to stay on for post-16 education is explained by a tendency to identify more strongly with the school or with the process of education. However this analysis of the reasons for staying and leaving does not add anything to the explanation of the higher staying-on rate among Afro–Caribbean students.

Students do not have a free choice at 16; they are constrained both by their material circumstances and their achievements to date. Among those whose families have the resources and the will to support a child in education beyond compulsory schooling, and who are persistent enough, taking further GCSEs in the sixth form, and then taking A-levels or going to college, is an option. However, those for whom education is not of value as an end in itself, who have not done very well at school so far, and who have the opportunity to start work right away, may prefer to call it quits at 16.

But even those who have achieved more may need an extra incentive to remain within the education system beyong the end of compulsory schooling. Perhaps paradoxically among those who are still attending school regularly towards the end of their fifth year, this extra incentive seems to be more available or perhaps more obvious to Afro–Caribbean and Bangladeshi students than to white students.

Notes

1. This research project was funded by a grant from British Petroleum plc.
2. This figure does not include the small number of students who entered colleges of further education at 16 and who subsequently were offered places in higher education. However, these students would probably add less than one percentage point to the total participation rate.
3. A national longitudinal data base.

Chapter 16

Doublespeak: The New Vocationalism, Bilingual Learners and the World of Work

Eddy Adams

It is a measure of the extent to which our education system reflects wider social and political change that vocational and pre-vocational courses have now become established features on the educational landscape. At the same time, they have occupied a pivotal position in the shifting of recruitment patterns in employment, and as such have become, for many young people, the sole channel through which they have a realistic chance of entering the job market. Clearly then, the quality of the education and training which vocational and pre-vocational courses offer is a matter for concern, and in this chapter I intend to discuss their relevance and value to those students who are bilingual. I intend to focus primarily on courses of a pre-vocational nature.

According to the Inner London Education Authority (ILEA) Language Census of 1987, 22.7 per cent of the Authority's pupils had a language other than English as a mother tongue, and although similar statistics have not been recorded for students at further education (FE) colleges, the same document notes that a substantially higher percentage of bilingual students remain in full-time education beyond the age of 16. However, for our purposes it would be misleading to regard these students as forming part of a homogeneous group, for although there are certainly common denominators which affect all bilingual students, within the range of 172 identified languages spoken in London schools and colleges we must acknowledge the individuality of each student's experience, linked to the student's own ethnicity and linguistic background.

Yet to gauge the common experience of bilingual students, there are several considerations which might allow us to approach them as two separate groups. Generally speaking the first group consists of those ethnic minority communities which are now well-established in this country. Many of the students in this category are 'bilingual' in the literal sense of the word; that is to say that they speak English as well as, or almost as well as and sometimes even better than, their mother tongue. They belong to the 31 per cent of bilingual students classified as 'fluent' in English by the ILEA census, and it should be stressed that the academic educational system has by no means operated to the detriment of these students as a whole. In many cases, the families of children in this bilingual group enjoy what might be described as a middle-class lifestyle, and with it an awareness of the value of education and the power it conveys. Here, families transmit to their children what Bourdieu calls 'cultural capital' (Bourdieu and Passerson, 1977); that is, the values and ambitions of the educational middle class, a fact reflected in the ILEA's last set of exam statistics which showed that Indian (sic) children achieved the highest O-level results in 1985 and 1986.

The same statistics confirmed that Bangladeshi children had the poorest results of any identified ethnic group, and in many respects their experience is typical of those students who make up the second set. On the whole the young people in this category belong to ethnic communities which are relatively new to this country, many of whom are battling against the most virulent hardships in the form of poor housing, high unemployment, and racial abuse. As well as Bangladesh, they may come from Vietnam, Turkey, Somalia and other countries which have been subject to dramatic unheaval. Disoriented and uprooted, their disrupted educational backgrounds are only exacerbated by social and financial constraints (see Chapter 15).

For students in the latter category, the odds are heavily stacked against their managing to follow an academic education. In the first place, a high degree of English fluency remains a pre-requisite of academic achievement in this country, and while the statistics cited above confirm that many bilingual students possess such skills, a far greater number do not. Second, financial pressures require them to take up courses which will best prepare them for immediate employment. As already noted, the pre-vocational courses form the framework through which these students must pass if they wish to gain access to waged labour. Therefore in educational terms, they hope to cram enough into the space of a few short years to make themselves 'marketable' in the job sphere.

This is the real educational choice open to those who do not have the social or economic clout which carries the power to influence governments. And it is these considerations which have exercized influence over the bias of language support towards pre-vocational and technical courses at institutions like Hackney College, where many of the students belong to the second category. As Ann Janssen, English as a second language (ESL) Coordinator, puts it:

> In that limited amount of time you actually want people to achieve and succeed in something which will allow them to develop further.[1]

Given that access and achievement are inextricably linked to language, the choice for bilingual students is effectively between academic courses on which language provision is poor and where they may fail as a result, or less academic courses where the support will be better and prospects of success correspondingly higher. Clearly this will create a dilemma for those ESL students whose academic capabilities are not matched by their English language level, and there will be many cases where such students are directed on to inappropriate pre-vocational courses.

In the background to this is the information presented in the 1987 ILEA

Language Census that although the number of bilingual students increased between 1985 and 1987, both the number and percentage of those considered fluent actually dropped. As they point out, such statistics suggest that more resources are required for ESL teaching. However, this seems unlikely in the current climate, while following the break-up of the ILEA, there seems little reason to believe that the trend will be reversed with the transfer of responsibility to the boroughs.

Such misgivings might be misplaced however, if the lofty claims for the pre-vocational courses were a little more convincing. Wellington (1987) has noted the failure of such courses in Japan, where they were stigmatized as providing a second-rate education, yet there is little evidence to suggest that the same is not happening here. In a country where the management structure is still dominated by the 'old boy network' and where technical education has always been relegated to a poor second-best, the grounds for optimism are slim.

And yet the irony is that as language teachers, we cannot blind ourselves to the very positive features which pre-vocational courses offer bilingual students. Savita Kapoor has suggested (1985–6), that they may provide valuable scope for developing multi-ethnic, anti-racist (as well as anti-sexist) initiatives within their frameworks. As such they present an opportunity to challenge the way in which sections of our community have been largely ignored by the education system in this country, at the same time combatting the attempt to marginalize such issues, implicit in the outline of the national curriculum. Additionally, the fact that pre-vocational courses comprise a variety of components originally designed by progressive educationalists as part of a move towards student-centred language programmes, means that they retain valuable elements which are particularly relevant to the needs of ESL learners. Another case of the Right hijacking 'good means for bad ends'? Yet the bottom line is that in the current environment, with the concept of 'language across the curriculum' consigned to the back burner, for many bilingual students pre-vocational courses provide the *only* realistic means on offer.

Looking at those means, if we first consider the concepts of project work and collaborative learning, both being significant in pre-vocational courses, we find that they are also established features of successful work with ESL students. Here, language operates as a means to an end rather than as an end in itself, with students enjoying plenty of scope to interact with one another, moving freely about the class and working in groups. Of course this is merely an aspect of good teaching practice, allowing as it does for increasing students' responsibility for their own learning, but the element of peer contact which such techniques foster has been identified as an important feature of language learning; a fact which was noted by the Swann Report and one which hastened the winding down of the withdrawal system for ESL students.

Similarly, the shift towards an assessment programme based upon student profiling schemes is one which allows for a much fairer and more accurate examination of the bilingual student's abilities. As an integral part of academic courses, the 'all or nothing' written exam at the end of the year discriminates against those students whose written English language skills do not reflect the work they have produced during the course. Although the GCSE has gone some way to confronting this issue, A-level courses, still the principal gateway to higher education, remain entrenched in the old system and seem likely to remain so for some time.

Finally, we should consider the much criticized social and life skills (SLS) components of the pre-vocational courses. It is here that much of the flak has been directed, with suggestions that SLS is merely intended to inculcate working-class kids with subservient or middle-class manners. There may certainly be truth in this in the case of monolingual students, but I think the needs of bilingual students are quite distinct here. With first-language English speakers, SLS may indeed be catering for an 'imaginary deficit', but what it does provide is language practice in a way which is of particular value to ESL learners. It is the part of the course where they can acquire a wide variety of language skills, particularly when the use of situational videos consolidates the language with visual images. Extension work in the form of role plays and simulations gives students space to develop and practise the language for themselves – techniques which are ideally suited to teaching students through the medium of a second language and which have long been acknowledged as such.

Another integral part of the SLS programme which merits consideration is the residential visit, often the subject of enthusiastic student feedback. In many cases it can provide a welcome change for students who are living in run-down inner-city accommodation. As their community links are largely London-based, a substantial number may never have been out of the city before. Consequently, going on a residential course is something special. It can be a platform for developing and exploring peer relationships, for using language in an environment which is quite different from home in many respects, and for looking at themselves in a new light, away from domestic pressures. Quite frequently the tight ethnic bonding prevalent at college breaks down, as students sample each other's food, customs and values at first hand. This is especially true in the cases of the many young Muslim women for whom it is their first experience away from their families.

Yet although we can identify positive aspects for bilingual learners on such courses, we must shift our focus to the particularly thorny issue of work experience before committing ourselves to any overall conclusions. For the line dividing education from training is directly linked to work, and the most tangible expression of that division is the block of work experience which forms part of every pre-vocational course. This was made apparent by Lord Young in an article for the *Journal of the Institute of Directors* published in October 1982, when he argued that:

Training should not be confused with education. Training is about work-related skills and is intimately connected with employment. (Young, 1982, p. 34)

It is a connection that has been strengthened since the early 1980s, and it was Green (1986) who observed that since FE colleges have long occupied the strategic middle ground between school and work, it is hardly surprising that they have inherited the new generation of courses designed to smooth the passage from one to the other. However, it is a passage which has been irrecognizably changed from its forerunner. The apprenticeship system has been unceremoniously scrapped, while the pre-vocational courses have barely gone half-way to providing equivalent training skills. Meanwhile, outside the narrow provision of the skilled trades, many of the larger organizations, along with the high street giants like Marks and Spencer, Sainsburys and Rumbelows, now use variations of work-experience schemes, Youth Training Schemes (YTS) or whatever, as a way of checking out new staff, measures which certainly get away from the old half-hour interview. As a YTS Coordinator pointed out:

I think it probably loses people jobs who would have got them on an interview, but it gets kids jobs who can't handle interviews and who do have skills . . . and bilingual students come very strongly there, because it's difficult for them to perform well in an interview.[2]

This is particularly true in cases where language difficulties are compounded by cultural differences. Many Chinese and Vietnamese students, for example, find standard 'interviewee' behaviour offensive, coming as they do from cultures where modesty is still regarded as a virtue. By encouraging these students to 'sell themselves', teachers are asking them to go against the cultural grain.

Such issues raise fundamental questions about the work done on courses with bilingual students, questions which do not lend themselves to facile answers. Clearly, both Right and Left pin their hopes on Britain's post-Fordist economic future on the expansion of the service sector (where communication and 'personality' are crucially important), so as teachers we are left to ponder our part in a system which actively contributes to the 'Taiwanization' of the United Kingdom where bilingual students are encouraged to set their sights on supermarket management as the apex of their career goals.

It is expected that the 1990s will see a workforce increasingly composed of non-unionized, part-time or casual employees located in service sector jobs. But although traineeship may have become an integral part of the workplace, we should remember that the half-hour selection process has now been replaced by one which may last up to two years, at the end of which the employer can still decide that the candidate is 'unsuitable' for the post.

The employers have nothing to lose. As the Department of Education and

Science (DES) itself acknowledged in its introduction to the two-year YTS course:

They [the employers] have a great deal to gain from it: an assured supply of qualified young workers; a more versatile, more readily acceptable, more highly motivated and therefore more productive workforce. (DES, 1985e)

'Versatile', 'acceptable', and 'productive' – the trainees will thus be ideally prepared for a lifetime of insecure, short-term jobs. But in theory at least, it is a three-way bargain struck between the student, the college and the employer who may get cheap labour, but at a price. That price is time and supervision, yet evidence suggests that employers are loathe to take on bilingual students because they suspect that doing so will involve them in extra work.

According to guidelines issued by the ILEA FHCE Inspectorate:

It is particularly important that bilingual students on MSC-funded courses are provided with work experience, as few if any of them have worked in this country, and there is some evidence that students are failing to get work because of this.

This is all very well, but it fails to acknowledge the difficulty in finding work placements for these students in boroughs like Hackney and Tower Hamlets. As one ESL coordinator has put it:

If you can actually set up a pilot scheme with the high street banks or whoever, and say 'Look, we can actually provide you with trainees who are bilingual', it is not a problem. In Aldgate you'd do well to have 80% of your staff Sylheti speaking.[3]

So in yet another area of their lives ESL students receive messages telling them that their bilingualism is a handicap rather than a valuable resource.

The period of work placement, when it does get off the ground, is the ideal Thatcherite learning experience. Students are pitched in at the deep end where they sink or swim according to their own resources. Although every effort may be taken to cushion the impact, the experience is inevitably fraught with potential hazards for all trainees, but particularly for bilingual students who may not have the language, cultural awareness or plain 'street sense' of their monolingual peers. They are required to process an enormous amount of ungraded language, often in situations unconducive to clear communication, yet the perhaps surprising outcome is that the majority manage it, triumphing with a resilience often born out of earlier crises.

Naturally this fosters a great sense of achievement and there is no denying the possibilities of success. As a Hackney College coordinator noted:

When it [work experience] works well, then it's really valuable . . . more valuable arguably than anything else all year . . . in terms of confidence-building and the power it gives bilingual students. By the fact that they've gone out and done it.[4]

However, it is a fact that the success of work placements at that particular establishment rests largely on the efficient organization and selfless commitment of the ESL department, combined with the fact that funds have been hitherto available to ensure a relatively low student–staff ratio whenever possible. Experience has shown that unless this is so, then the entire operation may degenerate into petty exploitation, with trainees being lumbered with box-filling tasks where they learn nothing. So along the way teachers have become monitors, administrators and trainers, with increasing proportions of their timetables devoted to paperwork and non-teaching tasks. On the other hand, it is unfortunate that there is scant evidence to suggest that those in the workplace are becoming more like teachers, and it is striking how few employers or representatives visit colleges or take an active interest in the work they carry out.

So what conclusions can we draw from the information assembled in this chapter, and to what extent does it help us outline the future for bilingual students on such courses? My starting-point was that pre-vocational courses contain much that is particularly suited to the needs of bilingual students. The concern, however, is that these courses are labelled as locations for less-able students, with the concomitant worry that many ESL students will be shunted onto them due to a lack of language support provision elsewhere, poor pastoral care, lowered teacher expectation, or a combination of all three.

The indications are that the successful work carried out with ESL students at institutions like Hackney College will be threatened by further reductions in funding, and it would be unrealistic not to expect the abolition of the ILEA to increase financial hardship in those boroughs with fewer resources. Naturally, these are also the boroughs with greatest need in terms of ESL support. However, there are possible grounds for optimism. These are largely linked to the argument that the individual boroughs now have to become more responsive to the needs of the immediate community, and it is here that they have an opportunity to challenge the Tories' appropriation of the concept of educational choice. By making themselves accountable to the ethnic groups in the borough, and by forging stronger links with the local business community, the new LEAs may be able to maintain and improve the benefits bilingual students derive from such courses. However, should they fail, there will be nothing to prevent such students becoming mere 'job fodder' on what will continue to be identified as 'dead-end' courses.

Notes

1. Interview with Ann Janssen, ESL Coordinator, Hackney College, 26 April 1988.
2. Interview with Helen Casey, YTS Coordinator, 26 April 1988.

3. Interview with Ann Jannsen, 26 April 1988.
4. Interview with Helen Casey, 26 April 1988.

References

Ahier, J and Flude, M (eds) (1983), *Contemporary Education Policy*. London and Canberra: Croom Helm.

Alexander, W (1969), *Towards a New Education Act*. London: Councils and Education Press.

Anderson, J D and Johnson, A (1981), 'Birth of a tertiary system: a case-study', *Forum* 23, 3, pp. 71–73.

—— (1985), 'Adolescence of a tertiary system: a case-study', *Forum* 27, 3, pp. 81–83.

Ashby, B, Morrison, A and Butcher, H J (1970), 'The abilities and attainments of immigration children', *Research in Education* 4, pp. 73–80.

Austin, G M (1982), 'The tertiary college solution', *Forum* 25, 1, pp. 24–26.

—— (1987), 'The opportunity of tertiary', *Education* 27 February, p. 196.

Baker, K (1989), 'Further education: a new strategy', speech to the Association of Colleges of Further and Higher Education, February.

Ballard, J (1985), 'Tertiary synthesis', in F Janes et al (eds), pp. 60–64).

Ballard, R and Vellins, S (1985), 'South Asian entrants to British universities: a comparative note, *New Community* 12, 2, pp. 260–65.

Bangladesh Youth League (1988), *The Future Organisation of Inner London Education: a Bangladeshi perspective*. London: Bangladesh Youth League.

Banks, O (1955), *Parity and Prestige in English Secondary Education*. London: Routledge & Kegan Paul.

Barker, B (1987), 'Pre-vocationalism and schooling', in M Holt (ed) *Skills and Vocationalism: the Easy Answer*. Milton Keynes: Open University Press, pp. 5–11.

Barnett, C (1986), *The Audit of War*. London: Macmillan.

Becker, H S (1952), 'Social class variations in teacher–pupil relationships', *Journal of Educational Sociology* 25, pp. 451–65.

Benn, C (1984), 'Learning your place', *Teaching London Kids* no. 22, pp. 7–9.

Benn, C and Fairley, J (eds) (1986), *Challenging the MSC: on jobs, education and training*. London: Pluto Press.

Bernbaum, G (1979), 'Editorial Introduction', in G Bernbaum (ed) *Schooling in Decline*. London: Macmillan, pp. 1–16).

Bernstein, B (1958), 'Some sociological determinants of perception', *British Journal of Sociology* IX, pp. 159–74.

—— (1962), 'Social class, linguistic codes and grammatical elements', *Language and Speech* 5, pp. 221–40.

(1970), 'Education cannot compensate for society', *New Society* 26 February, pp. 344–47.

Blackman, S J (1987), 'The labour market in school: new vocationalism and issues of socially ascribed discrimination', in P Brown and D N Ashton (eds) *Education, Unemployment and Labour Markets*. Lewes: Falmer Press, pp. 27–56.

Board of Education (1926), *Report of the Consultative Committee on the Education of the Adolescent* (Hadow Report). London: HMSO.

(1943a), *Educational Reconstruction*, White Paper. London: HMSO.

(1943b), *Curriculum and Examinations in Secondary Schools* (Report of the Committee of the Secondary School Examinations Council – the Norwood Report). London: HMSO.

Boucher, L (1982), *Tradition and Change in Swedish Education*. Oxford: Pergamon Press.

Bourdieu, P and Passeron, J C (1977), *Reproduction in Education, Society and Culture*. London: Sage.

Bourner, T and Hamed, M (1987), *Entry Qualifications and Degree Performance*. CNAA Development Services Publication, 10.

Bowlby, J (1953), *Childcare and the Growth of Love*. Harmondsworth: Penguin Books.

Brewer, R I and Haslum, M N (1986), 'Ethnicity: the experience of socio-economic disadvantage and educational attainment', *British Journal of the Sociology of Education* 7, pp. 19–34.

Brockington, D, Pring, R and White, R (1985), *The 14–19 Curriculum: integrating CPVE, YTS, TVEI. A Discussion Document*. Bristol: Youth Education Service.

Brotherton, M S (1989), *The Implications of National Vocational Qualifications for Further Education*. Metropolitan Borough of Wirral, July.

Brown, P (1987), *Schooling Ordinary Kids*. London: Tavistock.

(1989), 'Education', in P Brown and R Sparks (eds) *Beyond Thatcherism*. Milton Keynes: Open University Press.

Burt, C (1909), 'Experimental tests of general intelligence', *British Journal of Psychology* 3, pp. 94–177.

(1921), *Mental and Scholastic Tests*. London: London County Council.

Cantor, L M and Roberts, I F (1986), *Further Education Today: a critical review* (3rd edn). London: Routledge & Kegan Paul.

Carey, S and Shukur, A (1985–86), 'A profile of the Bangladeshi community in East London', *New Community* 12, pp. 405–17.

Central Statistical Office (1988), *Social Trends*. London: HMSO.

Cherry, N and Gear, R (1987), 'Young people's perceptions of their vocational guidance needs: I priorities and preoccupations', *British Journal of Guidance and Counselling* 15, 1, pp. 59–71.

Chitty, C (1986), 'TVEI, the MSC's Trojan Horse', in C Benn and J Fairley (eds), pp. 76–98.

(1987a), 'The commodification of education', *Forum* 29, 3, pp. 66–69.

(1987b), 'City Technology Colleges: a bad idea in a bad cause', in C Chitty (ed) *Aspects of Vocationalism*. London: Post-16 Education Centre, Institute of Education, University of London, pp. 55–70.

(1989), *Towards a New Education System: the victory of the New Right?* Lewes: Falmer Press.

Chitty, C and Worgan, J (1987), 'TVEI: origins and transformation', in C Chitty (ed) *Aspects of Vocationalism*, pp. 19–36).

Clegg, M (1985), 'Mixed economy' in F Janes et al (eds), pp. 57–60).

Cockburn, C (1987), *Two Track Training*. London: Macmillan.

Cockroft Report (1982), *Mathematics Counts* (Report of the Committee of Inquiry into the teaching of mathematics in schools). London: HMSO.

Cohen, P (1984), 'Against the new vocationalism', in I Bates et al (eds) *Schooling for the Dole? The New Vocationalism*. London: Macmillan, pp. 104–69.

Coles, B (1988), Postscript to B Coles (ed) *Young Careers: the search for jobs and the New Vocationalism*. Milton Keynes: Open University Press, pp. 191–99.

Commission for Racial Equality (1988a), *Homelessness and Discrimination: report of the formal investigation into the allocation of housing by the London Borough of Tower Hamlets*. London: CRE.

(1988b), *Learning in Terror: a survey of racial harassment in schools and colleges in England, Scotland and Wales, 1985–1987*. London : CRE.

Communist Party of Great Britain (CPGB) (1985), 'Discussion paper on the CPVE'. London: CPGB.

Confederation of British Industry (CBI) (1985), 'CBI Work-Experience Workshop, 14 October.

(1989), *Towards a Skills Revolution – a Youth Charter*. London: CBI, July.

Coopers and Lybrand (1985), *A Challenge to Complacency*. Sheffield: MSC.

Corbett, A (1968), 'Sixth-form colleges', *New Society* 18 March, pp. 458–59.

Cotterell, A B and Heley, E W (eds) (1981), *Tertiary: a Radical Approach to Post-Compulsory Education*. Cheltenham: Stanley Thornes.

CPVE Joint Board (1988a), *CPVE Evaluation: general findings and recommendations.*

(1988b), *Issues of Practice: progression.*

Craft, M and Craft, A (1983), 'The participation of ethnic minority pupils in further and higher education', *Educational Research* 25, pp. 10–19.

Crisp, P and Melling, G (1988), 'Further and higher education: accountability, access . . . anarchy?', *Local Government Studies* Jan/Feb, pp. 31–38.

Cusick, P A (1983), *The Egalitarian Principle and the American High School*. New York: Longman.

Dale, R (1983), 'Thatcherism and education', in Ahier and Flude (eds), pp. 233–55.

(1985), 'The background and inception of the Technical and Vocational Education Initiative' in R Dale (ed) *Education, Training and Employment: towards a new vocationalism?* Oxford: Pergamon Press in association with the Open University, pp. 41–56.

Dean, J, Bradley, K, Choppin, B and Vincent, D (1979), *The Sixth Form and its Alternatives*. Windsor: National Foundation for Educational Research.

Deane, S (1985), *Celtic Revivals: Essays in Modern Irish Literature 1880–1980*. London: Faber.

Deem, R (1988), 'The Great Education Reform Bill – some issues and implications', *Journal of Educational Policy* 3, 2, pp. 181–89.

Dent, H C (1961), *Universities in Transition*. London: Cohen & West.

Department of Education and Science (DES) (1964), *Day Release* (Henniker Heaton Report). London: HMSO.

(1965), *The Organization of Secondary Education* (Circular 10/65). London: HMSO, July.

(1969a), *DES Report on Education No. 96: Trends in School Population*. London: DES, November.

(1969b), *Technician Courses and Examinations* (Haslegrave Report). London: HMSO.

(1972), *Education: a framework for expansion* (Cmnd 5174). London: HMSO, December.

(1976), *School Education in England: problems and initiatives* (Yellow Book). London: DES, July.

(1977), *Education in Schools: a consultative document* (Cmnd 6869). London: HMSO.

(1978), *Special Educational Needs* (Warnock Report) (Cmnd 7212). London: HMSO.

(1979), *Proposals for a Certificate of Extended Education* (Keohane Report) (Cmnd 7755). London: HMSO.

(1980a), *Examinations 16–18*. (Macfarlane Report). London: HMSO.

(1980b), *Education for 16–19 Year Olds*. London: DES/CLEA.

(1980c), *A Framework for the School Curriculum*. London: HMSO.

(1981a), *The School Curriculum*. London: HMSO.

(1981b), *The Legal Basis of Further Education* (Thompson Report). London: DES.

(1982a), *The Youth Training Scheme: implications for the education service* (Circular 6/82). London: HMSO.

(1982b), *17+: a new qualification*. London: HMSO.

(1985a), *Better Schools* (Cmnd 9469). London: HMSO, March.

(1985b), *Statistical Bulletin, 10/85*. London: HMSO.

(1985c), *Academic Validation in Public Sector Higher Education* (Lindop Report). London: HMSO.

(1985d), *Education for All – the Report of the Committee of Inquiry into the Education of Children from Ethnic Minority Groups* (Swann Report) (Cmnd 9453). London: HMSO.

(1985e), *Education and Training for Young People* (Cmnd 9482. London: HMSO, April.

(1987a), *Higher Education: meeting the challenge* (Cmnd 114). London: HMSO.

(1987b), *Providing for Quality: the pattern of organisation to age 19* (Circular 3/87). London: DES.

(1987c), *The National Curriculum 5–16: a consultation document*. London: HMSO, July.

(1987d), *Maintained Further Education: financing, Governance and Law* (Consultation Paper). London: HMSO.

(1987e), *Managing Colleges Efficiently*. London: DES.

(1988a), *National Curriculum Task Group on Assessment and Testing: a report*. London: DES and the Welsh Office.

(1988b), *Advancing A Levels* (Higginson Report. London: HMSO.

(1988c), *Education Reform Act: Local Management of Schools* (Circular 7/88). London: HMSO.

(1988d), *Education Reform Act: Governance of Maintained Further and Higher Education Colleges* (Circular 8/88). London: HMSO.

(1988e), *Education Reform Act 1988: Local Management of Further and Higher Education Colleges: Planning and Delegation Schemes and Articles of Government* (Circular 9/88). London: HMSO.

(1989), *The Widening of Access to Higher Education* (HMI report). London: HMSO, July.

Department of Employment (Doe) (1982), 'New technical education initiative'. Press Notice, 12 November.

(1984), *Training for Jobs*. Cmnd 9135. London: HMSO, February.

(1988), *Employment for the 1990s*. London: HMSO.

DoE and DES (1986), *Working Together – Education and Training* (Cmnd 9823). London: HMSO, July.

Department of the Environment, Inner Cities Directorate (1983), *Information Note no. 2, 1981 Census, Urban Deprivation*.

Devereux, W A (1982), *Adult Education in Inner London: 1870–1980*. London: Shepheard-Walwyn/ILEA.

Dewey, J (1916), *Democracy and Education*. New York: The Macmillan Company.

Docklands Forum (1987), *Housing in Docklands*. London: The Docklands Forum.

Driver, G and Ballard, R (1979), 'Comparing performance in multi-racial schools; South Asian pupils at 16-plus', *New Community* 7, 2, pp. 143–53.

Eagleton, T (1983), *Literary Theory: an introduction*. Oxford: Basil Blackwell.

Education Act (no. 2) 1986. London: HMSO.

Education Reform Act 1988. London: HMSO.

Eggleston, J, Dunn, D and Anjali, M (1986), *Education for Some: the educational and vocational experiences of 15–18 year old members of minority ethnic groups*. Stoke-on Trent: Trentham Books.

Elliott, D (1985), 'Higher education: towards a transbinary policy?' in M Hughes, P Ribbins and H Thomas (eds) *Managing Education: the system and the institution*. London: Cassell Education, pp. 198–220.

Engels, F (1969 edn), *The Condition of the Working Class in England*. Panther Books.

Essen, J and Ghodsian, M (1979), 'The children of immigrants: school performance', *New Community* 8, 3, 422–29.

Evans, N (1988), *Curriculum Opportunity*. London: FEU.

Fairbairn, A N (ed) (1980), *The Leicestershire Plan*. London: Heinemann Educational Books.

Fensham, P J (1985), 'Science for all: a reflective essay', *Journal of Curriculum Studies* 17, 4, pp. 415–35.

Field, J (1988), 'Further and adult education after the act', *Forum* 31, 1, pp. 17–18.

Finn, D (1984), 'The Manpower Services Commission and the Youth Training Scheme: the first year', *Comprehensive Education* 48, pp. 6–8.

(1985), 'The Manpower Services Commission and the Youth Training Scheme: a permanent bridge to work?' in R Dale (ed), pp. 111–25.

(1987), *Training without Jobs: new deals and broken promises*. London: Macmillan.

Floud, J (1962), 'Social class factors in educational achievement', in *Ability and Educational Opportunity*. OECD: HMSO, Chapter 4.

Forum Editorial Board (1988), 'The Education Bill', *Forum* 30, 2, p. 59.

Fowler, B, Littlewood, B and Madigan, R (1977), 'Immigrant school-leavers and the search for work', *Sociology* 11, 2, p. 69.

Fuller, M (1983), 'Qualified criticism, critical qualifications', in L Barton and S Walker (eds) *Race, Class and Education*. London: Croom Helm, pp. 166–90.

Fulton, O (1989), 'Time to be broadminded', *The Times Educational Supplement*, 19 May.

Further Education Unit (FEU) (1979), *A Basis for Choice: post-16 pre-employment courses*. London: FEU.

    (1980), *Signposts*. London: FEU.

    (1981), *ABC in Action: a report from an FEU/CGLI Working Party on the piloting of 'A Basis for Choice' 1979–81*. London: FEU.

    (1985a), *Signposts '85: a review of 16–19 education*. London: FEU.

    (1985b), *CPVE – Confusion or Deception*. London: FEU, March.

    (1985c), *CPVE in Action*. London: FEU.

    (1987a), *Progression from CPVE*. London: FEU.

    (1987b), *Relevance, Flexibility and Competence*. London: FEU.

    (1989), 'Access to FE for black adults', *Bulletin*, June.

Gamble, A (1985), *Britain in Decline: economic policy, political strategy and the British state* (2nd edn). London: Macmillan.

Giles, K and Woolfe, R (1977), 'Deprivation, disadvantage and compensation', *Schooling and Society* units 25–6. Milton Keynes: Open University Press.

Glass, D (ed) (1954), *Social Mobility in Britain*. London: Routledge & Kegan Paul.

Glass, D and Gray, J L (1938), 'Opportunity and the older universities', in L Hogben (ed), pp. 418–70.

Glazier, J (1985), 'The CEE is alive and kicking', *Education* 12 April, p. 332.

Gleeson, D (1985), 'Privatization of industry and the nationalization of youth', in R Dale (ed), pp. 57–72.

    (1987) (ed), *TVEI and Secondary Education: a critical appraisal*. Milton Keynes: Open University Press.

Gleeson, D and Mardle, G (1980), *Further Education or Training?* London: Routledge & Kegan Paul.

Goacher, B (1984), *Selection Post-16: the role of examination results* (Schools Council Examinations Bulletin 45). London: Methuen Educational.

Golby, M (1980), 'Perspectives on the core', in *Perspective 2: the Core Curriculum*. Exeter: University of Exeter School of Education, May, pp. 3–10.

Gray, J L and Moshinsky, P (1938a), 'Ability and educational opportunity in English education', in L Hogben (ed), pp. 334–76.

    (1938b), 'Ability and educational opportunity in relation to parental occupation', in L Hogben (ed), pp. 377–417.

Green, A (1986), 'The MSC and the three-tier structure of further education', in C Benn and J Fairley (eds), pp. 99–122.

    (1988), 'Lessons in standards', *Marxism Today* January, pp. 24–30.

    (1990), 'Education and training: a study in neglect', *Forum*, 32, 3, pp. 14–16.

    (1991), 'Education and training: a way forward', *Forum* 33, 2, pp. 60–61.

Green, P (1987), *A New Curriculum at 17? Some Issues in the Certificate of Pre-Vocational Education* (Occasional paper no. 1, Post-16 Education Centre). London: Post-16 Education Centre, Institute of Education, University of London.

Gupta, Y P (1977), 'The educational and vocational aspirations of Asian immigrant and English school-leavers – a comparative study', *British Journal of Sociology* 28, pp. 185–98.

Halsey, A H (1990), 'Slow blur of the binary line', *The Times Higher Education Supplement* 26 January.

Halsey, A H, Floud J E, and Anderson (eds) (1961), *Education, Economy and Society*. New York: Free Press of Glencoe.

Halsey, A H, Heath, A F and Ridge, J M (1980), *Origins and Destinations: family, class and education in modern Britain*. Oxford: Clarendon Press.

Harding, S (ed) (1987), *Feminism and Methodology*. Bloomington, Indianapolis and Milton Keynes: Indiana University Press and Open University Press.

Hargreaves, D H (1967), *Social Relations in a Secondary School*. London: Routledge & Kegan Paul.

(1982), *The Challenge for the Comprehensive School: culture, curriculum and community*. London: Routledge & Kegan Paul.

Harland, J (1987), 'The new INSET: a transformation scene', *Journal of Education Policy* 2, 3, pp. 235–44.

HM Inspectorate (1977), *Curriculum 11–16*. London: HMSO, December.

(1980), *A View of the Curriculum*. London: HMSO.

Hogben, L (ed) (1938), *Political Arithmetic*. London: Allen & Unwin.

Holland, G (1977), *Young People and Work: a report on the feasibility of a new programme of opportunities for unemployed young people*. London: HMSO.

Holland, J (1988), 'Girls and occupational choice: in search of meanings', in A Pollard, J Puris and G Walford (eds) *Education, Training and the New Vocationalism*. Milton Keynes: Open University Press, pp. 129–47.

Holt, M (1978), *The Common Curriculum: its structure and style in the comprehensive school*. London: Routledge & Kegan Paul.

(1983), 'Vocationalism: the new threat to universal education', *Forum* 25, 3, pp. 84–86.

Home Affairs Sub-Committee on Race Relations and Immigration (1987), *First Report, vol. I: Bangladeshis in Britain*. London: HMSO.

Hunter, C (1984), 'The Political devaluation of comprehensives: what of the future?', in S J Ball (ed) *Comprehensive Schooling: a reader*. Lewes: Falmer Press, pp. 273–92.

Industrial Training Research Unit (1981), *A – Z Study*. London: ITRU.

Inner London Education Authority (ILEA) (1970), *Evidence to the Russell Committee into Adult Education in England and Wales*. London: ILEA.

(1973a), *An Education Service for the Whole Community*. London: ILEA.

(1973b), *Review of Vocational Further and Higher Education*. London: ILEA.

(1980), *Statistical Information Bulletin No. 3. Staying On Rates 1977, 1978, 1979 and 1980*. London: ILEA.

(1981), *Analysis of Differences in School Staying-On Rates Between Girls and Boys and Different Divisions* (RS 809/81). London: ILEA.

(1983a), *Participation of Sixteen Year Olds in Full Time Education* (RS 867/83). London: ILEA.

(1983b), *Statistical Information Bulletin No. 8. Social and Ethnic Characteristics of ILEA Pupils 1981–82*. London: ILEA.

(1984), *Statistical Information Bulletin No. 12. Social and Ethnic Characteristics of ILEA Pupils 1983–84*. London: ILEA.

(1985), *School Examination Results in the ILEA 1984* (RS 977/85). London: ILEA.

(1986a), *16–19 Participation Rates* (RS1095/86). London: ILEA.

(1986b), *Bangladeshi Mothers' Views of Schooling in Tower Hamlets* (RS1029/86). London: ILEA.

(1986c), *1985 Language Census* (RS1026/86). London: ILEA.

(1987), *1987 Educational Priority Indices: changes in the characteristics of the school pupil population between 1985 and 1987* (RS1124/87). London: ILEA.

(1988), *School Examination Results in the ILEA 1987* (RS977/88). London: ILEA.

ILEA Careers Service, Division 5 – Tower Hamlets (1986), *Division 5 Destination Statistics 1985/1986*. London: ILEA.

(1987), *Division 5 Destination Statistics 1986/1987*. London: ILEA.

Institute for Public Policy Research (IPPR) (1990), *A British Baccalauréat: ending the division between education and training*. London: IPPR.

Institute of Manpower Studies (1984), *Competence and Competition: training and education in the Federal Republic of Germany, the United States and Japan*. London: NEDC/MSC.

Jackson, M (1989), 'Vocational courses attacked as narrow "trade training"', *The Times Educational Supplement* 20 October.

Janes, F (1979), 'Creating a tertiary college from scratch', *Education* 4 May, pp. 516–17.

Janes, F et al (eds) (1985), *Going Tertiary*. Yeovil: Tertiary Colleges Association.

Jones, K (1989), *Right Turn: the Conservative revolution in education*. London: Hutchinson Radius.

Joseph, K (1982), speech to the Institute of Directors, March, Supplement to *The Director*, May, pp. 3–5.

Jump, J (1982), 'Matthew Arnold', in B Ford (ed) *The New Pelican Guide to English Literature* vol. 6. Harmondsworth: Penguin Books, pp. 309–23.

Kapoor, S (1985–86), 'Multi-ethnic/anti-racist education and CPVE: an opportunity not to be missed', *ILEA Multi-Ethnic Review*. London: ILEA.

Karabel, T and Halsey, A H (1977), 'Educational research: a review and an interpretation', in T Karabel and A H Halsey (eds) *Power and Ideology in Education*. New York: Oxford University Press, pp. 1–85.

Kedney, B and Parkes, D (eds) (1988), *Planning the FE Curriculum*. London: FEU.

Keitel, C (1987), 'What are the goals of mathematics for all?', *Journal of Curriculum Studies* 19, 5, pp. 393–407.

Kelly, T (1970), *A History of Adult Education in Britain*. Liverpool: Liverpool University Press.

Kenyon, B (1987), 'A bleak outlook', *The Times Educational Supplement* 9 January.

Kogan, M (1971), *The Politics of Education: conversations with Edward Boyle and Anthony Crosland*. Harmondsworth: Penguin.

Krug, E A (1969), *The Shaping of the American High School, 1880–1920*. Madison: University of Wisconsin Press.

Labour Party (1982), *16–19: Learning for Life*. London: The Labour Party.

Labov, W (1969), '*The Logic of Non-Standard English*'. Georgetown Monographs on Language and Linguistics vol. 22, pp. 1–31.

Laclau, E and Mouffe, C (1985), *Hegemony and Socialist Strategy*. London: Verso.

Lambert, S (ed) (1988), *Managing Tertiary and Sixth Form Colleges*. London: Longman.

Lawton, D and Chitty, C (1988), *The National Curriculum* (University of London Bedford Way Papers 33). London: Institute of Education, University of London.

Layard, R, King, T and Moser, C (1969), *The Impact of Robbins*. Harmondsworth: Penguin Books.

Lees, S (1986), *Losing Out*. London: Hutchinson.

Lester Smith, WOL (1957), *Education*. Harmondsworth: Penguin Books.

Lindsay, K (1926), *Social Progress and Educational Wastage*. London: Routledge & Kegan Paul.

Lineham, P (1988), 'Liaison in post-16 education – an essential ingredient', in S Lambert (ed), pp. 58–76).

Locke, M and Pratt, J (1979), *A Guide to Learning After School*. Harmondsworth: Penguin Books.

Locke, M, Pratt, J and Bloomfield, J (1982), *Mapping and Reviewing the Pattern of 16–19 Education* (Schools Council Pamphlet 20). London: Schools Council.

London Borough of Tower Hamlets (1987), 'Memorandum submitted to the Home Affairs Sub-Committee on Race Relations and Immigration', in *The Bangladeshis in Britain, vol. 2: Minutes of Evidence Taken*. London: HMSO.

London Borough of Tower Hamlets Planning Department Directorate of Development (1987), *A Count of the Bangladeshi Population in Tower Hamlets*.

London Regional Manpower Intelligence Unit (1985), *Briefing Note No. 44: Employment Profile of Tower Hamlets*. Sheffield: MSC.

Low, G (1988), 'The MSC: a failure of democracy', in M Morris and C Griggs (eds) *Education: the wasted years? 1973–1986*. Lewes: Falmer Press, pp. 215–28.

Lowe, R (1988), *Education in the Post-War Years: a social history*. London: Routledge.

McCulloch, G (1987), 'History and policy; the politics of the TVEI', in Gleeson (ed), pp. 13–37.

McEwan, E C, Gipps, C V and Sumner, R (1975), *Language Proficiency in the Multi-Racial Junior School*. Windsor: NFER.

MacGregor, K (1990), 'Crosland's much-changed children', *The Times Higher Education Supplement* 6 April.

MacIntyre, A (1981), *After Virtue: a study of moral theory*. London: Duckworth.

McKnight, C C et al (1987), *The Underachieving Curriculum: assessing US school mathematics from an international perspective*. Champaign, Illinois: Stipes Publishing.

Maclure, S (1986), *Educational Documents: England and Wales: 1816 to the present day*. London: Methuen.

(1988), *Education Re-Formed*. London: Hodder & Stoughton.

Maden, M (1987), 'Towards a comprehensive model for 16–19 education', in C Chitty (ed), *Redefining the Comprehensive Experience* (Bedford Way Papers 32). London: Institute of Education, University of London, pp. 78–86.

Manpower Services Commission (MSC) (1982), *Youth Task Group Report*. Sheffield: MSC, April.

(1984), *TVEI Review 1984*. Sheffield: MSC.

(1986), *Review of Vocational Qualifications*. London: DES.

(1987), *Highly Qualified Manpower and Enterprise* (Commission paper MSC/87/28). Sheffield: MSC.

MSC and Local Authorities Association (1985), *Work Related NAFE: a guidance handbook*. Sheffield: MSC.

Merton, R K (1957), *Social Theory and Social Structure*. New York: John Wiley.

Mee, L G and Wiltshire, H C (1978), *Structure and Performance in Adult Education*. London: Longman.

Methven, Sir J (1976) 'What industry needs', *The Times Educational Supplement* 29 October.

Millins, P K C (1984), *Access Studies to Higher Education – September 1979–December 1983: a report*. Roehampton Institute of Higher Education.

(1986), 'Access and quality control: the Lindop onslaught', *Journal of Access Studies* 1, 2, pp. 68–71.

Ministry of Education (1956), *Technical Education* (Cmnd 9763). London: HMSO.

(1957), *Liberal Education in Technical Colleges* (Circular 323). London: Ministry of Education.

(1958), *Training for Skill* (Carr Report). London: HMSO.

(1959), *15–18: a report of the Central Advisory Council for Education (England) Vol. 1* (Crowther Report). London: HMSO.

(1961), *Better Opportunities in Technical Education* (Cmnd 1264). London: HMSO.

Ministry of Education, Victoria, Australia (1985), *Ministerial Review of Post-Compulsory Schooling*.

Mumford, D (1970), *Comprehensive Reorganisation and the Junior College*. Sheffield: Sheffield Polytechnic, ACFHE.

National Audit Office (1989), *Provision of Training through Managing Agents*. London: Department of Employment.

National Council for Vocational Qualifications (NCVQ) (1986), *Review of Vocational Qualifications in England and Wales* (DeVille Report). London: HMSO.

(1987), *The National Vocational Qualification Framework*. London: NCVQ, March.

(1989), *Generic Units and Common Learning Outcomes*. London: NCVQ, June.

(1989), *Vocational Qualifications: Criteria and Procedures*.

National Youth Employment Council (1974), *Unqualified, Untrained and Unemployed: Report of a Working Party set up by the National Youth Employment Council*, London: HMSO.

Norwood, C C (1929), *The English Tradition of Education*. London: Murray.

Oakley, A (1981), 'Interviewing women: a contradiction in terms', in H Roberts (ed), *Doing Feminist Research*. London: Routledge & Kegan Paul, pp. 30–61.

Office of Population Censuses and Surveys (OPCS) (1981), *Census of Population*. London: HMSO.

Organization for Economic Co-operation and Development (OECD) (1975), *Review of National Policies for Education: education development strategy in England and Wales*. Paris: OECD.

Ottaway, A K C (1953; 2nd revised edn 1962), *Education and Society*. London: Routledge & Kegan Paul.

Parkinson, B (1976), 'Adult education and working–class culture', in D Craig and M Heinemann (eds), *Experiments in English Teaching*. London: Edward Arnold, pp. 152–63.

Parry, G (1986), 'From patronage to partnership', *Journal of Access Studies* 1, 1, pp. 43–53.

Percy, Lord E (n.d., c. 1930), *Education at the Crossroads*. London: Evans.

Pollard, A (1988), *Education, Training and the New Vocationalism*. Oxford: Oxford University Press.

Popper, K R (1963), *Conjectures and Refutations: the growth of scientific knowledge*. London: Routledge & Kegan Paul.

Prais, S J and Wagner, K (1983), 'Schooling Standards in Britain and Germany: some summary comparisons bearing on economic efficiency'. National Institute of Economic and Social Research, discussion paper no. 60.

Pratley, B (1988), 'Who's driving the curriculum now?', in B Kedney and D Parkes (eds) *Planning the FE Curriculum*. London: FEU.

Pring, R (1985), 'In defence of TVEI', *Forum* 28, 1, pp. 14–18.

Radnor, H (1985), *Case Studies of Six Schools Related to Participation in a Pilot Scheme CPVE/CEE 1984/85*. University of Sussex/SREB Research Study.

Radnor, H et al (1989), 'The Certificate of Pre-Vocational Education', in A Hargreaves and D Reynolds (eds) *Education Policies: controversies and critiques*. Lewes: Falmer Press, pp. 95–119.

Raffe, D (1983), 'The end of the alternative route? The changing relationship of part-time education to work-life mobility among young male workers', in D Gleeson (ed) *Youth Training and the Search for Work*. London: Routledge & Kegan Paul.

   (1985), 'Content and context', in A G Watts (ed) *Education and Training 14–18*. Cambridge: CRAC Publications, pp. 19–24.

   (1985), 'The content and context of educational reform' in P Raggatt and G Weiner (eds), *Curriculum and Assessment*. Oxford: Pergamon Press in association with the Open University, pp. 67–73.

Raffe, D, and Tomes, N (1987), *The Organization and Content of Studies at the Post-Compulsory Level in Scotland*. Centre for Educational Sociology, Edinburgh University and OECD.

Raggatt, P and Evans, M (eds) (1977), *Urban Education 3: the political context*. London: Ward Lock Educational in association with the Open University Press.

Raison, T (1976), *The Act and the Partnership: an essay on educational adminisitration in England* (Centre for Studies in Social Policy). London: Bedford Square Press.

Ranson, S (1980), 'Changing relations between centre and locality in education', *Local Government Studies* 6, 6, pp. 3–23.

   (1984), 'Towards a tertiary tripartism: new codes of social control and the 17 plus', in P Broadfoot (ed) *Selection, Certification and Control: social issues in educational assessment*. Lewes: Falmer Press, pp. 221–44.

   (1988), 'From 1944 to 1988: education, citizenship and democracy', *Local Government Studies* Jan/Feb, pp. 1–19.

Rawls, J (1972), *A Theory of Justice*. Oxford: Oxford University Press.

Reeder, D (1979), 'A recurring debate: education and industry', in G Bernbaum (ed) *Schooling in Decline*. London: Macmillan, pp. 115–48.

Reid, I (1986), *The Sociology of the School and Education*. London: Fontana.

Reid, W A (1972), *The Universities and the Sixth Form Curriculum*. London: Macmillan.

   (1985), 'Curriculum change and the evolution of educational constituencies: the English sixth form in the nineteenth century', in I Goodson (ed) *Social Histories of the Secondary Curriculum*. Lewes: Falmer Press, pp. 289–311.

   (1988), 'The technological society and the concept of general education', in I Westbury and A C Purves (eds) *Cultural Literacy and the Idea of General Education* (87th Yearbook of the NSSE, Pt. 2). Chicago: University of Chicago Press.

Reid, W A and Filby, J (1982), *The Sixth: an essay in education and democracy*. Lewes: Falmer Press.

Reid, W A and Holt, M (1986), 'Structure and ideology in upper secondary education', in A Hartnett and M Naish (eds) *Education and Society Today*. Lewes: Falmer Press, pp. 89–108.

Rhoades, G (1987), 'Folk norms and school reforms: English secondary schools', *Sociology of Education* 60, pp. 44–53.

Ringer, F K (1979), *Education and Society in Modern Europe*. Bloomington: Indiana University Press.

Robbins Report (1963), *Higher Education: a report of the Committee appointed by the Prime Minister under the chairmanship of Lord Robbins, 1961–63* (Cmnd 2154). London: HMSO, October.

Robinson, E (1986), 'MSC and adult education', in C Benn and J Fairley (eds), pp. 123–33.

Robinson, V (1980), 'The achievement of Asian children', *Educational Research* 22, pp. 148–50.

Rogers, P (1987), 'Vocational education: first define the task', *Manpower Policy and Practice* 2, 3, Spring, pp. 17–18.

Rose, N (1979), 'The psychological complex: mental measurement and social administration', *Ideology and Consciousness* 5, p. 5–68.

Rothblatt, S (1988), 'General education on the American campus: an historical introduction in brief', in I Westbury and A C Purves (eds), *Cultural Literacy and the Idea of General Education* (87th Yearbook of the NSSE, Pt. 2). Chicago: University of Chicago Press.

Rubinstein, D and Simon, B (1973), *The Evolution of the Comprehensive School, 1926–1972* (2nd edn). London: Routledge & Kegan Paul.

Salter, B and Tapper, T (1981), *Education, Politics and the State: the theory and practice of educational change*. London: Grant McIntyre.

School Examinations and Assessment Council (SEAC) (1989), *Advancing A Levels: a response by the School Examinations and Assessment Council*: London: SEAC, August.

Schultz, T (1961), 'Investment in human capital', *American Economic Review* 51, March, pp. 1–17.

Scott, P (1988), 'Higher Education', in M Morris and C Griggs (eds) *Education: the wasted years? 1973–1986*. Lewes: Falmer Press, pp. 127–44.

Seale, C (1984), 'FEU and MSC: two curricular philosophies and their implications for the Youth Training Scheme', *The Vocational Aspect of Education* 36, 93, May, pp. 3–10.

Shannon, R (1974), *The Crisis in Imperialism, 1865–1915*. London: Hart-Davis/McGibbon.

Sharp, S (1984), 'Psychologists and intelligence testing in English education 1900–1940', in P Broadfoot (ed) *Selection, Certification and Control*. Lewes: Falmer Press, pp. 35–50.

Shilling, C (1989), *Schooling for Work in Capitalist Britain*. Lewes: Falmer Press.

Silver, H (1988), *Intentions and Outcomes*. London: Longman for FEU.

Simon, B (1974), *The Politics of Educational Reform 1920–1940*. London: Lawrence & Wishart.

(1988), *Bending the Rules: the Baker 'Reform' of Education*. London: Lawrence & Wishart.

Skilbeck, M (1982), *A Core Curriculum for the Common School* (An Inaugural Lecture). London: Institute of Education, University of London.

Slater, D (1985), 'Sixteen to nineteen: towards a coherent policy?' in M Hughes, P Ribbins and H Thomas (eds) *Managing Education: the system and the institution*. London: Cassell Education, pp. 177–97.

Smith, G D (1986), 'TVEI: replication and FE', *NATFHE Journal* 11, 8, pp. 18–20.

(1987a), 'TVEI: and FE: challenges and responses', *NATFHE Journal* 12, 2, pp. 16–22.

(1987b), 'TVEI update: extension developments', *NATFHE Journal* 13, 4, pp. 62–63.

Smithers, A (1988), 'Reshaping a fragmented system', *Education*, 29 July. p. 111.

Smithers, A. and Robinson, P (1989) *Increasing Participation in Higher Education*. London: B P Educational Service.

Sofer, A (1988), 'Damned statistics', *The Guardian* 26 July.

(1988), 'Skill passports needed for the 21st century', *The Guardian* 11 August.

Spours, K (1988a), *A Curricular Comparison of CPVE and BTEC First Diploma* (Post-16 Education Centre Working Paper No. 3, April). London: Post-16 Education Centre, Institute of Education, University of London.

(1988b), *Evaluation of Progression from CPVE in Newham Education Authority* (Post-16 Education Centre Report No. 4, December). London: Post-16 Education Centre, Institute of Education, University of London.

(1989), *Promoting Progression: prospects for a post-16 modular framework* (Post-16 Education Centre Conference Discussion Document). London: Post-16 Education Centre, Institute of Education, University of London.

(1990), *Politics of Progression: issues of access and continuity in the 14–19 curriculum*. Lewes: Falmer Press.

Spours, K and Baron, G (1988), *Progression from CPVE in Newham LEA* (Post-16 Education Centre Report No. 3, February). London: Post-16 Education Centre, Institute of Education, University of London.

Tait, T (1989), *NVQs and Progression: a 14–19 perspective*. NCVQ/Institute of Education Project Report, July.

Tawney, R H (1931), *Equality*. London: Unwin.

Taylor, J (1985), 'Preface' to 'Curriculum', in F Janes et al (eds). pp. 49–51.

Terry, D (1987), *The Tertiary College: Assuring Our Future*. Milton Keynes: Open University Press.

Thompson, J L (ed) (1980), *Adult Education for a Change*. London: Hutchinson.

Thomson, A and Rosenberg, H (1986), *A User's Guide to the Manpower Services Commission*. London: Kogan Page.

Times Higher Education Supplement (1989), 'Training Agency waters down YTS requirements', 3 February.

Times Newspapers (1971), *The British Economy: key statistics, 1900–1970*. London: *Times Newspapers*.

Titcombe, R (1986), 'CPVE and the sixth-form curriculum', *Forum* 28, 2, pp. 48–50.

Tomlinson, S (1980), 'The educational performance of ethnic minority children', *New Community* 8, pp. 213–234.

(1980b), 'Ethnic minority parents and education', in M Craft, J Raynor and L Cohen (eds), *Linking Home and School: a new review* (3rd edn). London: Harper and Row, pp. 186–99.

Tower Hamlets Homeless Families Campaign (1987), 'Evidence supplied as part of the Memorandum submitted by Tower Hamlets Association for Racial Equality to the Home Affairs Sub-Committee on Race Relations and Immigration', in *The Bangladeshis in Britain, Vol. 2: Minutes of Evidence Taken*. London: HMSO.

Trades Union Congress (1989), *Skills 2000*. TUC, August.

Turner, R H (1960), 'Sponsored and contest mobility and the school system', *American Sociological Review* 25, pp. 855–67.

Twomey, D (1988), 'Report of the Panel of Inquiry into Education in Division 5. Unpublished ILEA members' internal report.

United States Department of Education, National Commission on Excellence in Education (1983), *A Nation at Risk*. Washington DC: US Government Printing House.

Verma, G K and Ashworth, B (1986), *Ethnicity and Educational Achievement in British Schools*. London: Macmillan.

Wardle, D (1976), *English Popular Education*. Cambridge: Cambridge University Press.

Watkins, P (1982), *The Sixth Form College in Practice*. London: Edward Arnold.

Watts, A G (1983), *Education, Unemployment and the Future of Work*. Milton Keynes: Open University Press.

Watts, A G (ed) (1985) *Education and Training 14–18: Policy and Practice*. Cambridge: CRAC Publications.

Wellington, J (1987), 'Skills for the future?: vocational education and new technology', in M Holt (ed) *Skills and Vocationalism: the easy answer*. Milton Keynes: Open University Press, pp. 21–42.

White, J (1975), 'The end of the compulsory curriculum' in Paul H Hirst et al., *The Curriculum: The Doris Lee Lectures 1975*. Studies in Education (new series) 2. London: Institute of Education, University of London, pp. 22–39.

Whitfield, R (1980), 'Subject structures in a coherent curriculum', in M Holt (ed) *The Tertiary Sector*. London: Hodder & Stoughton, pp. 51–73.

Wiener, M (1981), *English Culture and the Decline of the Industrial Spirit, 1850–1980*. Cambridge: Cambridge University Press.

Williams, R (1961), *The Long Revolution*. Harmondsworth: Penguin Books.

(1980), 'A hundred years of culture and anarchy', in *Problems in Materialism and Culture*. London: Verso, pp. 3–8.

Willis, P (1982), 'Male school counterculture', *V203 Popular Culture*. Milton Keynes: Open University Press, block 7, unit 30, pp. 75–103.

Wragg, T (1986), 'The parliamentary version of the Great Debate', in M Golby (ed) *Ruskin Plus Ten* (Perspectives 26). Exeter: School of Education, University of Exeter, pp. 6–14.

Young, D (1982), 'Worried about unemployment? How you can help . . .', *The Director* October, pp. 34–35.

Young, M (1987), Introduction to C Chitty (ed) *Aspects of Vocationalism* (Post-16 Education Centre Occasional Paper No. 2). London: Post-16 Education Centre, Institute of Education, University of London, pp. 1–3.

Index